Hands-On Ensemble Learning with Python

Build highly optimized ensemble machine learning models using scikit-learn and Keras

George Kyriakides
Konstantinos G. Margaritis

BIRMINGHAM - MUMBAI

Hands-On Ensemble Learning with Python

Copyright © 2019 Packt Publishing

Commissioning Editor: Sunith Shetty
Acquisition Editor: Devika Battike
Content Development Editor: Athikho Sapuni Rishana
Senior Editor: Martin Whittemore
Technical Editor: Utkarsha S. Kadam
Copy Editor: Safis Editing
Project Coordinator: Kirti Pisat
Proofreader: Safis Editing
Indexer: Manju Arasan
Production Designer: Alishon Mendonsa

First published: July 2019

Production reference: 2300719

Published by Packt Publishing Ltd.
Livery Place
35 Livery Street
Birmingham
B3 2PB, UK.

ISBN 978-1-78961-285-1

www.packtpub.com

Packt.com

Subscribe to our online digital library for full access to over 7,000 books and videos, as well as industry leading tools to help you plan your personal development and advance your career. For more information, please visit our website.

Why subscribe?

- Spend less time learning and more time coding with practical eBooks and Videos from over 4,000 industry professionals

- Improve your learning with Skill Plans built especially for you

- Get a free eBook or video every month

- Fully searchable for easy access to vital information

- Copy and paste, print, and bookmark content

Did you know that Packt offers eBook versions of every book published, with PDF and ePub files available? You can upgrade to the eBook version at www.packt.com and as a print book customer, you are entitled to a discount on the eBook copy. Get in touch with us at customercare@packtpub.com for more details.

At www.packt.com, you can also read a collection of free technical articles, sign up for a range of free newsletters, and receive exclusive discounts and offers on Packt books and eBooks.

Contributors

About the authors

George Kyriakides is a Ph.D. researcher, studying distributed neural architecture search. His interests and experience include the automated generation and optimization of predictive models for a wide array of applications, such as image recognition, time series analysis, and financial applications. He holds an M.Sc. in computational methods and applications, and a B.Sc. in applied informatics, both from the University of Macedonia, Thessaloniki, Greece.

Konstantinos G. Margaritis has been a teacher and researcher in computer science for more than 30 years. His research interests include parallel and distributed computing, as well as computational intelligence and machine learning. He holds an M.Eng. in electrical engineering (Aristotle University of Thessaloniki, Greece), as well as an M.Sc. and a Ph.D. in computer science (Loughborough University, UK). He is a professor at the Department of Applied Informatics, University of Macedonia, Thessaloniki, Greece.

About the reviewers

Greg Walters has been involved with computers and computer programming since 1972. Currently, he is extremely well versed in Visual Basic, Visual Basic .NET, Python, and SQL using MySQL, SQLite, Microsoft SQL Server, Oracle, C++, Delphi, Modula-2, Pascal, C, 80x86 Assembler, COBOL, and Fortran. He is a programming trainer and has trained numerous people on many pieces of computer software, including MySQL, Open Database Connectivity, Quattro Pro, Corel Draw!, Paradox, Microsoft Word, Excel, DOS, Windows 3.11, Windows for Workgroups, Windows 95, Windows NT, Windows 2000, Windows XP, and Linux. He is currently retired and, in his spare time, is a musician and loves to cook, but he is also open to working as a freelancer on various projects.

Bhavesh Bhatt is a technology postgraduate at BITS Pilani with a keen interest in machine learning, data science, and computer vision. He currently works as a data scientist at Fractal Analytics. He has taught data science using the Python programming language to hundreds of students in the classroom. Additionally, Bhavesh hosts a machine learning-based educational YouTube channel with over 4,400 subscribers.

Packt is searching for authors like you

If you're interested in becoming an author for Packt, please visit `authors.packtpub.com` and apply today. We have worked with thousands of developers and tech professionals, just like you, to help them share their insight with the global tech community. You can make a general application, apply for a specific hot topic that we are recruiting an author for, or submit your own idea.

Table of Contents

Preface

Ensembling is a technique for combining two or more similar or dissimilar machine learning algorithms to create a model that delivers superior predictive power. This book will demonstrate how you can use a variety of weak algorithms to make a strong predictive model.

With its hands-on approach, you'll not only get up to speed on the basic theory, but also the application of various ensemble learning techniques. Using examples and real-world datasets, you'll be able to produce better machine learning models to solve supervised learning problems such as classification and regression. Later in the book, you'll go on to leverage ensemble learning techniques such as clustering to produce unsupervised machine learning models. As you progress, the chapters will cover different machine learning algorithms that are widely used in the practical world to make predictions and classifications. You'll even get to grips with using Python libraries such as scikit-learn and Keras to implement different ensemble models.

By the end of this book, you will be well versed in ensemble learning and have the skills you need to understand which ensemble method is required for which problem, in order to successfully implement them in real-world scenarios.

Who this book is for

This book is for data analysts, data scientists, machine learning engineers, and other professionals who are looking to generate advanced models using ensemble techniques.

What this book covers

Chapter 1, *A Machine Learning Refresher*, presents an overview of machine learning, including basic concepts such as training/test sets, performance measures, supervised and unsupervised learning, machine learning algorithms, and benchmark datasets.

Chapter 2, *Getting Started with Ensemble Learning*, introduces the concept of ensemble learning, highlighting the problems that it solves as well as the problems that it poses.

Chapter 3, *Voting*, introduces the most simple ensemble learning technique, voting, while explaining the difference between hard and soft voting. You will learn how to implement a custom classifier, as well as use scikit-learn's implementation of hard/soft voting.

Chapter 4, *Stacking*, covers meta learning (stacking) a more advanced ensemble learning method. After reading this chapter, you will be able to implement a stacking classifier in Python to use with scikit-learn classifiers.

Chapter 5, *Bagging*, introduces bootstrap resampling and the first generative ensemble learning technique, bagging. Furthermore, this chapter guides you through the process of implementing the technique in Python, as well as how to use the scikit-learn implementation.

Chapter 6, *Boosting*, touches on more advanced subjects in ensemble learning. This chapter explains how popular boosting algorithms work and are implemented. Furthermore, it presents XGBoost, a highly successful distributed boosting library.

Chapter 7, *Random Forests*, goes through the process of creating random decision trees by subsampling the instances and features of a dataset. Moreover, this chapter explains how to utilize an ensemble of random trees to create a random forest. Finally, this chapter presents scikit-learn's implementations and how to use them.

Chapter 8, *Clustering*, introduces to the possibility of using ensembles for unsupervised learning tasks, such as clustering. Furthermore, the OpenEnsembles Python library is introduced, along with guidance on using it.

Chapter 9, *Classifying Fraudulent Transactions*, presents an application for the classification of a real-world dataset, using ensemble learning techniques presented in earlier chapters. The dataset concerns fraudulent credit card transactions.

Chapter 10, *Predicting Bitcoin Prices*, presents an application for the regression of a real-world dataset, using ensemble learning techniques presented in earlier chapters. The dataset concerns the price of the popular cryptocurrency Bitcoin.

Chapter 11, *Evaluating Sentiment on Twitter*, presents an application for evaluating the sentiment of various tweets using a real-world dataset.

Chapter 12, *Recommending Movies with Keras*, presents the process of creating a recommender system using ensembles of neural networks.

Chapter 13, *Clustering World Happiness*, presents the process of using an ensemble learning approach to cluster data from the World Happiness Report 2018.

To get the most out of this book

This book is aimed at analysts, data scientists, engineers, and other professionals who have an interest in generating advanced models that describe and generalize datasets of interest to them. It is assumed that the reader has basic experience of programming in Python and is familiar with elementary machine learning models. Furthermore, a basic understanding of statistics is assumed, although key points and more advanced concepts are briefly presented. Familiarity with Python's scikit-learn module would be greatly beneficial, although it is not strictly required. A standard Python installation is required. Anaconda Distribution (https://www.anaconda.com/distribution/) greatly simplifies the task of installing and managing the various Python packages, although it is not necessary. Finally, a good **Integrated Development Environment (IDE)** is extremely useful for managing your code and debugging. In our examples, we usually utilize the Spyder IDE, which can be easily installed through Anaconda.

Download the example code files

You can download the example code files for this book from your account at www.packt.com. If you purchased this book elsewhere, you can visit www.packt.com/support and register to have the files emailed directly to you.

You can download the code files by following these steps:

1. Log in or register at www.packt.com.
2. Select the **SUPPORT** tab.
3. Click on **Code Downloads & Errata**.
4. Enter the name of the book in the **Search** box and follow the onscreen instructions.

Once the file is downloaded, please make sure that you unzip or extract the folder using the latest versions of the following:

- WinRAR/7-Zip for Windows
- Zipeg/iZip/UnRarX for macOS
- 7-Zip/PeaZip for Linux

The code bundle for the book is also hosted on GitHub at https://github.com/PacktPublishing/Hands-On-Ensemble-Learning-with-Python. In case there's an update to the code, it will be updated on the existing GitHub repository.

We also have other code bundles from our rich catalog of books and videos available at `https://github.com/PacktPublishing/`. Check them out!

Download the color images

We also provide a PDF file that has color images of the screenshots/diagrams used in this book. You can download it here: `https://static.packt-cdn.com/downloads/9781789612851_ColorImages.pdf`.

Code in action

Visit the following link to check out videos of the code being run: `http://bit.ly/2GfnRrv`.

Conventions used

There are a number of text conventions used throughout this book.

`CodeInText`: Indicates code words in text, database table names, folder names, filenames, file extensions, pathnames, dummy URLs, user input, and Twitter handles. Here is an example: "Mount the downloaded `WebStorm-10*.dmg` disk image file as another disk in your system."

A block of code is set as follows:

```
# --- SECTION 6 ---
# Accuracy of hard voting
print('-'*30)
print('Hard Voting:', accuracy_score(y_test, hard_predictions))
```

Bold: Indicates a new term, an important word, or words that you see onscreen. For example, words in menus or dialog boxes appear in the text like this. Here is an example: "Thus, the preferred approach is to utilize **K-fold cross validation**."

Warnings or important notes appear like this.

Tips and tricks appear like this.

Get in touch

Feedback from our readers is always welcome.

General feedback: If you have questions about any aspect of this book, mention the book title in the subject of your message and email us at customercare@packtpub.com.

Errata: Although we have taken every care to ensure the accuracy of our content, mistakes do happen. If you have found a mistake in this book, we would be grateful if you would report this to us. Please visit www.packt.com/submit-errata, selecting your book, clicking on the Errata Submission Form link, and entering the details.

Piracy: If you come across any illegal copies of our works in any form on the Internet, we would be grateful if you would provide us with the location address or website name. Please contact us at copyright@packt.com with a link to the material.

If you are interested in becoming an author: If there is a topic that you have expertise in and you are interested in either writing or contributing to a book, please visit authors.packtpub.com.

Reviews

Please leave a review. Once you have read and used this book, why not leave a review on the site that you purchased it from? Potential readers can then see and use your unbiased opinion to make purchase decisions, we at Packt can understand what you think about our products, and our authors can see your feedback on their book. Thank you!

For more information about Packt, please visit packt.com.

Section 1: Introduction and Required Software Tools

This section is a refresher on basic machine learning concepts and an introduction to ensemble learning. We will have an overview of machine learning and various concepts pertaining to it, such as train and test sets, supervised and unsupervised learning, and more. We will also learn about the concept of ensemble learning.

This section comprises the following chapters:

- Chapter 1, *A Machine Learning Refresher*
- Chapter 2, *Getting Started with Ensemble Learning*

A Machine Learning Refresher

Machine learning is a sub field of **artificial intelligence** (**AI**) focused on the aim of developing algorithms and techniques that enable computers to learn from massive amounts of data. Given the increasing rate at which data is produced, machine learning has played a critical role in solving difficult problems in recent years. This success was the main driving force behind the funding and development of many great machine learning libraries that make use of data in order to build predictive models. Furthermore, businesses have started to realize the potential of machine learning, driving the demand for data scientists and machine learning engineers to new heights, in order to design better-performing predictive models.

This chapter serves as a refresher on the main concepts and terminology, as well as an introduction to the frameworks that will be used throughout the book, in order to approach ensemble learning with a solid foundation.

The main topics covered in this chapter are the following:

- The various machine learning problems and datasets
- How to evaluate the performance of a predictive model
- Machine learning algorithms
- Python environment setup and the required libraries

Technical requirements

You will require basic knowledge of machine learning techniques and algorithms. Furthermore, a knowledge of python conventions and syntax is required. Finally, familiarity with the NumPy library will greatly help the reader to understand some custom algorithm implementations.

The code files of this chapter can be found on GitHub:

```
https://github.com/PacktPublishing/Hands-On-Ensemble-Learning-with-Python/
tree/master/Chapter01
```

Check out the following video to see the Code in Action: `http://bit.ly/30u8sv8`.

Learning from data

Data is the raw ingredient of machine learning. Processing data can produce information; for example, measuring the height of a portion of a school's students (data) and calculating their average (processing) can give us an idea of the whole school's height (information). If we process the data further, for example, by grouping males and females and calculating two averages – one for each group, we will gain more information, as we will have an idea about the average height of the school's males and females. Machine learning strives to produce the most information possible from any given data. In this example, we produced a very basic predictive model. By calculating the two averages, we can predict the average height of any student just by knowing whether the student is male or female.

The set of data that a machine learning algorithm is tasked with processing is called the problem's dataset. In our example, the dataset consists of height measurements (in centimeters) and the child's sex (male/female). In machine learning, input variables are called features and output variables are called targets. In this dataset, the features of our predictive model consist solely of the students' sex, while our target is the students' height in centimeters. The predictive model that is produced and maps features to targets will be referred to as simply the model from now on, unless otherwise specified. Each data point is called an instance. In this problem, each student is an instance of the dataset.

When the target is a continuous variable (a number), it presents a regression problem, as the aim is to regress the target on the features. When the target is a set of categories, it presents a classification problem, as we try to assign each instance to a category or class.

Note that, in classification problems, the target class can be represented by a number; this does not mean that it is a regression problem. The most useful way to determine whether it is a regression problem is to think about whether the instances can be ordered by their targets. In our example, the target is height, so we can order the students from tallest to shortest, as 100 cm is less than 110 cm. As a counter example, if the target was their favorite color, we could represent each color by a number, but we could not order them. Even if we represented red as one and blue as two, we could not say that red is "before" or "less than" blue. Thus, this counter example is a classification problem.

Popular machine learning datasets

Machine learning relies on data in order to produce high-performing models. Without data, it's not even possible to create models. In this section, we'll present some popular machine learning datasets, which we will utilize throughout this book.

Diabetes

The diabetes dataset concerns 442 individual diabetes patients and the progression of the disease one year after a baseline measurement. The dataset consists of 10 features, which are the patient's age, sex, **body mass index (bmi)**, average **blood pressure (bp)**, and six measurements of their blood serum. The dataset target is the progression of the disease one year after the baseline measurement. This is a regression dataset, as the target is a number.

In this book, the dataset features are mean-centered and scaled such that the dataset sum of squares for each feature equals one. The following table depicts a sample of the diabetes dataset:

age	sex	bmi	bp	s1	s2	s3	s4	s5	s6	target
0.04	0.05	0.06	0.02	-0.04	-0.03	-0.04	0.00	0.02	-0.02	151
0.00	-0.04	-0.05	-0.03	-0.01	-0.02	0.07	-0.04	-0.07	-0.09	75
0.09	0.05	0.04	-0.01	-0.05	-0.03	-0.03	0.00	0.00	-0.03	141
-0.09	-0.04	-0.01	-0.04	0.01	0.02	-0.04	0.03	0.02	-0.01	206

Breast cancer

The breast cancer dataset concerns 569 biopsies of malignant and benign tumors. The dataset provides 30 features extracted from images of fine-needle aspiration biopsies that describe cell nuclei. The images provide information about the shape, size, and texture of each cell nucleus. Furthermore, for each characteristic, three distinct values are provided. The mean, the standard error, and the worst or largest value. This ensures that, for each image, the cell population is adequately described.

The dataset target concerns the diagnosis, that is, whether a tumor is malignant or benign. Thus, this is a classification dataset. The available features are listed as follows:

- Mean radius
- Mean texture
- Mean perimeter
- Mean area
- Mean smoothness
- Mean compactness
- Mean concavity
- Mean concave points
- Mean symmetry
- Mean fractal dimension
- Radius error
- Texture error
- Perimeter error
- Area error
- Smoothness error
- Compactness error
- Concavity error
- Concave points error
- Symmetry error
- Fractal dimension error
- Worst radius
- Worst texture
- Worst perimeter
- Worst area
- Worst smoothness
- Worst compactness
- Worst concavity
- Worst concave points
- Worst symmetry
- Worst fractal dimension

Handwritten digits

The MNIST handwritten digit dataset is one of the most famous image recognition datasets. It consists of square images, 8 x 8 pixels, each containing a single handwritten digit. Thus, the dataset features are an 8 by 8 matrix, containing each pixel's color in grayscale. The target consists of 10 classes, one for each digit from 0 to 9. This is a classification dataset. The following figure is a sample from the handwritten digit dataset:

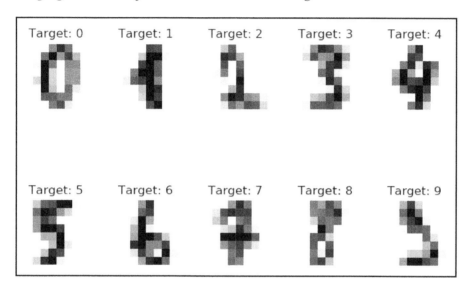

Sample of the handwritten digit dataset

Supervised and unsupervised learning

Machine learning can be divided into many subcategories; two broad categories are supervised and unsupervised learning. These categories contain some of the most popular and widely used machine learning methods. In this section, we present them, as well as some toy example uses of supervised and unsupervised learning.

Supervised learning

In examples such as those in the previous section, the data consisted of some features and a target; no matter whether the target was quantitative (regression) or categorical (classification). Under these circumstances, we call the dataset a labeled dataset. When we try to produce a model from a labeled dataset in order to make predictions about unseen or future data (for example, to diagnose a new tumor case), we make use of supervised learning. In simple cases, supervised learning models can be visualized as a line. This line's purpose is to either separate the data based on the target (in classification) or to closely follow the data (in regression).

The following figure illustrates a simple regression example. Here, y is the target and x is the dataset feature. Our model consists of the simple equation $y=2x-5$. As is evident, the line closely follows the data. In order to estimate the y value of a new unseen point, we calculate its value using the preceding formula. The following figure shows a simple regression with $y=2x-5$ as the predictive model:

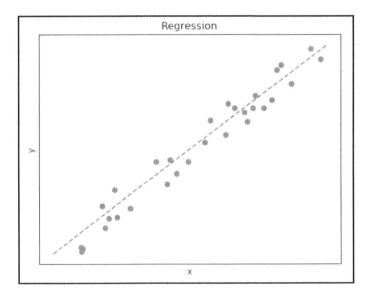

Simple regression with y=2x-5 as the predictive model

In the following figure, a simple classification problem is depicted. Here, the dataset features are *x* and *y*, while the target is the instance color. Again, the dotted line is $y=2x-5$, but this time we test whether the point is above or below the line. If the point's *y* value is lower than expected (smaller), then we expect it to be orange. If it is higher (greater), we expect it to be blue. The following figure is a simple classification with $y=2x-5$ as the boundary:

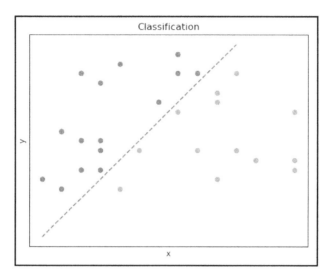

Simple classification with y=2x-5 as boundary

Unsupervised learning

In both regression and classification, we have a clear understanding of how the data is structured or how it behaves. Our goal is to simply model that structure or behavior. In some cases, we do not know how the data is structured. In those cases, we can utilize unsupervised learning in order to discover the structure, and thus information, within the data. The simplest form of unsupervised learning is clustering. As the name implies, clustering techniques attempt to group (or cluster) data instances. Thus, instances that belong to the same cluster share many similarities in their features, while they are dissimilar to instances that belong in separate clusters. A simple example with three clusters is depicted in the following figure. Here, the dataset features are *x* and *y*, while there is no target.

The clustering algorithm discovered three distinct groups, centered around the points (0, 0), (1, 1), and (2, 2):

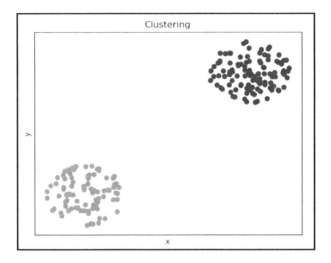

Clustering with three distinct groups

Dimensionality reduction

Another form of unsupervised learning is dimensionality reduction. The number of features present in a dataset equals the dataset's dimensions. Often, many features can be correlated, noisy, or simply not provide much information. Nonetheless, the cost of storing and processing data is correlated with a dataset's dimensionality. Thus, by reducing the dataset's dimensions, we can help the algorithms to better model the data.

Another use of dimensionality reduction is for the visualization of high-dimensional datasets. For example, using the t-distributed Stochastic Neighbor Embedding (t-SNE) algorithm, we can reduce the breast cancer dataset to two dimensions or components. Although it is not easy to visualize 30 dimensions, it is quite easy to visualize two.

Furthermore, we can visually test whether the information contained within the dataset can be utilized to separate the dataset's classes or not. The next figure depicts the two components on the y and x axis, while the color represents the instance's class. Although we cannot plot all of the dimensions, by plotting the two components, we can conclude that a degree of separability between the classes exists:

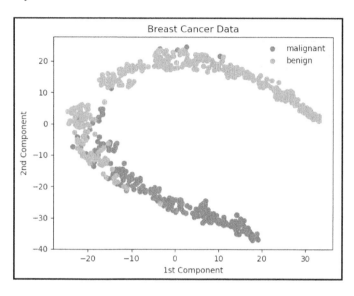

Using t-SNE to reduce the dimensionality of the breast cancer dataset

Performance measures

Machine learning is a highly quantitative field. Although we can gauge the performance of a model by plotting how it separates classes and how closely it follows data, more quantitative performance measures are needed in order to evaluate models. In this section, we present cost functions and metrics. Both of them are used in order to assess a model's performance.

Cost functions

A machine learning model's objective is to model our dataset. In order to assess each model's performance, we define an objective function. These functions usually express a cost, or how far from perfect a model is. These cost functions usually utilize a loss function to assess how well the model performed on each individual dataset instance.

Some of the most widely used cost functions are described in the following sections, assuming that the dataset has n instances, the target's true value for instance i is t_i and the model's output is y_i.

Mean absolute error

Mean absolute error (MAE) or L1 loss is the mean absolute distance between the target's real values and the model's outputs. It is calculated as follows:

$$MAE = \sum_{i=0}^{n} \frac{|y_i - t_i|}{n}$$

Mean squared error

Mean squared error (MSE) or L2 loss is the mean squared distance between the target's real values and the model's output. It is calculated as follows:

$$MSE = \sum_{i=0}^{n} \frac{(y_i - t_i)^2}{n}$$

Cross entropy loss

Cross entropy loss is used in models that output probabilities between 0 and 1, usually to express the probability that an instance is a member of a specific class. As the output probability diverges from the actual label, the loss increases. For a simple case where the dataset consists of two classes, it is calculated as follows:

$$CEL = -(t_i log(y_i) + (1 - t_i)log(1 - y_i))$$

Metrics

Cost functions are useful when we try to numerically optimize our models. But as humans, we need metrics that are useful and intuitive to understand and report. As such, there are a number of metrics available that give insight into a model's performance. The most common metrics are presented in the following sections.

Classification accuracy

The simplest and easiest to grasp of all, classification accuracy refers to the percentage of correct predictions. In order to calculate accuracy, we divide the number of correct predictions by the total number of instances:

$$Accuracy = \frac{Correct\ Predictions}{Total\ Instances}$$

In order for accuracy to hold any substantial value, the dataset must contain an equal number of instances belonging to each class. If the dataset is unbalanced, accuracy will be affected. For example, if a dataset consists of 90% class A and 10% class B, a model that predicts each instance as class A will have 90% accuracy, although it will hold zero predictive power.

Confusion matrix

In order to tackle the preceding problem, it is possible to utilize a confusion matrix. Confusion matrices present the number of instances correctly or incorrectly predicted as each possible class. In a dataset with only two classes (Yes and No), a confusion matrix has the following form:

n = 200	Predicted: Yes	Predicted: No
Target: Yes	80	70
Target: No	20	30

There are four cells, each corresponding to one of the following:

- **True Positives** (**TP**): When the target belongs to the Yes class and the model predicted Yes
- **True Negatives** (**TN**): When the target belongs to the No class and the model predicted No
- **False Positives** (**FP**): When the target belongs to the No class and the model predicted Yes
- **False Negatives** (**FN**): When the target belongs to the Yes class and the model predicted No

Confusion matrices provide information about the balance of the true and predicted classes. In order to calculate the accuracy from a confusion matrix, we divide the sum of TP and TN by the total number of instances:

$$Accuracy = \frac{TP + TN}{n}$$

Sensitivity, specificity, and area under the curve

Area under the curve (AUC) concerns binary classification datasets, and it depicts the probability that the model will rank any given instance correctly. In order to define it, we must first define sensitivity and specificity:

- **Sensitivity (True Positive Rate)**: Sensitivity is the percentage of positive instances correctly predicted as positive, relative to all positive instances. It is calculated as follows:

$$Sensitivity = \frac{TP}{FN + TP}$$

- **Specificity (False Positive Rate)**: Specificity is the percentage of negative instances incorrectly predicted as positive, relative to all negative instances. It is calculated as follows:

$$Specificity = \frac{FN}{FP + TN}$$

By iteratively computing (1-specificity) and sensitivity at specific intervals (for example, in 0.05 increments), we can see how the model behaves. The intervals concern the model's output probability for each instance; for example, we first compute them for all instances with an estimated probability of belonging to the Yes class of less than 0.05. Then, we re-compute for all instances with an estimated probability of less than 0.1 and so on. The result is depicted here:

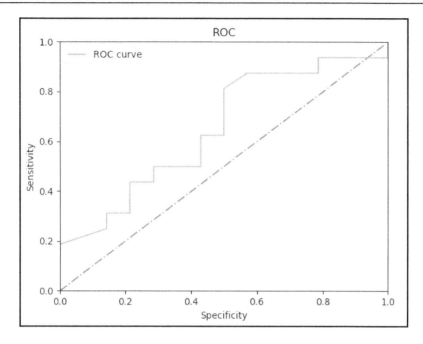

Receiver operator characteristic curve

The straight line represents an equal probability of ranking an instance correctly or incorrectly: a random model. The orange line (ROC curve) depicts the model's probability. If the ROC curve is below the straight line, it means that the model performs worse than a random, uninformed model.

Precision, recall, and the F1 score

Precision gauges how a model behaves by quantifying the percentage of instances correctly classified as a specific class, relative to all instances predicted as the same class. It is calculated as follows:

$$Precision = \frac{TP}{TP + FP}$$

Recall is another name for sensitivity. The harmonic mean of precision and recall is called the F1 score and is calculated as follows:

$$F1 = 2\frac{Recall \times Precision}{Recall + Precision}$$

The reason to use the harmonic mean instead of a simple average is that the harmonic mean is greatly affected by imbalances between the two values (precision and recall). Thus, if either precision or recall is significantly smaller than the other, the F1 score will reflect this imbalance.

Evaluating models

Although there are various metrics that indicate a model's performance, it is important to carefully set the testing environment. One of the most important things is to split the dataset into two parts. One part of the dataset will be utilized by the algorithm in order to generate a model; the second part will be utilized to assess the model. These are usually called the train and test set.

The train set is available to the algorithm to generate and optimize a model, using any cost function. After the algorithm is finished, the produced model is tested on the test set, in order to assess its predictive ability on unseen data. While the algorithm may produce a model that performs well on the train set (in-sample performance), it may not be able to generalize and perform as well on the test set (out-of-sample performance). This can be attributed to many factors – covered in the next chapter. Some of the problems that arise can be tackled with the use of ensembles. Nonetheless, if the algorithm is presented with low-quality data, there is little that can be done to improve out-of-sample performance.

In order to obtain a fair estimate, we sometimes iteratively split different parts of a dataset into fixed-size train and test sets, say, 90% train and 10% test, until we have tested the whole dataset. This is called K-fold cross validation. In the case of a 90% to 10% split, it is called 10-fold cross validation, because we need to perform it 10 times in order to get an estimate for the whole dataset.

Machine learning algorithms

There are a number of machine learning algorithms, for both supervised and unsupervised learning. In this book, we will cover some of the most popular algorithms that can be utilized within ensembles. In this chapter, we will go over the key concepts behind each algorithm, the basic algorithms, and the libraries that implement them in Python.

Python packages

In order to leverage the power of any programming language, libraries are essential. They provide a convenient and tested implementation of many algorithms. In this book, we will be using Python 3.6 along with the following libraries: NumPy, for its excellent implementation of numerical operators and matrices; Pandas, for its convenient data manipulation methods; Matplotlib, to visualize our data; scikit-learn, for its excellent implementations of various machine learning algorithms, and Keras to build neural networks, utilizing its Pythonic, intuitive interface. Keras is an interface for other frameworks, such as TensorFlow, PyTorch, and Theano. The specific versions of each library used in this book are listed as follows:

- numpy==1.15.1
- pandas==0.23.4
- scikit-learn==0.19.1
- matplotlib==2.2.2
- Keras==2.2.4

Supervised learning algorithms

The most common class of machine learning algorithm is supervised learning algorithms. These concern problems where data has a known structure. This means that each data point has a specific value related to it that we wish to model or predict.

Regression

Regression is one of the simplest machine learning algorithms. The **Ordinary Least Squares** (**OLS**) regression of the form $y=ax+b$ attempts to optimize the a and b parameters in order to fit the data. It uses MSE as its cost function. As the name implies, it is able to solve regression problems.

We can use the scikit-learn implementation of OLS to try and model the diabetes dataset (the dataset is provided with the library):

```
# --- SECTION 1 ---
# Libraries and data loading
from sklearn.datasets import load_diabetes
from sklearn.linear_model import LinearRegression
from sklearn import metrics
diabetes = load_diabetes()
```

The first section deals with importing libraries and loading data. We use the
`LinearRegression` implementation that exists in the `linear_model` package:

```
# --- SECTION 2 ---
# Split the data into train and test set
train_x, train_y = diabetes.data[:400], diabetes.target[:400]
test_x, test_y = diabetes.data[400:], diabetes.target[400:]
```

The second section splits the data into a train and a test set. For this example, we used the
first 400 instances as the train set and the other 42 as the test set:

```
# --- SECTION 3 ---
# Instantiate, train and evaluate the model
ols = LinearRegression()
ols.fit(train_x, train_y)
err = metrics.mean_squared_error(test_y, ols.predict(test_x))
r2 = metrics.r2_score(test_y, ols.predict(test_x))
```

The next section instantiates a linear regression object with `ols = LinearRegression()`.
It then optimizes the parameters, or fits the model with our training instances, using
`ols.fit(train_x, train_y)`. Finally, by using the `metrics` package, we calculate the
MSE and R^2 of our model, using the test data in Section 4:

```
# --- SECTION 4 ---
# Print the model
print('---OLS on diabetes dataset.---')
print('Coefficients:')
print('Intercept (b): %.2f'%ols.intercept_)
for i in range(len(diabetes.feature_names)):
 print(diabetes.feature_names[i]+': %.2f'%ols.coef_[i])
print('-'*30)
print('R-squared: %.2f'%r2, ' MSE: %.2f \n'%err)
```

The code's output is the following:

```
---OLS on diabetes dataset.---
Coefficients:
Intercept (b): 152.73
age: 5.03
sex: -238.41
bmi: 521.63
bp: 299.94
s1: -752.12
s2: 445.15
s3: 83.51
s4: 185.58
s5: 706.47
```

```
s6: 88.68
-----------------------------
R-squared: 0.70 MSE: 1668.75
```

Another form of regression, logistic regression, attempts to model the probability that an instance belongs to one of two classes. Again, it attempts to optimize the *a* and *b* parameters in order to model $p=1/(1+e^{-(ax+b)})$. Once again, using scikit-learn and the breast cancer dataset, we can create and evaluate a simple logistic regression. The following code sections are similar to the preceding ones, but this time we'll use classification accuracy and a confusion matrix rather than R^2 as a metric:

```python
# --- SECTION 1 ---
# Libraries and data loading
from sklearn.linear_model import LogisticRegression
from sklearn.datasets import load_breast_cancer
from sklearn import metrics
bc = load_breast_cancer()

# --- SECTION 2 ---
# Split the data into train and test set
train_x, train_y = bc.data[:400], bc.target[:400]
test_x, test_y = bc.data[400:], bc.target[400:]

# --- SECTION 3 ---
# Instantiate, train and evaluate the model
logit = LogisticRegression()
logit.fit(train_x, train_y)
acc = metrics.accuracy_score(test_y, logit.predict(test_x))

# --- SECTION 4 ---
# Print the model
print('---Logistic Regression on breast cancer dataset.---')
print('Coefficients:')
print('Intercept (b): %.2f'%logit.intercept_)
for i in range(len(bc.feature_names)):
 print(bc.feature_names[i]+': %.2f'%logit.coef_[0][i])
print('-'*30)
print('Accuracy: %.2f \n'%acc)
print(metrics.confusion_matrix(test_y, logit.predict(test_x)))
```

The test classification accuracy achieved with this model is 95%, which is quite good. Furthermore, the confusion matrix that follows here indicates that the model does not try to take advantage of class imbalances. Later in this book, we will learn how to further increase the classification accuracy with the use of ensemble methods. The following table shows the logit model confusion matrix:

n = 169	Predicted: Malignant	Predicted: Benign
Target: Malignant	38	1
Target: Benign	8	122

Support vector machines

Support vector machines or SVMs use a subset of training data, specifically data points near the edge of each class, in order to define a separating hyperplane (in two dimensions, a line). These edge cases are called support vectors. The goal of an SVM is to find the hyperplane that maximizes the margin (distance) between the support vectors (depicted in the following figure). In order to classify nonlinear separable classes, SVMs use the kernel trick to map data in a higher dimensional space, where it can become linearly separable:

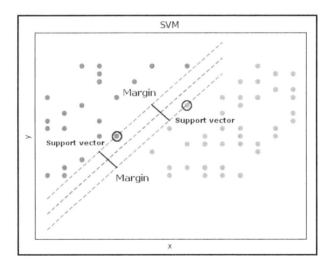

SVM margins and support vectors

 If you want to learn more about the kernel trick, this is a good starting point: https://en.wikipedia.org/wiki/Kernel_method#Mathematics:_the_ kernel_trick.

In scikit-learn, an SVM is implemented under `sklearn.svm`, both for regression with `sklearn.svm.SVR` and classification with `sklearn.svm.SVC`. Once again, we'll test the algorithm's potential using scikit-learn and the code utilized in the regression examples. Using an SVM with a linear kernel on the breast cancer dataset results in 95% accuracy and the following confusion matrix:

n = 169	Predicted: Malignant	Predicted: Benign
Target: Malignant	39	0
Target: Benign	9	121

On the diabetes dataset, by fine-tuning the C parameter to 1,000 during the (`svr = SVR(kernel='linear', C=1e3)`) object instantiation, we are able to achieve an R2 of 0.71 and an MSE of 1622.36, marginally better than the logit model.

Neural networks

Neural networks, inspired by the way biological brains are connected, consist of many neurons, or computational modules, organized in layers. Data is provided at the input layer and predictions are produced at the output layer. All intermediate layers are called hidden layers. Neurons that belong to the same layer are not connected to each other, only to neurons that belong in other layers. Each neuron can have multiple inputs, where each input is multiplied by a specific weight and the sum of multiplied inputs is passed to an activation function that defines the neuron's output. Common activation functions include the following:

Sigmoid	Tanh	ReLU	Linear
$f(z) = \dfrac{1}{1 + e^{-z}}$	$f(z) = \dfrac{e^z - e^{-z}}{e^z + e^{-z}}$	$f(z) = max(0, z)$	$f(z) = z$

The network's goal is to optimize each neuron's weights, such that the cost function is minimized. Neural networks can be either used for regression, where the output layer consists of a single neuron, or classification, where it consists of many neurons, usually equal to the number of classes. There are a number of optimizing algorithms or optimizers available for neural networks. The most common is stochastic gradient descent or SGD. The main idea is that the weights are updated based on the direction and magnitude (first derivative) of the error's gradient, multiplied by a factor called the learning rate.

Variations and extensions have been proposed that take into account the second derivative, adapt the learning rate, or use the momentum of previous weight changes to update the weights.

Although the concept of neural networks has existed for a long time, recently their popularity has greatly increased with the advent of deep learning. Modern architectures consist of convolutional layers, where each layer's weights consist of matrices, and the output is calculated by sliding the weight matrix onto the input. Another type of layers, max pooling layers, calculates the output as the maximum input element again by sliding a fixed-size window onto the input. Recurrent layers retain information about their previous states. Finally, fully connected layers are traditional neurons, as described previously.

Scikit-learn implements traditional neural networks, under the `sklearn.neural_network` package. Once again, using the preceding examples, we'll try to model the diabetes and breast cancer datasets. On the diabetes dataset, we'll use `MLPRegressor` with **Stochastic Gradient Descent (SGD)** as the optimizer, with `mlpr = MLPRegressor(solver='sgd')`. Without any further fine-tuning, we achieve an R^2 of 0.64 and an MSE of 1977. On the breast cancer dataset, using the **Limited-memory Broyden–Fletcher–Goldfarb–Shanno (LBFGS)** optimizer, with `mlpc = MLPClassifier(solver='lbfgs')`, we get a classification accuracy of 93% and a competent confusion matrix. The following table shows the neural network confusion matrix for the breast cancer dataset:

n = 169	Predicted: Malignant	Predicted: Benign
Target: Malignant	35	4
Target: Benign	8	122

A very important note on neural networks: the initial weights of a network are randomly initialized. Thus, the same code can perform differently if it is executed several times. In order to ensure non-random (non-stochastic) execution, the initial random state of the network must be fixed. The two scikit-learn classes implement this feature through the `random_state` parameter in the object constructor. In order to set the random state to a specific seed value, the constructor must be called as follows: `mlpc = MLPClassifier(solver='lbfgs', random_state=12418)`.

Decision trees

Decision trees are less of a black box than other machine learning algorithms. They can easily explain how they produce a prediction, which is called **interpretability**. The main concept is that they produce rules by splitting the training set using the provided features. By iteratively splitting the data, a tree form is produced, thus this is where their name derives from. Let's consider a dataset where the instances are individual persons deciding on their vacations.

The dataset features consist of the person's age and available money, while the target is their preferred destination, one of either **Summer Camp**, **Lake**, or **Bahamas**. A possible decision tree model is depicted in the following figure:

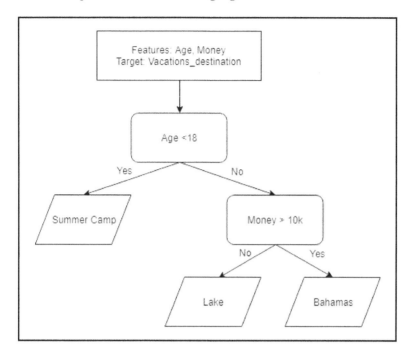

Decision tree model for the vacation destination problem

As is evident, the model can explain how it produces any predictions. The way that the model itself is built is by trying to select the feature and threshold that maximize the information produced. Roughly, this means that the model will try to iteratively split the dataset in a way that separates the greatest number of remaining instances.

Although intuitive to understand, decision trees can produce unreasonable models, with the extreme being the generation of so many rules that, eventually, each rule combination leads to a single instance. In order to avoid such models, we can restrict the model by requiring that it does not exceed a specific depth (maximum number of consecutive rules), or that each node has at least a minimum number of instances before it can be further split.

In scikit-learn, decision trees are implemented under the `sklearn.tree` package, with `DecisionTreeClassifier` and `DecisionTreeRegressor`. In our examples, using `DecisionTreeRegressor` with `dtr = DecisionTreeRegressor(max_depth=2)`, we achieve an R^2 of 0.52 and an MSE of 2655. On the breast cancer dataset, using `dtc = DecisionTreeClassifier(max_depth=2)`, we achieve 89% accuracy and the following confusion matrix:

n = 169	Predicted: Malignant	Predicted: Benign
Target: Malignant	37	2
Target: Benign	17	113

Although not the best-performing algorithm so far, we can clearly see how each individual was classified, by exporting the tree to the `graphviz` format with `export_graphviz(dtc, feature_names=bc.feature_names, class_names=bc.target_names, impurity=False)`:

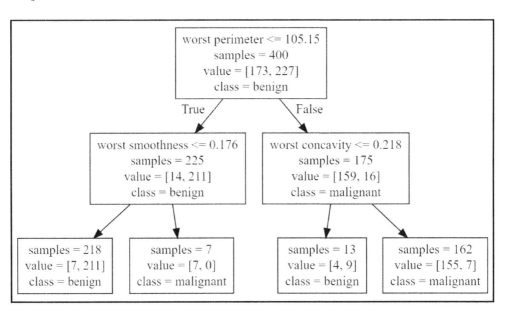

The decision tree generated for the breast cancer dataset

K-Nearest Neighbors

k-Nearest Neighbors (k-NN) is a relatively simple machine learning algorithm. Each instance is classified by comparing it to its K-nearest examples as the majority class. In regression, the average value of neighbors is used. Scikit-learn's implementation lies within the `sklearn.neighbors` package of the library. As it is the naming convention of the library, `KNeighborsClassifier` implements the classification and `KNeighborsRegressor` implements the regression version of the algorithm. Using them in our examples, the regressor generates an R^2 of 0.58 with an MSE of 2342, while the classifier achieves 93% accuracy. The following table shows the k-NN confusion matrix for the breast cancer dataset:

n = 169	Predicted: Malignant	Predicted: Benign
Target: Malignant	37	2
Target: Benign	9	121

K-means

K-means is a clustering algorithm that presents similarities to k-NN. A number of cluster centers are produced, and each instance is assigned to its nearest cluster. After all instances are assigned to a cluster, the centroid of the cluster becomes the new center, until the algorithm converges to a stable solution. In scikit-learn, this algorithm is implemented in `sklearn.cluster.KMeans`. We can try to cluster the first two features of the breast cancer dataset: the mean radius and the texture of the FNA imaging.

First, we load the required data and libraries, while retaining only the first two features of the dataset:

```
# --- SECTION 1 ---
# Libraries and data loading
import numpy as np
import matplotlib.pyplot as plt

from sklearn.datasets import load_breast_cancer
from sklearn.cluster import KMeans
bc = load_breast_cancer()
bc.data=bc.data[:,:2]
```

Then, we fit the cluster on the data. Note that we don't have to split the data into train and test sets:

```
# --- SECTION 2 ---
# Instantiate and train
km = KMeans(n_clusters=3)
km.fit(bc.data)
```

Following that, we create a two-dimensional mesh and cluster every point, in order to plot the cluster areas and boundaries:

```
# --- SECTION 3 ---
# Create a point mesh to plot cluster areas
# Step size of the mesh.
h = .02
# Plot the decision boundary. For that, we will assign a color to each
x_min, x_max = bc.data[:, 0].min() - 1, bc.data[:, 0].max() + 1
y_min, y_max = bc.data[:, 1].min() - 1, bc.data[:, 1].max() + 1
# Create the actual mesh and cluster it
xx, yy = np.meshgrid(np.arange(x_min, x_max, h), np.arange(y_min, y_max,
h))
Z = km.predict(np.c_[xx.ravel(), yy.ravel()])
# Put the result into a color plot
Z = Z.reshape(xx.shape)
plt.figure(1)
plt.clf()
plt.imshow(Z, interpolation='nearest',
 extent=(xx.min(), xx.max(), yy.min(), yy.max()),
 aspect='auto', origin='lower',)
```

Finally, we plot the actual data, color-mapped to its respective clusters:

```
 --- SECTION 4 ---
# Plot the actual data
c = km.predict(bc.data)
r = c == 0
b = c == 1
g = c == 2
plt.scatter(bc.data[r, 0], bc.data[r, 1], label='cluster 1')
plt.scatter(bc.data[b, 0], bc.data[b, 1], label='cluster 2')
plt.scatter(bc.data[g, 0], bc.data[g, 1], label='cluster 3')
plt.title('K-means')
plt.xlim(x_min, x_max)
plt.ylim(y_min, y_max)
plt.xticks(())
plt.yticks(())
plt.xlabel(bc.feature_names[0])
plt.ylabel(bc.feature_names[1])
```

```
` ()
plt.show()
```

The result is a two-dimensional image with color-coded boundaries of each cluster, as well as the instances:

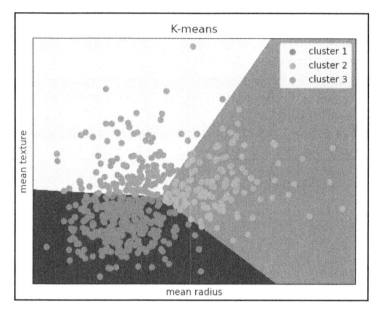

K-means clustering of the first two features of the breast cancer dataset

Summary

In this chapter, we presented the basic datasets, algorithms, and metrics that we will use throughout the book. We talked about regression and classification problems, where datasets have not only features but also targets. We called these labeled datasets. We also talked about unsupervised learning, in the form of clustering and dimensionality reduction. We introduced cost functions and model metrics that we will use to evaluate the models that we generate. Furthermore, we presented the basic learning algorithms and Python libraries that we will utilize in the majority of our examples.

In the next chapter, we will introduce the concepts of bias and variance, as well as the concept of ensemble learning. Some key points to remember are as follows:

- We try to solve a regression problem when the target variable is a continuous number and its values have a meaning in terms of magnitude, such as speed, cost, blood pressure, and so on. Classification problems can have their targets coded as numbers, but we cannot treat them as such. There is no meaning in trying to sort colors or foods based on the number they are assigned during a problem's encoding.
- Cost functions are a way to quantify how far away a predictive model is from modelling data perfectly. Metrics provide information that is easier for humans to understand and report.
- All of the algorithms presented in this chapter have implementations for both classification and regression problems in scikit-learn. Some are better suited to particular tasks, at least without tuning their hyper parameters. Decision trees produce models that are easily interpreted by humans.

Getting Started with Ensemble Learning

2

Ensemble learning involves a combination of techniques that allows multiple machine learning models, called base learners (or, sometimes, weak learners), to consolidate their predictions and output a single, optimal prediction, given their respective inputs and outputs.

In this chapter, we will give an overview of the main problems that ensembles try to solve, namely, bias and variance, as well as the relationship between them. This will help us understand the motivation behind identifying the root cause of an under-performing model and using an ensemble to address it. Furthermore, we will go over the basic categories of the methodologies available, as well as the difficulties we can expect to encounter when implementing ensembles.

The main topics covered in this chapter are the following:

- Bias, variance, and the trade-off between the two
- The motivation behind using ensemble learning
- Identifying the root cause of an under-performing model
- Ensemble learning methods
- Difficulties in applying ensemble learning successfully

Technical requirements

You will require basic knowledge of machine learning techniques and algorithms. Furthermore, a knowledge of python conventions and syntax is required. Finally, familiarity with the NumPy library will greatly help the reader to understand some custom algorithm implementations.

The code files of this chapter can be found on GitHub:

`https://github.com/PacktPublishing/Hands-On-Ensemble-Learning-with-Python/tree/master/Chapter02`

Check out the following video to see the Code in Action: `http://bit.ly/2JKkWYS`.

Bias, variance, and the trade-off

Machine learning models are not perfect; they are prone to a number of errors. The two most common sources of errors are bias and variance. Although two distinct problems, they are interconnected and relate to a model's available degree of freedom or complexity.

What is bias?

Bias refers to the inability of a method to correctly estimate the target. This does not only apply to machine learning. For example, in statistics, if we want to measure a population's average and do not sample carefully, the estimated average will be biased. In simple terms, the method's (sampling) estimation will not closely match the actual target (average).

In machine learning, bias refers to the difference between the expected prediction and its target. Biased models cannot properly fit the training data, resulting in poor in-sample performance and out-of-sample performance. A good example of a biased model arises when we try to fit a sine function with a simple linear regression. The model cannot fit the sine function, as it lacks the required complexity to do so. Thus, it will not be able to perform well in-sample or out-of-sample. This problem is called underfitting. A graphical example is illustrated in the following figure :

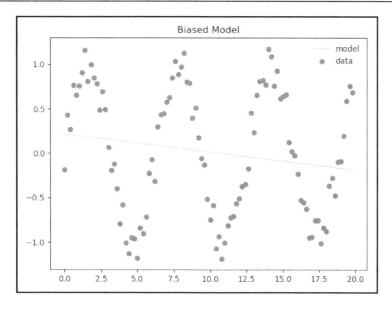

A biased linear regression model for sine function data

The mathematical formula for bias is the difference between the target value and the expected prediction:

$$Bias - E[y] - t$$

What is variance?

Variance refers to how much individuals vary within a group. Again, variance is a concept from statistics. Taking a sample from a population, variance indicates how much each individual's value differs from the mean.

In machine learning, variance refers to the model's variability or sensitivity to data changes. This means that high-variance models can generally fit the training data well and so achieve high in-sample performance, but perform poorly out-of-sample. This is due to the model's complexity. For example, a decision tree can have high variance if it creates a rule for every single instance in the training dataset. This is called **overfitting**. The following figure depicts a decision tree trained on the preceding dataset. Blue dots represent the training data and orange dots represent the test data.

As is evident, the model fits the training data perfectly but does not perform on the test data so well:

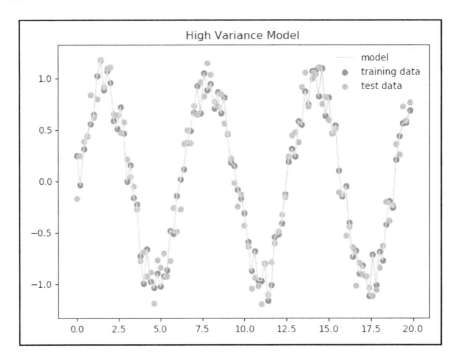

A high-variance decision tree model on the sine function

The mathematical formula for variance is depicted as follows:

$$Variance = E\left[\left(y - E[y]\right)^2\right]$$

Essentially, this is the standard formula for population variance, assuming that our population is comprised of our models, as they have been produced by the machine learning algorithm. For example, as we saw earlier in Chapter 1, *A Machine Learning Refresher*, neural networks can have different training outcomes, depending on their initial weights. If we consider all the neural networks with the same architecture, but different initial weights, by training them, we will have a population of different models.

Trade-off

Bias and variance are two of the three major components that comprise a model's error. The third is called the irreducible error and can be attributed to inherent randomness or variability in the data. The total error of a model can be decomposed as follows:

$$Error = Bias^2 + Variance + Irrecducible\ Error$$

As we saw earlier, bias and variance stem from the same source: model complexity. While bias arises from too little complexity and freedom, variance thrives in complex models. Thus, it is not possible to reduce bias without increasing variance and vice versa. Nevertheless, there is an optimal point of complexity, where the error is minimized as bias and variance are at an optimal trade-off point. When the model's complexity is at this optimal point (the red dotted line in the next figure), then the model performs best both in-sample and out-of-sample. As is evident in the next figure, the error can never be reduced to zero.

Furthermore, although some may think that it is better to reduce the bias, even at the cost of increased variance, it is clear that the model would not perform better, even if it was unbiased, due to the error that variance inevitably induces:

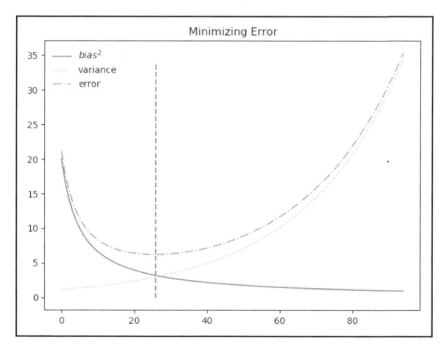

Bias-variance trade-off and its effect on the error

The following figure depicts the perfect model, with a minimum amount of combined bias and variance, or reducible error. Although the model does not fit the data perfectly, this is due to noise that is inherent in the dataset. If we try to fit the training data better, we will induce overfitting (variance). If we try to simplify the model further, we will induce underfitting (bias):

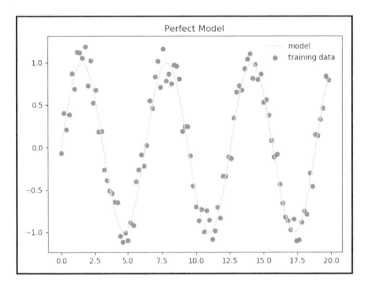

Perfect model for our data, a sine function

Ensemble learning

Ensemble learning involves a collection of machine learning methods aimed at improving the predictive performance of algorithms by combining many models. We will analyze the motivation behind using such methods to solve problems that arise from high bias and variance. Furthermore, we will present methods that allow the identification of bias and variance in machine learning models, as well as basic classes of ensemble learning methods.

Motivation

Ensemble learning aims to solve the problems of bias and variance. By combining many models, we can reduce the ensemble's error, while retaining the individual models' complexities. As we saw earlier, there is a certain lower limit imposed on each model error, which is related to the model complexity.

Furthermore, we mentioned that the same algorithm can produce different models, due to the initial conditions, hyperparameters, and other factors. By combining different, diverse models, we can reduce the expected error of the group, while each individual model remains unchanged. This is due to statistics, rather than pure learning.

In order to better demonstrate this, let's consider an ensemble of 11 base learners for a classification, each with a probability of misclassification (error) equal to *err*=0.15 or 15%. Now, we want to create a simple ensemble. We always assume that the output of most base learners is the correct answer. Assuming that they are diverse (in statistics, uncorrelated), the probability that the majority of them is wrong is 0.26%:

$$\sum_{k=6}^{11} \binom{11}{k} err^k (1 - error)^{25-k} = 0.0026$$

As is evident, the more base learners we add to the ensemble, the more accurate the ensemble will be, under the condition that each learner is uncorrelated to the others. Of course, this is increasingly difficult to achieve. Furthermore, the law of diminishing returns applies. Each new uncorrelated base learner contributes less to the overall error reduction than the previously added base learner. The following figure shows the ensemble error percentage for a number of uncorrelated base learners. As is evident, the greatest reduction is applied when we add two uncorrelated base learners:

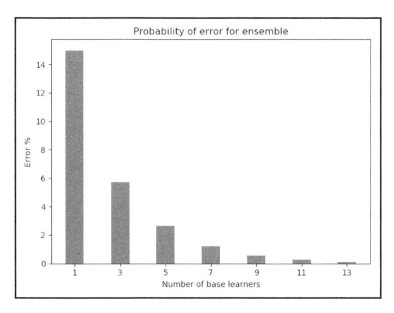

The relation between the number of base learners and the ensemble error

Identifying bias and variance

Although bias and variance have theoretical formulas, it is difficult to calculate their actual values. A simple way to estimate them empirically is with learning and validation curves.

Validation curves

Validation curves refer to an algorithm's achieved performance, given different hyperparameters. For each hyperparameter value, we perform k-fold cross validations and store the in-sample performance and out-of-sample performance. We then calculate and plot the mean and standard deviation of in-sample and out-of-sample performance for each hyperparameter value. By examining the relative and absolute performance, we can gauge the level of bias and variance in our model.

Borrowing the `KNeighborsClassifier` example from Chapter 1, *A Machine Learning Refresher*, we modify it in order to experiment with different neighbor numbers. We start by loading the required libraries and data. Notice that we import `validation_curve` from `sklearn.model_selection`. This is scikit-learn's own implementation of validation curves:

```
# --- SECTION 1 ---
# Libraries and data loading
import numpy as np
import matplotlib.pyplot as plt

from sklearn.datasets import load_breast_cancer
from sklearn.model_selection import validation_curve
from sklearn.neighbors import KNeighborsClassifier
bc = load_breast_cancer()
```

Next, we define our features and targets (x and y), as well as our base learner. Furthermore, we define our parameter search space with `param_range = [2,3,4,5]` and use `validation_curve`. In order to use it, we must define our base learner, our features, targets, the parameter's name that we wish to test, as well as the parameter's values to test. Furthermore, we define the cross-validation's K folds with `cv=10`, as well as the metric that we wish to calculate, with `scoring="accuracy"`:

```
# --- SECTION 2 ---
# Create in-sample and out-of-sample scores
x, y = bc.data, bc.target
learner = KNeighborsClassifier()
param_range = [2,3,4,5]
train_scores, test_scores = validation_curve(learner, x, y,
                                        param_name='n_neighbors',
```

```
                    param_range=param_range,
                    cv=10,
                    scoring="accuracy")
```

Afterward,we calculate the mean and standard deviation for both in-sample performance (`train_scores`) as well as out-of-sample performance (`test_scores`):

```
# --- SECTION 3 ---
# Calculate the average and standard deviation for each hyperparameter
train_scores_mean = np.mean(train_scores, axis=1)
train_scores_std = np.std(train_scores, axis=1)
test_scores_mean = np.mean(test_scores, axis=1)
test_scores_std = np.std(test_scores, axis=1)
```

Finally, we plot the means and deviations. We plot the means as curves, using `plt.plot`. In order to plot the standard deviations, we create a transparent rectangle surrounding the curves, with a width equal to the standard deviation at each hyperparameter value point. This is achieved with the use of `plt.fill_between`, by passing the value points as the first parameter, the lowest rectangle's point as the second parameter, and the highest point as the third. Furthermore, `alpha=0.1` instructs `matplotlib` to make the rectangle transparent (combining the rectangle's color with the background in a 10%-90% ratio, respectively):

Sections 3 and 4 are adapted from the scikit-learn examples found `https:/ /scikit-learn.org/stable/auto_examples/model_selection/plot_ validation_curve.html`.

```
# --- SECTION 4 ---
# Plot the scores
plt.figure()
plt.title('Validation curves')
# Plot the standard deviations
plt.fill_between(param_range, train_scores_mean - train_scores_std,
                 train_scores_mean + train_scores_std, alpha=0.1,
                 color="C1")
plt.fill_between(param_range, test_scores_mean - test_scores_std,
                 test_scores_mean + test_scores_std, alpha=0.1, color="C0")

# Plot the means
plt.plot(param_range, train_scores_mean, 'o-', color="C1",
         label="Training score")
plt.plot(param_range, test_scores_mean, 'o-', color="C0",
         label="Cross-validation score")
plt.xticks(param_range)
plt.xlabel('Number of neighbors')
```

```
plt.ylabel('Accuracy')
plt.legend(loc="best")
plt.show()
```

The script finally outputs the following. As the curves close the distance between them, the variance generally reduces. The further away they both are from the desired accuracy (taking into account the irreducible error), the bias increases.

Furthermore, the relative standard deviations are also an indicator of variance:

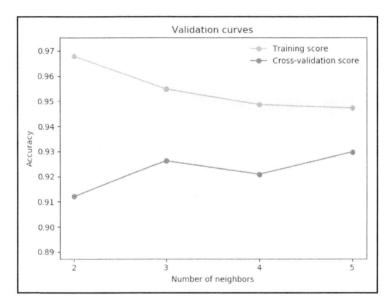

Validation curves for K-Nearest-Neighbors, 2 to 5 neighbor

The following table presents the bias and variance identification based on validation curves:

	Great	**Small**
Distance between curves	High Variance	Low Variance
Distance from desired accuracy	High Bias	Low Bias
Relative rectangle area ratio	High Variance	Low Variance

Bias and variance identification based on validation curves

Learning curves

Another way to identify bias and variance is to generate learning curves. Like validation curves, we generate a number of in-sample and out-of-sample performance statistics with cross-validation. Instead of experimenting with different hyperparameter values, we utilize different amounts of training data. Again, by examining the means and standard deviations of in-sample and out-of-sample performance, we can get an idea about the amount of bias and variance inherent in our models.

Scikit-learn implements learning curves in the `sklearn.model_selection` module as `learning_curve`. Once again, we will use the `KNeighborsClassifier` example from `Chapter 1`, *A Machine Learning Refresher.* First, we import the required libraries and load the breast cancer dataset:

```
# --- SECTION 1 ---
# Libraries and data loading
import numpy as np
import matplotlib.pyplot as plt

from sklearn.datasets import load_breast_cancer
from sklearn.neighbors import KNeighborsClassifier
from sklearn.model_selection import learning_curve
bc = load_breast_cancer()
```

Following that, we define the amount of training instances that will be used at each cross-validation set with `train_sizes = [50, 100, 150, 200, 250, 300]`, instantiate the base learner, and call `learning_curve`. The function returns a tuple of the train set sizes, the in-sample performance scores, and out-of-sample performance scores. The function accepts the base learner, the dataset features and targets, and the train set sizes as parameters in a list with `train_sizes=train_sizes` and the number of cross-validation folds with `cv=10`:

```
# --- SECTION 2 ---
# Create in-sample and out-of-sample scores
x, y = bc.data, bc.target
learner = KNeighborsClassifier()
train_sizes = [50, 100, 150, 200, 250, 300]
train_sizes, train_scores, test_scores = learning_curve(learner, x,
y,  train_sizes=train_sizes, cv=10)
```

Again, we calculate the mean and standard deviation of in-sample and out-of-sample performance:

```
# --- SECTION 3 ---
# Calculate the average and standard deviation for each hyperparameter
train_scores_mean = np.mean(train_scores, axis=1)
train_scores_std = np.std(train_scores, axis=1)
test_scores_mean = np.mean(test_scores, axis=1)
test_scores_std = np.std(test_scores, axis=1)
```

Finally, we plot the means and standard deviations as curves and rectangles, as we did before:

```
# --- SECTION 4 ---
# Plot the scores
plt.figure()
plt.title('Learning curves')
# Plot the standard deviations
plt.fill_between(train_sizes, train_scores_mean - train_scores_std,
 train_scores_mean + train_scores_std, alpha=0.1,
 color="C1")
plt.fill_between(train_sizes, test_scores_mean - test_scores_std,
 test_scores_mean + test_scores_std, alpha=0.1, color="C0")

# Plot the means
plt.plot(train_sizes, train_scores_mean, 'o-', color="C1",
 label="Training score")
plt.plot(train_sizes, test_scores_mean, 'o-', color="C0",
 label="Cross-validation score")

plt.xticks(train_sizes)
plt.xlabel('Size of training set (instances)')
plt.ylabel('Accuracy')
plt.legend(loc="best")
plt.show()
```

The final output is depicted as follows. The model seems to reduce its variance for the first 200 training samples. After that, it seems that the means diverge, as well as the standard deviation of the cross-validation score increasing, thus indicating an increase in variance.

Note that, although both curves have above 90% accuracy for training sets with at least 150 instances, this does not imply low bias. Datasets that are highly separable (good quality data with low noise) tend to produce such curves—no matter what combination of algorithms and hyperparameters we choose. Moreover, noisy datasets (for example, instances with the same features that have different targets) will not be able to produce high accuracy models—no matter what techniques we use.

Thus, bias must be measured by comparing the learning and validation curves to a desired accuracy (one that is considered achievable, given the dataset quality), rather than its absolute value:

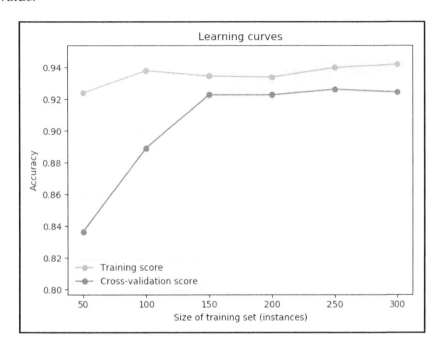

Learning curves for K-Nearest-Neighbors. 50 to 300 training instances

Ensemble methods

Ensemble methods are divided into two major classes or taxonomies: generative and non-generative methods. Non-generative methods are focused on combining the predictions of a set of pretrained models. These models are usually trained independently of one another, and the ensemble algorithm dictates how their predictions will be combined. Base classifiers are not affected by the fact that they exist in an ensemble.

In this book, we will cover two main non-generative methods: voting and stacking. Voting, as the name implies(see Chapter 3, *Voting*), refers to techniques that allow models to vote in order to produce a single answer, similar to how individuals vote in national elections. The most popular (most voted for) answer is selected as the winner. Chapter 4, *Stacking*, on the other hand, refers to methods that utilize a model (the meta-learner) that learns how to best combine the base learner's predictions. Although stacking entails the generation of a new model, it does not affect the base learners, thus it is a non-generative method.

Generative methods, on the other hand, are able to generate and affect the base learners that they use. They can either tune their learning algorithm or the dataset used to train them, in order to ensure diversity and high model performance. Furthermore, some algorithms can induce randomness in models, in order to further enforce diversity.

The main generative methods that we will cover in this book are bagging, boosting, and random forests. Boosting is a technique mainly targeting biased models. Its main idea is to sequentially generate models, such that each new model addresses biases inherent in the previous models. Thus, by iteratively correcting previous errors, the final ensemble has a significantly lower bias. Bagging aims to reduce variance. The bagging algorithm resamples instances of the training dataset, creating many individual and diverse datasets, originating from the same dataset. Afterward, a separate model is trained on each sampled dataset, forcing diversity between the ensemble models. Finally, Random Forests, is similar to bagging, in that it resamples from the training dataset. Instead of sampling instances, it samples features, thus creating even more diverse trees, as features strongly correlated to the target may be absent in many trees.

Difficulties in ensemble learning

Although ensemble learning can greatly increase the performance of machine learning models, it comes at a cost. There are difficulties and drawbacks in correctly implementing it. Some of these difficulties and drawbacks will now be discussed.

Weak or noisy data

The most important ingredient of a successful model is the dataset. If the data contains noise or incomplete information, there is not a single machine learning technique that will generate a highly performant model.

Let's illustrate this with a simple example. Suppose we study populations (in the statistical sense) of cars and we gather data about the color, shape, and manufacturer. It is difficult to generate a very accurate model for either variable, as a lot of cars are the same color and shape but are made by a different manufacturer. The following table depicts this sample dataset.

The best any model can do is achieve 33% classification accuracy, as there are three viable choices for any given feature combination. Adding more features to the dataset can greatly improve the model's performance. Adding more models to an ensemble cannot improve performance:

Color	Shape	Manufacturer
Black	Sedan	BMW
Black	Sedan	Audi
Black	Sedan	Alfa Romeo
Blue	Hatchback	Ford
Blue	Hatchback	Opel
Blue	Hatchback	Fiat

Car dataset

Understanding interpretability

By employing a large number of models, interpretability is greatly reduced. For example, a single decision tree can easily explain how it produced a prediction, by simply following the decisions made at each node. On the other hand, it is difficult to interpret why an ensemble of 1,000 trees predicted a single value. Moreover, depending on the ensemble method, there may be more to explain than the prediction process itself. How and why did the ensemble choose to train these specific models. Why did it not choose to train other models? Why did it not choose to train more models?

When the model's results are to be presented to an audience, especially a not-so-highly-technical audience, simpler but more easily explainable models may be a better solution.

Furthermore, when the prediction must also include a probability (or confidence level), some ensemble methods (such as boosting) tend to deliver poor probability estimates:

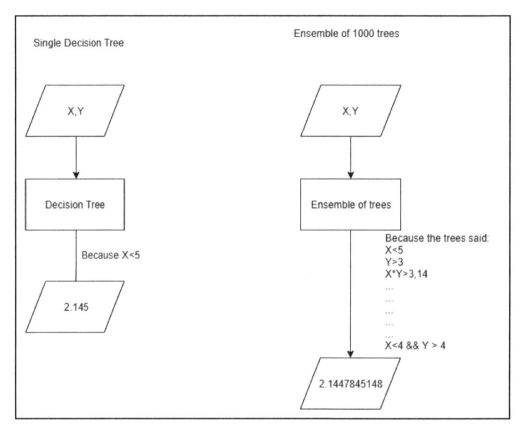

Interpretability of a single tree versus a 1000

Computational cost

Another drawback of ensembles is the computational cost they impose. Training a single neural network is computationally expensive. Training a 1000 of them requires a 1000 times more computational resources. Furthermore, some methods are sequential by nature. This means that it is not possible to harness the power of distributed computing. Instead, each new model must be trained when the previous model is completed. This imposes time penalties on the model's development process, on top of the increased computational cost.

Computational costs do not only hinder the development process; when the ensemble is put into production, the inference time will suffer as well. If the ensemble consists of 1,000 models, then all of those models must be fed with new data, produce predictions, and then those predictions must be combined in order to produce the ensemble output. In latency-sensitive settings (financial exchanges, real-time systems, and so on), sub-millisecond execution times are expected, thus a few microseconds of added latency can make a huge difference.

Choosing the right models

Finally, the models that comprise the ensemble must possess certain characteristics. There is no point in creating any ensemble from a number of identical models. Generative methods may produce their own models, but the algorithm used as well as its initial hyperparameters are usually selected by the analyst. Furthermore, the model's achievable diversity depends on a number of factors, such as the size and quality of the dataset, and the learning algorithm itself.

A single model that is similar in behavior to the data-generating process will usually outperform any ensemble, both in terms of accuracy as well as latency. In our bias-variance example, the simple sine function will always outperform any ensemble, as the data is generated from the same function with some added noise. An ensemble of many linear regressions may be able to approximate the sine function, but it will always require more time to train and execute. Furthermore, it will not be able to generalize (predict out-of-sample) as well as the sine function.

Summary

In this chapter, we presented the concepts of bias and variance, as well as the trade-off between them. They are essential in understanding how and why a model may under-perform, either in-sample or out-of-sample. We then introduced the concept and motivation of ensemble learning, how to identify bias and variance in models, as well as basic categories of ensemble learning methods. We presented ways to measure and plot bias and variance, using scikit-learn and matplotlib. Finally, we talked about the difficulties and drawbacks of implementing ensemble learning methods. Some key points to remember are the following.

High-bias models usually have difficulty performing well in-sample. This is also called **underfitting**. It is due to the model's simplicity (or lack of complexity). High-variance models usually have difficulty generalizing or performing well out-of-sample, while they perform reasonably well in-sample. This is called **overfitting**. It is usually due to the model's unnecessary complexity. The **bias-variance trade-off** refers to the fact that as the model's complexity increases, its bias decreases, while its variance increases. Ensemble learning aims to address high bias or variance, by combining the predictions of many diverse models. These models are usually called **base-learners**. For model selection, **validation curves** indicate how a model performs in-sample and out-of-sample for a given set of hyperparameters. **Learning curves** are the same as validation curves but instead of a set of hyperparameters, they use different train set sizes. Substantial distance between the train and test curves indicates high variance. A big rectangle area around the test curve also indicates high variance. A substantial distance between both curves from the target accuracy indicates high bias. Generative methods have control over the generation and training of their base learners; non-generative methods do not. Ensemble learning can have a negligible or negative impact on performance when data is poor or models are correlated. It can impact negatively on the interpretability of models and the computational resources required.

In the next chapter, we will present the Voting ensemble, as well as how to use it for both regression and classification problems.

2
Section 2: Non-Generative Methods

In this section, we will cover the simplest methods of ensemble learning.

This section comprises the following chapters:

- Chapter 3, *Voting*
- Chapter 4, *Stacking*

3
Voting

The most intuitive of all ensemble learning methods is **majority voting**. It is intuitive, as the aim is to output the most popular (or most voted for) of the base learner's predictions. This chapter covers the basic theory as well as practical implementations concerning majority voting. By the end of this chapter, you will be able to do the following:

- Understand majority voting
- Understand the difference between hard and soft majority voting and their respective strengths and weaknesses
- Implement both versions in Python
- Utilize the voting technique to improve the performance of classifiers on the breast cancer dataset

Technical requirements

You will require basic knowledge of machine learning techniques and algorithms. Furthermore, a knowledge of python conventions and syntax is required. Finally, familiarity with the NumPy library will greatly help the reader to understand some custom algorithm implementations.

The code files of this chapter can be found on GitHub:

https://github.com/PacktPublishing/Hands-On-Ensemble-Learning-with-Python/tree/master/Chapter03

Check out the following video to see the Code in Action: http://bit.ly/2M52VY7.

Hard and soft voting

Majority voting is the simplest ensemble learning technique that allows the combination of multiple base learner's predictions. Similar to how elections work, the algorithm assumes that each base learner is a voter and each class is a contender. The algorithm takes votes into consideration in order to elect a contender as the winner. There are two main approaches to combining multiple predictions with voting: one is hard voting and the other is soft voting. We present both approaches here.

Hard voting

Hard voting combines a number of predictions by assuming that the most voted class is the winner. In a simple case of two classes and three base learners, if a target class has at least two votes, it becomes the ensemble's output, as shown in the following diagram. Implementing a hard voting classifier is as simple as counting the votes for each target class:

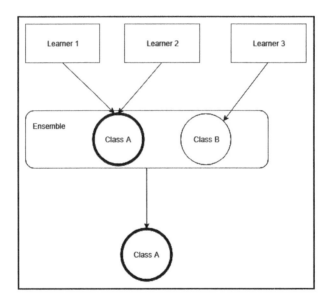

Voting with two classes and three base learners

For example, let's say that there are three different base learners, who are predicting whether a sample belongs to one of three classes with a certain probability (*Table 1*).

In the following table, each learner predicts the probability that the instance belongs to a certain class:

	Class A	Class B	Class C
Learner 1	0.5	0.3	0.2
Learner 2	0	0.48	0.52
Learner 3	0.4	0.3	0.3

Assigned class probabilities

In this example, class A has two votes, while class C has only one. According to hard voting, class A will be the prediction of the ensemble. It's a fairly robust method of combining many base learners, although it doesn't take into account that some classes may be chosen by a base learner only because they are marginally better than the others.

Soft voting

Soft voting takes into account the probability of the predicted classes. In order to combine the predictions, soft voting calculates the average probability of each class and assumes that the winner is the class with the highest average probability.In the simple case of three base learners and two classes, we must take into consideration the predicted probability for each class and average them across the three learners:

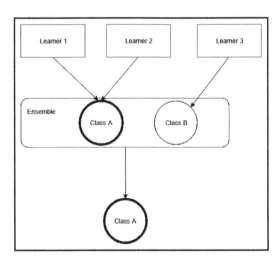

Soft voting with two classes and three base learners

Using our previous example, and by taking the average of each column for *Table 1*, we can expand it, adding a row for the average probability.

The following table shows the predicted probabilities for each class by each learner, as well as the average probability:

	Class A	Class B	Class C
Learner 1	0.5	0.3	0.2
Learner 2	0	0.48	0.52
Learner 3	0.4	0.3	0.3
Average	0.3	0.36	0.34

Predicted probabilities for each class by each learner, as well as the average probability

As we can see, class A has an average probability of 0.3, class B has an average probability of 0.36, and class C has an average probability of 0.34, making class B the winner. Note that class B is not selected by any base learner as the predicted class, but by combining the predicted probabilities, class B arises as the best compromise between the predictions.

In order for soft voting to be more effective than hard voting, the base classifiers must produce good estimates regarding the probability that a sample belongs to a specific class. If the probabilities are meaningless (for example, if they are always 100% for one class and 0% for all others), soft voting could be even worse than hard voting.

A note on voting: it is impossible to have a perfect voting system, as has been proved by Dr. Kenneth Arrow with his impossibility theorem. Nonetheless, certain types of voting systems can better reflect the preferences of a population. Soft voting better reflects the individual learner's preferences, as it takes into account the rating (probabilities) instead of the ranking (predicted class).

For more on the impossibility theorem, see A difficulty in the concept of social welfare. *Arrow, K.J., 1950. Journal of political economy*, 58(4), pp.328-346.

Python implementation

The simplest way to implement hard voting in Python is to use scikit-learn to create base learners, train them on some data, and combine their predictions on test data. In order to do so, we will go through the following steps:

1. Load the data and split it into train and test sets
2. Create some base learners
3. Train them on the train data
4. Produce predictions for the test data
5. Combine predictions using hard voting
6. Compare the individual learner's predictions as well as the combined predictions with the ground truth (actual correct classes)

Although scikit-learn has implementations for voting, by creating a custom implementation, it will be easier to understand how the algorithm works. Furthermore, it will enable us to better understand how to process and analyze a base learner's outputs.

Custom hard voting implementation

In order to implement a custom hard voting solution, we will use three base learners: a **Perceptron** (a neural network with a single neuron), a **Support Vector Machine** (**SVM**), and a **Nearest Neighbor**. These are contained in the sklearn.linear_model, sklearn.svm, and sklearn.neighbors packages. Furthermore, we will use the argmax function from NumPy. This function returns the index of an array's (or array-like data structure) element with the highest value. Finally, accuracy_score will calculate the accuracy of each classifier on our test data:

```
# --- SECTION 1 ---
# Import the required libraries
from sklearn import datasets, linear_model, svm, neighbors
from sklearn.metrics import accuracy_score
from numpy import argmax
# Load the dataset
breast_cancer = datasets.load_breast_cancer()
x, y = breast_cancer.data, breast_cancer.target
```

We then instantiate our base learners. We hand-picked their hyperparameters to ensure that they are diverse in order to produce a well-performing ensemble. As `breast_cancer` is a classification dataset, we use `SVC`, the classification version of SVM, along with `KNeighborsClassifier` and `Perceptron`. Furthermore, we set the random state of `Perceptron` to 0 in order to ensure the reproducibility of our example:

```
# --- SECTION 2 ---
# Instantiate the learners (classifiers)
learner_1 = neighbors.KNeighborsClassifier(n_neighbors=5)
learner_2 = linear_model.Perceptron(tol=1e-2, random_state=0)
learner_3 = svm.SVC(gamma=0.001)
```

We split the data into train and test sets, using 100 instances for our test set and train our base learners on the train set:

```
# --- SECTION 3 ---
# Split the train and test samples
test_samples = 100
x_train, y_train = x[:-test_samples], y[:-test_samples]
x_test, y_test = x[-test_samples:], y[-test_samples:]

# Fit learners with the train data
learner_1.fit(x_train, y_train)
learner_2.fit(x_train, y_train)
learner_3.fit(x_train, y_train)
```

By storing each base learner's prediction in `predictions_1`, `predictions_2`, and `predictions_3`, we can further analyze and combine them into our ensemble. Note that we trained each classifier individually; additionally, as well as that each classifier produces predictions for the test data autonomously. As mentioned in `Chapter 2`, *Getting Started with Ensemble Learning*, this is the main characteristic of non-generative ensemble methods:

```
#--- SECTION 4 ---
# Each learner predicts the classes of the test data
predictions_1 = learner_1.predict(x_test)
predictions_2 = learner_2.predict(x_test)
predictions_3 = learner_3.predict(x_test)
```

Following the predictions, we combine the predictions of each base learner for each test instance. The `hard_predictions` list will contain the ensemble's predictions (output). By iterating over every test sample with `for i in range(test_samples)`, we count the total number of votes that each class has received from the three base learners. As the dataset contains only two classes, we need a list of two elements: `counts = [0 for _ in range(2)]`. In `# --- SECTION 3 ---`, we stored each base learner's predictions in an array. Each one of those array's elements contains the index of the instance's predicted class (in our case, 0 and 1). Thus, we increase the corresponding element's value in `counts[predictions_1[i]]` by one to count the base learner's vote. Then, `argmax(counts)` returns the element (class) with the highest number of votes:

```
# --- SECTION 5 ---
# We combine the predictions with hard voting
hard_predictions = []
# For each predicted sample
for i in range(test_samples):
    # Count the votes for each class
    counts = [0 for _ in range(2)]
    counts[predictions_1[i]] = counts[predictions_1[i]]+1
    counts[predictions_2[i]] = counts[predictions_2[i]]+1
    counts[predictions_3[i]] = counts[predictions_3[i]]+1
    # Find the class with most votes
    final = argmax(counts)
    # Add the class to the final predictions
    hard_predictions.append(final)
```

Finally, we calculate the accuracy of the individual base learners as well as the ensemble with `accuracy_score`, and print them on screen:

```
# --- SECTION 6 ---
# Accuracies of base learners
print('L1:', accuracy_score(y_test, predictions_1))
print('L2:', accuracy_score(y_test, predictions_2))
print('L3:', accuracy_score(y_test, predictions_3))
# Accuracy of hard voting
print('-'*30)
print('Hard Voting:', accuracy_score(y_test, hard_predictions))
```

The final output is as follows:

```
L1: 0.94
L2: 0.93
L3: 0.88
----------------------------
Hard Voting: 0.95
```

Analyzing our results using Python

The final accuracy achieved is 1% better than the best of the three classifiers (the **k-Nearest Neighbors** (**k-NN**) classifier). We can visualize the learner's errors in order to examine why the ensemble performs in this specific way.

First, we import `matplotlib` and use a specific `seaborn-paper` plotting style with `mpl.style.use('seaborn-paper')`:

```
# --- SECTION 1 ---
# Import the required libraries
import matplotlib as mpl
import matplotlib.pyplot as plt
mpl.style.use('seaborn-paper')
```

Then, we calculate the errors by subtracting our prediction from the actual target. Thus, we get a -1 each time the learner predicts a positive (1) when the true class is negative (0), and a 1 when it predicts a negative (0) while the true class is positive (1). If the prediction is correct, we get a zero (0):

```
# --- SECTION 2 ---
# Calculate the errors
errors_1 = y_test-predictions_1
errors_2 = y_test-predictions_2
errors_3 = y_test-predictions_3
```

For each base learner, we plot the instances where they have predicted the wrong class. Our aim is to scatter plot the x and y lists. These lists will contain the instance number (the x list) and the type of error (the y list). With `plt.scatter`, we can specify the coordinates of our points using the aforementioned lists, as well as specify how these points are depicted. This is important in order to ensure that we can simultaneously visualize all the errors of the classifiers as well as the relationship between them.

The default shape for each point is a circle. By specifying the `marker` parameter, we can alter this shape. Furthermore, with the `s` parameter, we can specify the marker's size. Thus, the first learner (k-NN) will have a round shape of size 120, the second learner (Perceptron) will have an x shape of size 60, and the third learner (SVM) will have a round shape of size 20. The `if not errors_*[i] == 0` guard ensures that we will not store correctly classified instances:

```
# --- SECTION 3 ---
# Discard correct predictions and plot each learner's errors
x=[]
y=[]
for i in range(len(errors_1)):
    if not errors_1[i] == 0:
        x.append(i)
        y.append(errors_1[i])
plt.scatter(x, y, s=120, label='Learner 1 Errors')

x=[]
y=[]
for i in range(len(errors_2)):
    if not errors_2[i] == 0:
        x.append(i)
        y.append(errors_2[i])
plt.scatter(x, y, marker='x', s=60, label='Learner 2 Errors')

x=[]
y=[]
for i in range(len(errors_3)):
    if not errors_3[i] == 0:
        x.append(i)
        y.append(errors_3[i])
plt.scatter(x, y, s=20, label='Learner 3 Errors')
```

Finally, we specify the figure's title and labels, and plot the legend:

```
plt.title('Learner errors')
plt.xlabel('Test sample')
plt.ylabel('Error')
plt.legend()
plt.show()
```

As the following shows, there are five samples where at least two learners predict the wrong class. These are the 5 cases out of the 100 that the ensemble predicts wrong, as the most voted class is wrong, thus producing a 95% accuracy. In all other cases, two out of three learners predict the correct class, thus the ensemble predicts the correct class as it is the most voted:

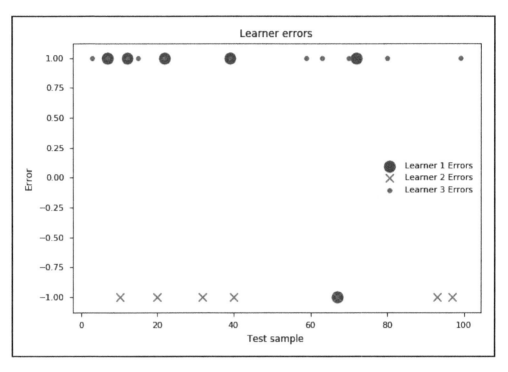

Learner errors on the test set

Using scikit-learn

The scikit-learn library includes many ensemble learning algorithms, including voting. In order to implement hard voting, we will follow the same procedure as we did previously, except this time, we will not implement the individual fitting, predicting, and voting ourselves. Instead, we will use the provided implementation, which enables quick and easy training and testing.

Hard voting implementation

Similarly to our custom implementation, we import the required libraries, split our train and test data, and instantiate our base learners. Furthermore, we import scikit-learn's `VotingClassifier` voting implementation from the `sklearn.ensemble` package, as follows:

```
# --- SECTION 1 ---
# Import the required libraries
from sklearn import datasets, linear_model, svm, neighbors
from sklearn.ensemble import VotingClassifier
from sklearn.metrics import accuracy_score
# Load the dataset
breast_cancer = datasets.load_breast_cancer()
x, y = breast_cancer.data, breast_cancer.target

# Split the train and test samples
test_samples = 100
x_train, y_train = x[:-test_samples], y[:-test_samples]
x_test, y_test = x[-test_samples:], y[-test_samples:]

# --- SECTION 2 ---
# Instantiate the learners (classifiers)
learner_1 = neighbors.KNeighborsClassifier(n_neighbors=5)
learner_2 = linear_model.Perceptron(tol=1e-2, random_state=0)
learner_3 = svm.SVC(gamma=0.001)
```

Following the above code, we instantiate the `VotingClassifier` class, passing as a parameter a list of tuples with the names and objects of our base classifiers. Note that passing the parameters outside of a list will result in an error:

```
# --- SECTION 3 ---
# Instantiate the voting classifier
voting = VotingClassifier([('KNN', learner_1),
                           ('Prc', learner_2),
                           ('SVM', learner_3)])
```

Now, having instantiated the classifier, we can use it in the same way as any other classifier, without having to tend to each base learner individually. The following two sections execute the fitting and prediction for all base learners as well as the calculation of the most voted class for each test instance:

```
# --- SECTION 4 ---
# Fit classifier with the training data
voting.fit(x_train, y_train)

# --- SECTION 5 ---
# Predict the most voted class
hard_predictions = voting.predict(x_test)
```

Finally, we can print the accuracy of the ensemble:

```
# --- SECTION 6 ---
# Accuracy of hard voting
print('-'*30)
print('Hard Voting:', accuracy_score(y_test, hard_predictions))
```

This is the same as our custom implementation:

```
------------------------------
Hard Voting: 0.95
```

Note that `VotingClassifier` will not fit the objects that you pass as parameters, but will, instead, clone them and fit the cloned objects. Thus, if you try to print the accuracy of each individual base learner on the test set, you will get `NotFittedError`, as the objects that you have access to are, in fact, not fitted. This is the only drawback of using scikit-learn's implementation over a custom one.

Soft voting implementation

Scikit-learn's implementation allows for soft voting as well. The only requirement is that the base learners implement the `predict_proba` function. In our example, `Perceptron` does not implement the function at all, while `SVC` only produces probabilities when it is passed the `probability=True` argument. Having these limitations in mind, we swap our `Perceptron` with a Naive Bayes classifier implemented in the `sklearn.naive_bayes` package.

To actually use soft voting, the `VotingClassifier` object must be initialized with the `voting='soft'` argument. Except for the changes mentioned here, the majority of the code remains the same. Load the libraries and datasets, and produce a train/test split as follows:

```
# --- SECTION 1 ---
# Import the required libraries
from sklearn import datasets, naive_bayes, svm, neighbors
from sklearn.ensemble import VotingClassifier
from sklearn.metrics import accuracy_score
# Load the dataset
breast_cancer = datasets.load_breast_cancer()
x, y = breast_cancer.data, breast_cancer.target

# Split the train and test samples
test_samples = 100
x_train, y_train = x[:-test_samples], y[:-test_samples]
x_test, y_test = x[-test_samples:], y[-test_samples:]
```

Instantiate the base learners and voting classifier. We use a Gaussian Naive Bayes implemented as `GaussianNB`. Note that we use `probability=True` in order for the `GaussianNB` object to be able to produce probabilities:

```
# --- SECTION 2 ---
# Instantiate the learners (classifiers)
learner_1 = neighbors.KNeighborsClassifier(n_neighbors=5)
learner_2 = naive_bayes.GaussianNB()
learner_3 = svm.SVC(gamma=0.001, probability=True)

# --- SECTION 3 ---
# Instantiate the voting classifier
voting = VotingClassifier([('KNN', learner_1),
                           ('NB', learner_2),
                           ('SVM', learner_3)],
                           voting='soft')
```

We fit both `VotingClassifier` and the individual learners. We want to analyze our results, and, as mentioned earlier, the classifier will not fit the objects that we pass as arguments, but will instead clone them. Thus, we have to manually fit our learners as follows:

```
# --- SECTION 4 ---
# Fit classifier with the training data
voting.fit(x_train, y_train)
learner_1.fit(x_train, y_train)
learner_2.fit(x_train, y_train)
learner_3.fit(x_train, y_train)
```

We predict the test set's targets using both the voting ensemble and the individual learners:

```
# --- SECTION 5 ---
# Predict the most probable class
hard_predictions = voting.predict(x_test)

# --- SECTION 6 ---
# Get the base learner predictions
predictions_1 = learner_1.predict(x_test)
predictions_2 = learner_2.predict(x_test)
predictions_3 = learner_3.predict(x_test)
```

Finally, we print the accuracy of each base learner and the soft voting ensemble's accuracy:

```
# --- SECTION 7 ---
# Accuracies of base learners
print('L1:', accuracy_score(y_test, predictions_1))
print('L2:', accuracy_score(y_test, predictions_2))
print('L3:', accuracy_score(y_test, predictions_3))
# Accuracy of hard voting
print('-'*30)
print('Hard Voting:', accuracy_score(y_test, hard_predictions))
```

The final output is as follows:

```
L1: 0.94
L2: 0.96
L3: 0.88
------------------------------
Hard Voting: 0.94
```

Analyzing our results

As is evident, the accuracy achieved by soft voting is 2% worse than the best learner and on par with the second-best learner. We would like to analyze our results similarly to how we analyzed the performance of our hard voting custom implementation. But as soft voting takes into account the predicted class probabilities, we cannot use the same approach. Instead, we will plot the predicted probability for each instance to be classified as positive by each base learner as well as the average probability of the ensemble.

Again, we `import matplotlib` and set the plotting style:

```
# --- SECTION 1 ---
# Import the required libraries
import matplotlib as mpl
import matplotlib.pyplot as plt
mpl.style.use('seaborn-paper')
```

We calculate the ensemble's errors with `errors = y_test-hard_predictions` and get the predicted probabilities of each base learner with the `predict_proba(x_test)` function. All base learners implement this function, as it is a requirement for utilizing them in a soft voting ensemble:

```
# --- SECTION 2 ---
# Get the wrongly predicted instances
# and the predicted probabilities for the whole test set
errors = y_test-hard_predictions

probabilities_1 = learner_1.predict_proba(x_test)
probabilities_2 = learner_2.predict_proba(x_test)
probabilities_3 = learner_3.predict_proba(x_test)
```

Following this, for each wrongly classified instance, we store the predicted probability that the instance belongs to in class 0. We also implement this for each base learner, as well as their average. Each `probabilities_*` array, is a two-dimensional array. Each row contains the predicted probability that the corresponding instance belongs to class 0 or class 1. Thus, storing one of the two is sufficient. In the case of a dataset with N classes, we would have to store at least N-1 probabilities in order to get a clear picture:

```
# --- SECTION 2 ---
# Store the predicted probability for
# each wrongly predicted instance, for each base learner
# as well as the average predicted probability
#
x=[]
y_1=[]
y_2=[]
```

```
y_3=[]
y_avg=[]

for i in range(len(errors)):
    if not errors[i] == 0:
        x.append(i)
        y_1.append(probabilities_1[i][0])
        y_2.append(probabilities_2[i][0])
        y_3.append(probabilities_3[i][0])
        y_avg.append((probabilities_1[i][0]+
                    probabilities_2[i][0]+probabilities_3[i][0])/3)
```

Finally, we plot the probabilities as bars of different widths with `plt.bar`. This ensures that any overlapping bars will still be visible. The third `plt.bar` argument dictates the bar's width. We scatter plot the average probability as a black 'X' and ensure that it will be plotted over any bar with `zorder=10`. Finally, we plot a threshold line at 0.5 probability with `plt.plot(y, c='k', linestyle='--')`, ensuring that it will be a black dotted line with `c='k', linestyle='--'`. If the average probability is above the line, the sample is classified as positive, as follows:

```
# --- SECTION 3 ---
# Plot the predicted probaiblity of each base learner as
# a bar and the average probability as an X
plt.bar(x, y_1, 3, label='KNN')
plt.bar(x, y_2, 2, label='NB')
plt.bar(x, y_3, 1, label='SVM')
plt.scatter(x, y_avg, marker='x', c='k', s=150,
            label='Average Positive', zorder=10)

y = [0.5 for x in range(len(errors))]
plt.plot(y, c='k', linestyle='--')

plt.title('Positive Probability')
plt.xlabel('Test sample')
plt.ylabel('probability')
plt.legend()
plt.show()
```

The preceding code outputs the following:

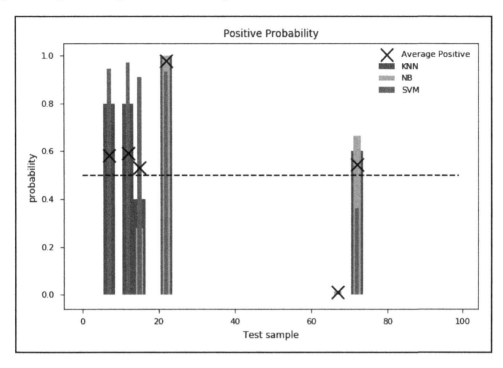

Predicted and average probabilities for the test set

As we can see, only two samples have an extreme average probability (sample 22 with p = 0.98 and 67 with p = 0.001). The other four are quite close to 50%. For three out of these four samples, SVM seems to assign a very high probability to the wrong class, thus greatly affecting the average probability. If SVM did not overestimate the probability of these samples as much, the ensemble could well out perform each individual learner. For the two extreme cases, nothing can be done, as all three learners agree on the miss classification. We can try to swap our SVM for another k-NN with a significantly higher number of neighbors. In this case, (`learner_3 = neighbors.KNeighborsClassifier(n_neighbors=50)`), we can see that the ensemble's accuracy is greatly increased. The ensemble's accuracies and errors are as follows:

```
L1: 0.94
L2: 0.96
L3: 0.95
-------------------------------
Hard Voting: 0.97
```

Take a look at the following screenshot:

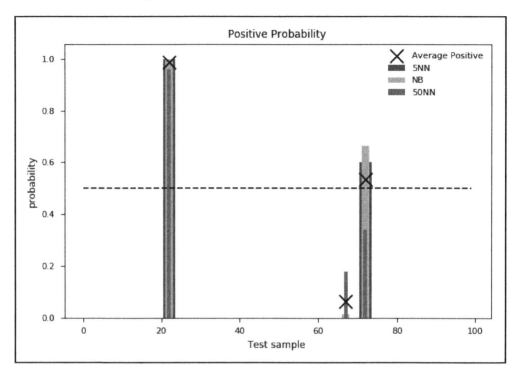

Predicted and average probabilities for the test set with two k-NNs

Summary

In this chapter, we presented the most basic ensemble learning method: voting. Although it is quite simple, it can prove to be effective and an easy way to combine many machine learning models. We presented hard and soft voting, a custom implementation for hard voting, and scikit-learn implementations for both hard and soft voting. Finally, we presented a way to analyze the ensemble's performance by plotting each base learner's errors using `matplotlib`. The chapter's key points are summarized below.

Hard voting assumes that the most voted class is the winner. **Soft voting** assumes that the class with the highest average probability is the winner. **Soft voting** requires that the base classifiers predict the **probability** of each class for every instance with a relatively high accuracy. Scikit-learn implements voting ensembles using the `VotingClassifier` class. An array of tuples in the form of `[(learner_name, learner_object),...]` is passed to `VotingClassifier`. The `VotingClassifier` does not train the objects passed as arguments. Instead, a copy is generated and trained. The default mode of `VotingClassifier` implements hard voting. To use soft voting, pass the `voting='soft'` argument to the constructor. Soft voting requires that the base learners return probabilities for each prediction. If a base learner greatly takes over or underestimates the probabilities, the ensemble's predictive ability will suffer.

In the next chapter, we will discuss about another non-generative method, Stacking, and how it can be utilized in both regression and classification problems.

4
Stacking

Stacking is the second ensemble learning technique that we will study. Together with voting, it belongs to the non-generative methods class, as they both use individually trained classifiers as base learners.

In this chapter, we will present the main ideas behind stacking, its strengths and weaknesses, and how to select base learners. Furthermore, we will go through the processes of implementing stacking for both regression and classification problems with scikit-learn.

The main topics covered in this chapter are as follows:

- The methodology of stacking and using a meta-learner to combine predictions
- The motivation behind using stacking
- The strengths and weaknesses of stacking
- Selecting base learners for an ensemble
- Implementing stacking for regression and classification problems

Technical requirements

You will require basic knowledge of machine learning techniques and algorithms. Furthermore, a knowledge of python conventions and syntax is required. Finally, familiarity with the NumPy library will greatly help the reader to understand some custom algorithm implementations.

The code files of this chapter can be found on GitHub:

`https://github.com/PacktPublishing/Hands-On-Ensemble-Learning-with-Python/tree/master/Chapter04`

Check out the following video to see the Code in Action: `http://bit.ly/2XJgyD2`.

Meta-learning

Meta-learning is a broad machine learning term. It has a number of meanings, but it generally entails utilizing metadata for a specific problem in order to solve it. Its applications range from solving a problem more efficiently, to designing entirely new learning algorithms. It is a growing research field that has recently yielded impressive results by designing novel deep learning architectures.

Stacking

Stacking is a form of meta-learning. The main idea is that we use base learners in order to generate metadata for the problem's dataset and then utilize another learner called a meta-learner, in order to process the metadata. Base learners are considered to be level 0 learners, while the meta learner is considered a level 1 learner. In other words, the meta learner is stacked on top of the base learners, hence the name stacking.

A more intuitive way to describe the ensemble is to present an analogy with voting. In voting, we combined a number of base learners' predictions in order to increase their performance. In stacking, instead of explicitly defining the combination rule, we train a model that learns how to best combine the base learners' predictions. The meta-learner's input dataset consists of the base learners' predictions (metadata), as shown in figure:

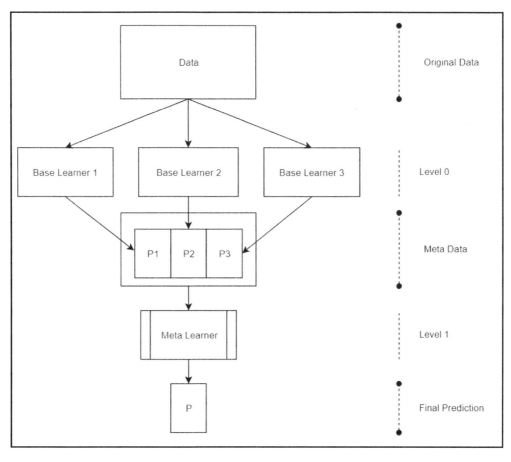

Stacking ensemble data flow, from original data to the base learners, creating metadata for the meta-learner

Creating metadata

As mentioned earlier, we need metadata in order to both train and operate our ensemble. During the operation phase, we simply pass the data from our base learners. On the other hand, the training phase is a little more complicated. We want our meta-learner to discover strengths and weaknesses between our base learners. Although some would argue that we could train the base learners on the train set, predict on it, and use the predictions in order to train our meta-learner, this would induce variance. Our meta-learner would discover the strengths and weaknesses of data that has already been seen (by the base learners). As we want to generate models with decent predictive (out-of-sample) performance, instead of descriptive (in-sample) capabilities, another approach must be utilized.

Another approach would be to split our training set into a base learner train set and a meta-learner train (validation) set. This way, we would still retain a true test set where we can measure the ensemble's performance. The drawback of this approach is that we must donate some of the instances to the validation set. Furthermore, both the validation set size and the train set size will be smaller than the original train set size. Thus, the preferred approach is to utilize **K-fold cross validation**. For each K, the base learners will be trained on the K-1 folds and predict on the Kth fold, generating $100/K$ percent of the final training metadata. By repeating the process K times, one for each fold, we will have generated metadata for the whole training dataset. The process is depicted in the following diagram. The final result is a set of metadata for the whole dataset, where the metadata is generated on out-of-sample data (from the perspective of the base learners, for each fold):

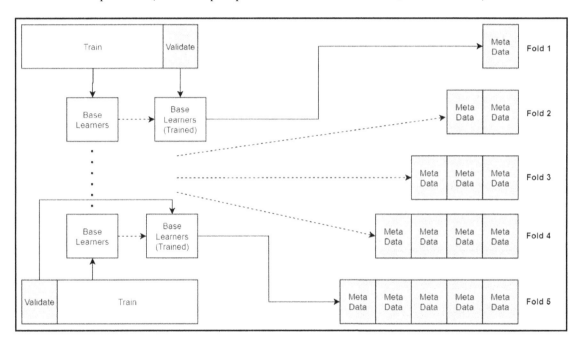

Creating metadata with five-fold cross-validation

Deciding on an ensemble's composition

We described stacking as an advanced form of voting. Similarly to voting (and most ensemble learning techniques for that matter), stacking is dependent on the diversity of its base learners. If the base learners exhibit the same characteristics and performance throughout the problem's domain, it will be difficult for the meta-learner to dramatically improve their collective performance. Furthermore, a complex meta-learner will be needed. If the base learners are diverse and exhibit different performance characteristics in different domains of the problem, even a simple meta-learner will be able to greatly improve their collective performance.

Selecting base learners

It is generally a good idea to mix different learning algorithms, in order to capture both linear and non-linear relationships between the features themselves, as well as the target variable. Take, for example, the following dataset, which exhibits both linear and non-linear relationships between the feature (x) and the target variable (y). It is evident that neither a single linear nor a single non-linear regression will be able to fully model the data. A stacking ensemble with a linear and non-linear regression will be able to greatly outperform either of the two models. Even without stacking, by hand-crafting a simple rule, (for example "use the linear model if x is in the spaces [0, 30] or [60, 100], else use the non-linear") we can greatly outperform the two models:

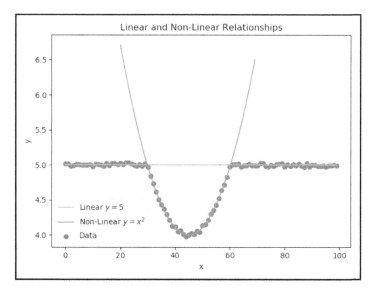

Combination of x=5 and x-squared for the example dataset

Selecting the meta-learner

Generally, the meta-learner should be a relatively simple machine learning algorithm, in order to avoid overfitting. Furthermore, additional steps should be taken in order to regularize the meta-learner. For example, if a decision tree is used, then the tree's maximum depth should be limited. If a regression model is used, a regularized regression (such as elastic net or ridge regression) should be preferred. If there is a need for more complex models in order to increase the ensemble's predictive performance, a multi-level stack could be used, in which the number of models and each individual model's complexity reduces as the stack's level increases:

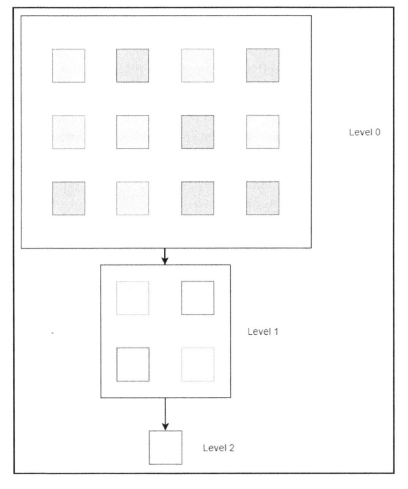

Level stacking ensemble. Each level has simpler models than the previous level

Another really important characteristic of the meta-learner should be the ability to handle correlated inputs and especially to not make any assumptions about the independence of features from one another, as naive Bayes classifiers do. The inputs to the meta-learner (metadata) will be highly correlated. This happens because all base learners are trained to predict the same target. Thus, their predictions will come from an approximation of the same function. Although the predicted values will vary, they will be close to each other.

Python implementation

Although scikit-learn does implement most ensemble methods that we cover in this book, stacking is not one of them. In this section, we will implement custom stacking solutions for both regression and classification problems.

Stacking for regression

Here, we will try to create a stacking ensemble for the diabetes regression dataset. The ensemble will consist of a 5-neighbor **k-Nearest Neighbors** (**k-NN**), a decision tree limited to a max depth of four, and a ridge regression (a regularized form of least squares regression). The meta-learner will be a simple **Ordinary Least Squares** (**OLS**) linear regression.

First, we have to import the required libraries and data. Scikit-learn provides a convenient method to split data into K-folds, with the KFold class from the sklearn.model_selection module. As in previous chapters, we use the first 400 instances for training and the remaining instances for testing:

```
# --- SECTION 1 ---
# Libraries and data loading
from sklearn.datasets import load_diabetes
from sklearn.neighbors import KNeighborsRegressor
from sklearn.tree import DecisionTreeRegressor
from sklearn.linear_model import LinearRegression, Ridge
from sklearn.model_selection import KFold
from sklearn import metrics
import numpy as np
diabetes = load_diabetes()

train_x, train_y = diabetes.data[:400], diabetes.target[:400]
test_x, test_y = diabetes.data[400:], diabetes.target[400:]
```

In the following code, we instantiate the base and meta-learners. In order to have ease of access to the individual base learners later on, we store each base learner in a list, called `base_learners`:

```
# --- SECTION 2 ---
# Create the ensemble's base learners and meta-learner
# Append base learners to a list for ease of access
base_learners = []
knn = KNeighborsRegressor(n_neighbors=5)

base_learners.append(knn)
dtr = DecisionTreeRegressor(max_depth=4 , random_state=123456)

base_learners.append(dtr)
ridge = Ridge()

base_learners.append(ridge)
meta_learner = LinearRegression()
```

After instantiating our learners, we need to create the metadata for the training set. We split the training set into five folds by first creating a `KFold` object, specifying the number of splits (K) with `KFold(n_splits=5)`, and then calling `KF.split(train_x)`. This, in turn, returns a generator for the train and test indices of the five splits. For each of these splits, we use the data indicated by `train_indices` (four folds) to train our base learners and create metadata on the data corresponding to `test_indices`. Furthermore, we store the metadata for each classifier in the `meta_data` array and the corresponding targets in the `meta_targets` array. Finally, we transpose `meta_data` in order to get a (instance, feature) shape:

```
# --- SECTION 3 ---
# Create the training metadata

# Create variables to store metadata and their targets
meta_data = np.zeros((len(base_learners), len(train_x)))
meta_targets = np.zeros(len(train_x))

# Create the cross-validation folds
KF = KFold(n_splits=5)
meta_index = 0
for train_indices, test_indices in KF.split(train_x):
    # Train each learner on the K-1 folds
    # and create metadata for the Kth fold
    for i in range(len(base_learners)):
        learner = base_learners[i]
        learner.fit(train_x[train_indices], train_y[train_indices])
        predictions = learner.predict(train_x[test_indices])
```

```
        meta_data[i][meta_index:meta_index+len(test_indices)] = \
                            predictions

    meta_targets[meta_index:meta_index+len(test_indices)] = \
                            train_y[test_indices]
    meta_index += len(test_indices)

# Transpose the metadata to be fed into the meta-learner
meta_data = meta_data.transpose()
```

For the test set, we do not need to split it into folds. We simply train the base learners on the whole train set and predict on the test set. Furthermore, we evaluate each base learner and store the evaluation metrics, in order to compare them with the ensemble's performance. As this is a regression problem, we use R-squared and **Mean Squared Error (MSE)** as evaluation metrics:

```
# --- SECTION 4 ---
# Create the metadata for the test set and evaluate the base learners
test_meta_data = np.zeros((len(base_learners), len(test_x)))
base_errors = []
base_r2 = []
for i in range(len(base_learners)):
  learner = base_learners[i]
  learner.fit(train_x, train_y)
  predictions = learner.predict(test_x)
  test_meta_data[i] = predictions

  err = metrics.mean_squared_error(test_y, predictions)
  r2 = metrics.r2_score(test_y, predictions)

  base_errors.append(err)
  base_r2.append(r2)

test_meta_data = test_meta_data.transpose()
```

Now, that we have the metadata for both the train and test sets, we can train our meta-learner on the train set and evaluate on the test set:

```
# --- SECTION 5 ---
# Fit the meta-learner on the train set and evaluate it on the test set
meta_learner.fit(meta_data, meta_targets)
ensemble_predictions = meta_learner.predict(test_meta_data)

err = metrics.mean_squared_error(test_y, ensemble_predictions)
r2 = metrics.r2_score(test_y, ensemble_predictions)

# --- SECTION 6 ---
# Print the results
```

```
print('ERROR R2 Name')
print('-'*20)
for i in range(len(base_learners)):
  learner = base_learners[i]
  print(f'{base_errors[i]:.1f} {base_r2[i]:.2f}
{learner.__class__.__name__}')
print(f'{err:.1f} {r2:.2f} Ensemble')
```

We get the following output:

```
ERROR R2 Name
--------------------
2697.8 0.51 KNeighborsRegressor
3142.5 0.43 DecisionTreeRegressor
2564.8 0.54 Ridge
2066.6 0.63 Ensemble
```

As is evident, r-squared has improved by over 16% from the best base learner (ridge regression), while MSE has improved by almost 20%. This is a considerable improvement.

Stacking for classification

Stacking is a viable method for both regression and classification. In this section, we will use it to classify the breast cancer dataset. Again, we will use three base learners. A 5-neighbor k-NN, a decision tree limited to a max depth of 4, and a simple neural network with 1 hidden layer of 100 neurons. For the meta-learner, we utilize a simple logistic regression.

Again, we load the required libraries and split the data into a train and test set:

```
# --- SECTION 1 ---
# Libraries and data loading
from sklearn.datasets import load_breast_cancer
from sklearn.neighbors import KNeighborsClassifier
from sklearn.tree import DecisionTreeClassifier
from sklearn.neural_network import MLPClassifier
from sklearn.naive_bayes import GaussianNB
from sklearn.linear_model import LogisticRegression
from sklearn.model_selection import KFold
from sklearn import metrics
import numpy as np
bc = load_breast_cancer()

train_x, train_y = bc.data[:400], bc.target[:400]
test_x, test_y = bc.data[400:], bc.target[400:]
```

We instantiate the base learners and the meta-learner. Note that MLPClassifier has a hidden_layer_sizes =(100,) parameter, which specifies the number of neurons for each hidden layer. Here, we have a single layer of 100 neurons:

```
# --- SECTION 2 ---
# Create the ensemble's base learners and meta-learner
# Append base learners to a list for ease of access
base_learners = []

knn = KNeighborsClassifier(n_neighbors=2)
base_learners.append(knn)

dtr = DecisionTreeClassifier(max_depth=4, random_state=123456)
base_learners.append(dtr)

mlpc = MLPClassifier(hidden_layer_sizes =(100, ),
            solver='lbfgs', random_state=123456)
base_learners.append(mlpc)

meta_learner = LogisticRegression(solver='lbfgs')
```

Again, using KFolds, we split the train set into five folds in order to train on four folds and generate metadata for the remaining fold, repeated five times. Note that we use learner.predict_proba(train_x[test_indices])[:,0] in order to get the predicted probability that the instance belongs to in the first class. Given that we have only two classes, this is sufficient. For *N* classes, we would have to either save *N*-1 features or simply use learner.predict, in order to save the predicted class:

```
# --- SECTION 3 ---
# Create the training metadata

# Create variables to store metadata and their targets
meta_data = np.zeros((len(base_learners), len(train_x)))
meta_targets = np.zeros(len(train_x))

# Create the cross-validation folds
KF = KFold(n_splits=5)
meta_index = 0
for train_indices, test_indices in KF.split(train_x):
    # Train each learner on the K-1 folds and create
    # metadata for the Kth fold
    for i in range(len(base_learners)):
    learner = base_learners[i]

    learner.fit(train_x[train_indices], train_y[train_indices])
    predictions = learner.predict_proba(train_x[test_indices])[:,0]
```

```
      meta_data[i][meta_index:meta_index+len(test_indices)] = predictions

      meta_targets[meta_index:meta_index+len(test_indices)] = \
                            train_y[test_indices]
      meta_index += len(test_indices)

  # Transpose the metadata to be fed into the meta-learner
  meta_data = meta_data.transpose()
```

Then, we train the base classifiers on the train set and create metadata for the test set, as well as evaluating their accuracy with `metrics.accuracy_score(test_y, learner.predict(test_x))`:

```
  # --- SECTION 4 ---
  # Create the metadata for the test set and evaluate the base learners
  test_meta_data = np.zeros((len(base_learners), len(test_x)))
  base_acc = []
  for i in range(len(base_learners)):
    learner = base_learners[i]
    learner.fit(train_x, train_y)
    predictions = learner.predict_proba(test_x)[:,0]
    test_meta_data[i] = predictions

    acc = metrics.accuracy_score(test_y, learner.predict(test_x))
    base_acc.append(acc)
  test_meta_data = test_meta_data.transpose()
```

Finally, we fit the meta-learner on the train metadata, evaluate its performance on the test data, and print both the ensemble's and the individual learner's accuracy:

```
  # --- SECTION 5 ---
  # Fit the meta-learner on the train set and evaluate it on the test set
  meta_learner.fit(meta_data, meta_targets)
  ensemble_predictions = meta_learner.predict(test_meta_data)

  acc = metrics.accuracy_score(test_y, ensemble_predictions)

  # --- SECTION 6 ---
  # Print the results
  print('Acc Name')
  print('-'*20)
  for i in range(len(base_learners)):
    learner = base_learners[i]
    print(f'{base_acc[i]:.2f} {learner.__class__.__name__}')
  print(f'{acc:.2f} Ensemble')
```

The final output is as follows:

```
Acc Name
-------------------
0.86 KNeighborsClassifier
0.88 DecisionTreeClassifier
0.92 MLPClassifier
0.93 Ensemble
```

Here, we can see that the meta-learner was only able to improve the ensemble's performance by 1%, compared to the best performing base learner. If we try to utilize the `learner.predict` method to generate our metadata, we see that the ensemble actually under performs, compared to the neural network:

```
Acc Name
-------------------
0.86 KNeighborsClassifier
0.88 DecisionTreeClassifier
0.92 MLPClassifier
0.91 Ensemble
```

Creating a stacking regressor class for scikit-learn

We can utilize the preceding code in order to create a reusable class that orchestrates the ensemble's training and prediction. All scikit-learn classifiers use the standard `fit(x, y)` and `predict(x)` methods, in order to train and predict respectively. First, we import the required libraries and declare the class and its constructor. The constructor's argument is a list of lists of scikit-learn classifiers. Each sub-list contains the level's learners. Thus, it is easy to construct a multi-level stacking ensemble. For example, a three-level ensemble can be constructed with `StackingRegressor([ [111, 112, 113],[ 121, 122], [131] ])`. We create a list of each stacking level's size (the number of learners) and also create deep copies of the base learners. The classifier in the last list is considered to be the meta-learner:

 All of the following code, up to (not including) Section 5 (comment labels), is part of the `StackingRegressor` class. It should be properly indented if it is copied to a Python editor.

```
# --- SECTION 1 ---
# Libraries
import numpy as np
```

```
from sklearn.model_selection import KFold
from copy import deepcopy

class StackingRegressor():
  # --- SECTION 2 ---
  # The constructor
  def __init__(self, learners):
    # Create a list of sizes for each stacking level
    # And a list of deep copied learners
    self.level_sizes = []
    self.learners = []
    for learning_level in learners:
      self.level_sizes.append(len(learning_level))
      level_learners = []
      for learner in learning_level:
        level_learners.append(deepcopy(learner))
      self.learners.append(level_learners)
```

In following the constructor definition, we define the `fit` function. The only difference from the simple stacking script we presented in the preceding section is that instead of creating metadata for the meta-learner, we create a list of metadata, one for each stacking level. We save the metadata and targets in the `meta_data`, `meta_targets` lists and use `data_z`, `target_z` as the corresponding variables for each level. Furthermore, we train the level's learners on the metadata of the previous level. We initialize the metadata lists with the original training set and targets:

```
  # --- SECTION 3 ---
  # The fit function. Creates training metadata for every level
  # and trains each level on the previous level's metadata
  def fit(self, x, y):
    # Create a list of training metadata, one for each stacking level
    # and another one for the targets. For the first level,
    # the actual data is used.
    meta_data = [x]
    meta_targets = [y]
    for i in range(len(self.learners)):
      level_size = self.level_sizes[i]

      # Create the metadata and target variables for this level
      data_z = np.zeros((level_size, len(x)))
      target_z = np.zeros(len(x))

      train_x = meta_data[i]
      train_y = meta_targets[i]

      # Create the cross-validation folds
      KF = KFold(n_splits=5)
```

```
    meta_index = 0
    for train_indices, test_indices in KF.split(x):
      # Train each learner on the K-1 folds and create
      # metadata for the Kth fold
      for j in range(len(self.learners[i])):

        learner = self.learners[i][j]
        learner.fit(train_x[train_indices],
            train_y[train_indices])
        predictions = learner.predict(train_x[test_indices])

        data_z[j][meta_index:meta_index+len(test_indices)] = \
                        predictions

      target_z[meta_index:meta_index+len(test_indices)] = \
                    train_y[test_indices]
      meta_index += len(test_indices)

    # Add the data and targets to the metadata lists
    data_z = data_z.transpose()
    meta_data.append(data_z)
    meta_targets.append(target_z)


    # Train the learner on the whole previous metadata
    for learner in self.learners[i]:
      learner.fit(train_x, train_y)
```

Finally, we define the `predict` function, which creates metadata for each level for the provided test set, using the same logic as was used in `fit` (storing each level's metadata). The function returns the metadata for each level, as they are also the predictions of each level. The ensemble's output can be accessed with `meta_data[-1]`:

```
# --- SECTION 4 ---
# The predict function. Creates metadata for the test data and returns
# all of them. The actual predictions can be accessed with
# meta_data[-1]
def predict(self, x):

  # Create a list of training metadata, one for each stacking level
  meta_data = [x]
  for i in range(len(self.learners)):
    level_size = self.level_sizes[i]

    data_z = np.zeros((level_size, len(x)))

    test_x = meta_data[i]
```

```
    # Create the cross-validation folds
    KF = KFold(n_splits=5)
    for train_indices, test_indices in KF.split(x):
        # Train each learner on the K-1 folds and create
        # metadata for the Kth fold
        for j in range(len(self.learners[i])):

            learner = self.learners[i][j]
            predictions = learner.predict(test_x)
            data_z[j] = predictions

        # Add the data and targets to the metadata lists
        data_z = data_z.transpose()
        meta_data.append(data_z)

    # Return the meta_data the final layer's prediction can be accessed
    # With meta_data[-1]
    return meta_data
```

If we instantiate StackingRegressor with the same meta-learner and base learners as our regression example, we can see that it performs exactly the same! In order to access intermediate predictions, we must access the level's index plus one, as the data in meta_data[0] is the original test data:

```
# --- SECTION 5 ---
# Use the classifier
from sklearn.datasets import load_diabetes
from sklearn.neighbors import KNeighborsRegressor
from sklearn.tree import DecisionTreeRegressor
from sklearn.linear_model import LinearRegression, Ridge
from sklearn import metrics
diabetes = load_diabetes()

train_x, train_y = diabetes.data[:400], diabetes.target[:400]
test_x, test_y = diabetes.data[400:], diabetes.target[400:]

base_learners = []

knn = KNeighborsRegressor(n_neighbors=5)
base_learners.append(knn)

dtr = DecisionTreeRegressor(max_depth=4, random_state=123456)
base_learners.append(dtr)

ridge = Ridge()
base_learners.append(ridge)

meta_learner = LinearRegression()
```

```
# Instantiate the stacking regressor
sc = StackingRegressor([[knn,dtr,ridge],[meta_learner]])

# Fit and predict
sc.fit(train_x, train_y)
meta_data = sc.predict(test_x)

# Evaluate base learners and meta-learner
base_errors = []
base_r2 = []
for i in range(len(base_learners)):
  learner = base_learners[i]
  predictions = meta_data[1][:,i]
  err = metrics.mean_squared_error(test_y, predictions)
  r2 = metrics.r2_score(test_y, predictions)
  base_errors.append(err)
  base_r2.append(r2)

err = metrics.mean_squared_error(test_y, meta_data[-1])
r2 = metrics.r2_score(test_y, meta_data[-1])

# Print the results
print('ERROR R2 Name')
print('-'*20)
for i in range(len(base_learners)):
  learner = base_learners[i]
  print(f'{base_errors[i]:.1f} {base_r2[i]:.2f}
      {learner.__class__.__name__}')
print(f'{err:.1f} {r2:.2f} Ensemble')
```

The results match with our previous example's result:

```
ERROR R2 Name
-------------------
2697.8 0.51 KNeighborsRegressor
3142.5 0.43 DecisionTreeRegressor
2564.8 0.54 Ridge
2066.6 0.63 Ensemble
```

In order to further clarify the relationships between the `meta_data` and `self.learners` lists, we graphically depict their interactions as follows. We initialize `meta_data[0]` for the sake of code simplicity. While it can be misleading to store the actual input data in the `meta_data` list, it avoids the need to handle the first level of base learners in a different way than the rest:

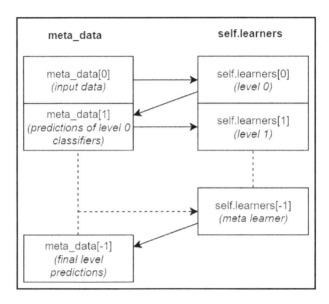

The relationships between each level of meta_data and self.learners

Summary

In this chapter, we presented an ensemble learning method called stacking (or stacked generalization). It can be seen as a more advanced method of voting. We first presented the basic concept of stacking, how to properly create the metadata, and how to decide on the ensemble's composition. We presented one regression and one classification implementation for stacking. Finally, we presented an implementation of an ensemble class (implemented similarly to scikit-learn classes), which makes it easier to use multi-level stacking ensembles. The following are some key points to remember from this chapter.

Stacking can consist of many **levels**. Each level generates **metadata** for the next. You should create each level's metadata by splitting the train set into **K folds** and iteratively **train on K-1 folds**, while creating **metadata for the Kth fold**. After creating the metadata, you should train the current level on the whole train set. Base learners must be diverse. The meta-learner should be a relatively simple algorithm that is resistant to overfitting. If possible, try to induce regularization in the meta-learner. For example, limit the maximum depth if you use a decision tree or use a regularized regression. The meta-learner should be able to handle correlated inputs relatively well. You should not be afraid to **add under-performing models** to the ensemble, as long as they introduce new information to the metadata (that is, they handle the dataset differently from the other models). In the next chapter, we will introduce the first generative ensemble method, Bagging.

Section 3: Generative Methods 3

In this section, we will cover more advanced ensemble learning methods.

This section comprises the following chapters:

- Chapter 5, *Bagging*
- Chapter 6, *Boosting*
- Chapter 7, *Random Forests*

5
Bagging

Bagging, or bootstrap aggregating, is the first generative ensemble learning technique that this book will present. It can be a useful tool to reduce variance as it creates a number of base learners by sub-sampling the original train set. In this chapter, we will discuss the statistical method on which bagging is based, bootstrapping. Next, we will present bagging, along with its strengths and weaknesses. Finally, we will implement the method in Python, as well as use the scikit-learn implementation, to solve regression and classification problems.

The main topics covered in this chapter are as follows:

- The bootstrapping method from computational statistics
- How bagging works
- Strengths and weaknesses of bagging
- Implementing a custom bagging ensemble
- Using the scikit-learn implementation

Technical requirements

You will require basic knowledge of machine learning techniques and algorithms. Furthermore, a knowledge of python conventions and syntax is required. Finally, familiarity with the NumPy library will greatly help the reader to understand some custom algorithm implementations.

The code files of this chapter can be found on GitHub:

https://github.com/PacktPublishing/Hands-On-Ensemble-Learning-with-Python/tree/master/Chapter05

Check out the following video to see the Code in Action: http://bit.ly/2JKcokD.

Bootstrapping

Bootstrapping is a resampling method. In statistics, resampling entails the use of many samples, generated from an original sample. In machine learning terms, the sample is our training data. The main idea is to use the original sample as the population (the whole domain of our problem) and the generated sub-samples as samples.

In essence, we are simulating how a statistic would behave if we collected many samples from the original population, as shown in the following diagram:

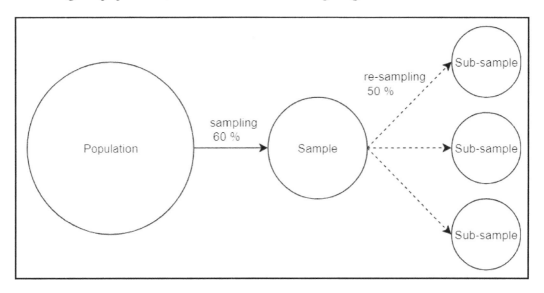

A representation of how resampling works

Creating bootstrap samples

In order to create bootstrap samples, we resample with replacement (each instance may be selected multiple times) from our original sample. This means that a single instance can be selected multiple times. Suppose we have data for 100 individuals. The data contains the weight and height of each individual. If we generate random numbers from 1 to 100 and add the corresponding data to a new dataset, we have essentially created a bootstrap sample.

In Python, we can use `numpy.random.choice`to create a sub-sample of a given size. We can try to create bootstrap samples and estimates about the mean and standard deviation of the diabetes dataset. First, we load the dataset and libraries and print the statistics of our sample, as in the following example:

```
# --- SECTION 1 ---
# Libraries and data loading
import numpy as np
import matplotlib.pyplot as plt
from sklearn.datasets import load_diabetes

diabetes = load_diabetes()

# --- SECTION 2 ---
# Print the original sample's statistics
target = diabetes.target

print(np.mean(target))
print(np.std(target))
```

We then create the bootstrap samples and statistics and store them in `bootstrap_stats`. We could store the whole bootstrap samples, but it is not memory-efficient to do so. Furthermore, we only care about the statistics, so it makes sense only to store them. Here, we create 10,000 bootstrap samples and statistics:

```
# --- SECTION 3 ---
# Create the bootstrap samples and statistics
bootstrap_stats = []
for _ in range(10000):
    bootstrap_sample = np.random.choice(target, size=len(target))
    mean = np.mean(bootstrap_sample)
    std = np.std(bootstrap_sample)
    bootstrap_stats.append((mean, std))
bootstrap_stats = np.array(bootstrap_stats)
```

We can now plot the histograms of the mean and standard deviation, as well as calculate the standard error (that is, the standard deviation of the statistic's distributions) for each:

```
# --- SECTION 4 ---
# plot the distributions
plt.figure()
plt.subplot(2,1,1)
std_err = np.std(bootstrap_stats[:,0])
plt.title('Mean, Std. Error: %.2f'%std_err)
plt.hist(bootstrap_stats[:,0], bins=20)

plt.subplot(2,1,2)
```

```
std_err = np.std(bootstrap_stats[:,1])
plt.title('Std. Dev, Std. Error: %.2f'%std_err)
plt.hist(bootstrap_stats[:,1], bins=20)
plt.show()
```

We get the output shown in the following diagram:

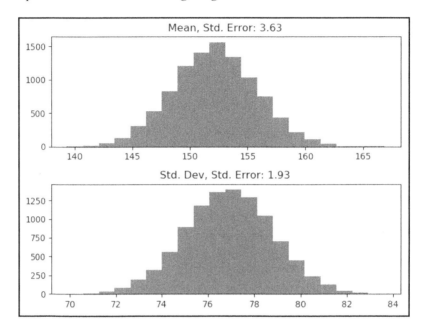

Bootstrap distributions for mean and standard deviation

Note that due to the inherent randomness of the process (for which instances will be selected for each bootstrap sample), the results may vary each time the procedure is executed. A higher number of bootstrap samples will help to stabilize the results. Nonetheless, it is a useful technique to calculate the standard error, confidence intervals, and other statistics without making any assumptions about the underlying distribution.

Bagging

Bagging makes use of bootstrap samples in order to train an array of base learners. It then combines their predictions using voting. The motivation behind this method is to produce diverse base learners by diversifying the train sets. In this section, we discuss the motivation, strengths, and weaknesses of this method.

Creating base learners

Bagging applies bootstrap sampling to the train set, creating a number of N bootstrap samples. It then creates the same number N of base learners, using the same machine learning algorithm. Each base learner is trained on the corresponding train set and all base learners are combined by voting (hard voting for classification, and averaging for regression). The procedure is depicted as follows:

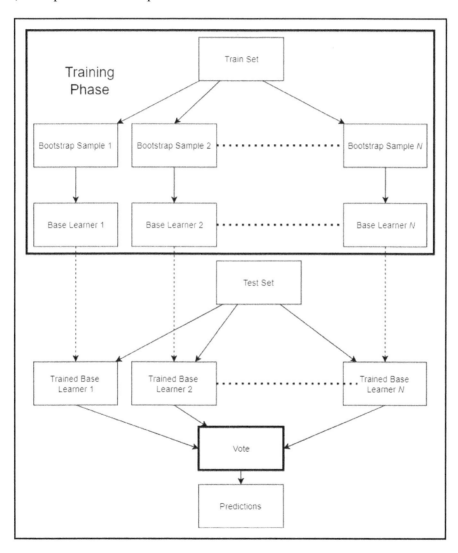

Creating base learners through bagging

By using bootstrap samples with the same size as the original train set, each instance has a probability of 0.632 of appearing in any given bootstrap sample. Thus, in many cases, this type of bootstrap estimate is referred to as the 0.632 bootstrap estimate. In our case, this means that we can use the remaining 36.8% of the original train set in order to estimate the individual base learner's performance. This is called the **out-of-bag score**, and the 36.8% of instances are called **out-of-bag instances**.

Strengths and weaknesses

Bagging is usually utilized with decision trees as its base learners, but it can be used with any machine learning algorithm. Bagging reduces variance greatly and it has been proved that it is most effective when unstable base learners are used. Unstable learners generate models with great inter-model variance, even when the respective train sets vary only slightly. Furthermore, bagging converges as the number of base learners grows. Similar to estimating a bootstrap statistic, by increasing the number of base learners, we also increase the number of bootstrap samples. Finally, bagging allows for easy parallelization, as each model is trained independently.

The main disadvantage of bagging is the loss of interpretability and transparency of our models. For example, using a single decision tree allows for great interpretability, as the decision of each node is readily available. Using a bagging ensemble of 100 trees makes the individual decisions less important, while the collective predictions define the ensemble's final output.

Python implementation

To better understand the process of creating the ensemble, as well as its merits, we will implement it in Python using decision trees. In this example, we will try to classify the MNIST dataset of handwritten digits. Although we have used the cancer dataset for classification examples up until now, it contains only two classes, while the number of examples is relatively small for effective bootstrapping. The digits dataset contains a considerable number of examples and is also more complex, as there is a total of 10 classes.

Implementation

For this example, we will use 1500 instances as the train set, and the remaining 297 as the test set. We will generate 10 bootstrap samples, and consequently 10 decision-tree models. We will then combine the base predictions using hard voting:

1. We load the libraries and data as shown in the following example:

```
# --- SECTION 1 ---
# Libraries and data loading
from sklearn.datasets import load_digits
from sklearn.tree import DecisionTreeClassifier
from sklearn import metrics
import numpy as np
digits = load_digits()

train_size = 1500
train_x, train_y = digits.data[:train_size],
digits.target[:train_size]
test_x, test_y = digits.data[train_size:],
digits.target[train_size:]
```

2. We then create our bootstrap samples and train the corresponding models. Note, that we do not use `np.random.choice`. Instead, we generate an array of indices with `np.random.randint(0, train_size, size=train_size)`, as this will enable us to choose both the features and the corresponding targets for each bootstrap sample. We store each base learner in the `base_learners` list, for ease of access later on:

```
# --- SECTION 2 ---
# Create our bootstrap samples and train the classifiers

ensemble_size = 10
base_learners = []

for _ in range(ensemble_size):
  # We sample indices in order to access features and targets
  bootstrap_sample_indices = np.random.randint(0, train_size,
size=train_size)
  bootstrap_x = train_x[bootstrap_sample_indices]
  bootstrap_y = train_y[bootstrap_sample_indices]
  dtree = DecisionTreeClassifier()
  dtree.fit(bootstrap_x, bootstrap_y)
  base_learners.append(dtree)
```

3. Next, we predict the targets of the test set with each base learner and store their predictions as well as their evaluated accuracy, as shown in the following code block:

```
# --- SECTION 3 ---
# Predict with the base learners and evaluate them

base_predictions = []
base_accuracy = []
for learner in base_learners:
 predictions = learner.predict(test_x)
 base_predictions.append(predictions)
 acc = metrics.accuracy_score(test_y, predictions)
 base_accuracy.append(acc)
```

4. Now that we have each base learner's predictions in `base_predictions`, we can combine them with hard voting, as we did in Chapter 3, *Voting*, for individual base learners. Furthermore, we evaluate the ensemble's accuracy:

```
# Combine the base learners' predictions

ensemble_predictions = []
# Find the most voted class for each test instance
for i in range(len(test_y)):
    counts = [0 for _ in range(10)]
    for learner_predictions in base_predictions:
        counts[learner_predictions[i]] =
counts[learner_predictions[i]]+1
    # Find the class with most votes
    final = np.argmax(counts)
    # Add the class to the final predictions
    ensemble_predictions.append(final)

ensemble_acc = metrics.accuracy_score(test_y, ensemble_predictions)
```

5. Finally, we print the accuracy of each base learner, as well as the ensemble's accuracy, sorted in ascending order:

```
# --- SECTION 5 ---
# Print the accuracies
print('Base Learners:')
print('-'*30)
for index, acc in enumerate(sorted(base_accuracy)):
 print(f'Learner {index+1}: %.2f' % acc)
print('-'*30)
print('Bagging: %.2f' % ensemble_acc)
```

The final output is shown in the following example:

```
Base Learners:
------------------------------
Learner 1: 0.72
Learner 2: 0.72
Learner 3: 0.73
Learner 4: 0.73
Learner 5: 0.76
Learner 6: 0.76
Learner 7: 0.77
Learner 8: 0.77
Learner 9: 0.79
Learner 10: 0.79
------------------------------
Bagging: 0.88
```

It is evident that the ensemble's accuracy is almost 10% higher than the best-performing base model. This is a considerable improvement, especially if we take into account that this ensemble consists of identical base learners (considering the machine learning method used).

Parallelizing the implementation

We can easily parallelize our bagging implementation using from concurrent.futures import ProcessPoolExecutor. This executor allows the user to spawn a number of tasks to be executed and executes them in parallel processes. It only needs to be passed a target function and its parameters. In our example, we only need to create functions out of code sections (sections 2 and 3):

```
def create_learner(train_x, train_y):
  # We sample indices in order to access features and targets
  bootstrap_sample_indices = np.random.randint(0, train_size,
size=train_size)
  bootstrap_x = train_x[bootstrap_sample_indices]
  bootstrap_y = train_y[bootstrap_sample_indices]
  dtree = DecisionTreeClassifier()
  dtree.fit(bootstrap_x, bootstrap_y)
  return dtree

def predict(learner, test_x):
  return learner.predict(test_x)
```

Then, in the original sections 2 and 3, we modify the code as follows:

```
# Original Section 2
with ProcessPoolExecutor() as executor:
 futures = []
 for _ in range(ensemble_size):
 future = executor.submit(create_learner, train_x, train_y)
 futures.append(future)

 for future in futures:
 base_learners.append(future.result())

# Original Section 3
base_predictions = []
 base_accuracy = []
 with ProcessPoolExecutor() as executor:
 futures = []
 for learner in base_learners:
 future = executor.submit(predict, learner, test_x)
 futures.append(future)

 for future in futures:
 predictions = future.result()
 base_predictions.append(predictions)
 acc = metrics.accuracy_score(test_y, predictions)
 base_accuracy.append(acc)
```

The `executor` returns an object (in our case `future`), which contains the results of our function. The rest of the code remains unchanged with the exception that it is enclosed in `if __name__ == '__main__'` guard, as each new process will import the whole script. This guard prevents them from re-executing the rest of the code. As our example is small, with six processes available, we need to have at least 1,000 base learners to see any considerable speedup in the execution times. For a fully working version, please refer to `'bagging_custom_parallel.py'` from the provided codebase.

Using scikit-learn

Scikit-learn has a great implementation of bagging for both regression and classification problems. In this section, we will go through the process of using the provided implementations to create ensembles for the digits and diabetes datasets.

Bagging for classification

Scikit-learn's implementation of bagging lies in the `sklearn.ensemble` package.
`BaggingClassifier` is the corresponding class for classification problems. It has a
number of interesting parameters, allowing for greater flexibility. It can use any scikit-learn
estimator by specifying it with `base_estimator`. Furthermore, `n_estimators` dictates the
ensemble's size (and, consequently, the number of bootstrap samples that will be
generated), while `n_jobs` dictates how many jobs (processes) will be used to train and
predict with each base learner. Finally, if set to `True`, `oob_score` calculates the out-of-bag
score for the base learners.

Using the actual classifier is straightforward and similar to all other scikit-learn estimators.
First, we load the required data and libraries, as shown in the following example:

```
# --- SECTION 1 ---
# Libraries and data loading
from sklearn.datasets import load_digits
from sklearn.tree import DecisionTreeClassifier
from sklearn.ensemble import BaggingClassifier
from sklearn import metrics

digits = load_digits()

train_size = 1500
train_x, train_y = digits.data[:train_size], digits.target[:train_size]
test_x, test_y = digits.data[train_size:], digits.target[train_size:]
```

We then create, train, and evaluate the estimator:

```
# --- SECTION 2 ---
# Create the ensemble
ensemble_size = 10
ensemble = BaggingClassifier(base_estimator=DecisionTreeClassifier(),
 n_estimators=ensemble_size,
 oob_score=True)

# --- SECTION 3 ---
# Train the ensemble
ensemble.fit(train_x, train_y)

# --- SECTION 4 ---
# Evaluate the ensemble
ensemble_predictions = ensemble.predict(test_x)

ensemble_acc = metrics.accuracy_score(test_y, ensemble_predictions)
```

```
# --- SECTION 5 ---
# Print the accuracy
print('Bagging: %.2f' % ensemble_acc)
```

The final achieved accuracy is 88%, the same as our own implementation. Furthermore, we can access the out-of-bag score through `ensemble.oob_score_`, which in our case is equal to 89.6%. Generally, the out-of-bag score slightly overestimates the out-of-sample predictive capability of the ensemble, which is what we observe in this example.

In our examples, we chose an `ensemble_size` of 10. Suppose we would like to test how different ensemble sizes affect the ensemble's performance. Given that the bagging classifier accepts the size as a constructor's parameter, we can use validation curves from Chapter 2, *Getting Started with Ensemble Learning*, to conduct the test. We test 1 to 39 base learners, with a step of 2. We observe an initial decrease in bias and variance. For ensembles with more than 20 base learners, there seems to be zero benefit in increasing the ensemble's size. The results are depicted in the following diagram:

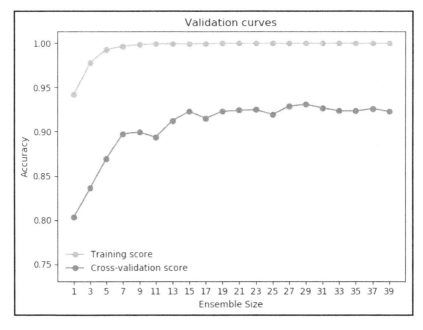

Validation curves for 1 to 39 base learners

Bagging for regression

For regression purposes, we will use the `BaggingRegressor` class from the same `sklearn.ensemble` package. We will also instantiate a single `DecisionTreeRegressor` to compare the results. We start by loading the libraries and data, as usual:

```
# --- SECTION 1 ---
 # Libraries and data loading
 from sklearn.datasets import load_diabetes
 from sklearn.tree import DecisionTreeRegressor
 from sklearn.ensemble import BaggingRegressor
 from sklearn import metrics
 import numpy as np
 diabetes = load_diabetes()

np.random.seed(1234)

train_x, train_y = diabetes.data[:400], diabetes.target[:400]
test_x, test_y = diabetes.data[400:], diabetes.target[400:]
```

We instantiate the single decision tree and the ensemble. Note that we allow for a relatively deep decision tree, by specifying `max_depth=6`. This allows the creation of diverse and unstable models, which greatly benefits bagging. If we restrict the maximum depth to 2 or 3 levels, we will see that bagging does not perform better than a single model. Training and evaluating the ensemble and the model follows the standard procedure:

```
# --- SECTION 2 ---
# Create the ensemble and a single base learner for comparison
estimator = DecisionTreeRegressor(max_depth=6)
ensemble = BaggingRegressor(base_estimator=estimator,
n_estimators=10)

# --- SECTION 3 ---
# Train and evaluate both the ensemble and the base learner
ensemble.fit(train_x, train_y)
ensemble_predictions = ensemble.predict(test_x)

estimator.fit(train_x, train_y)
single_predictions = estimator.predict(test_x)

ensemble_r2 = metrics.r2_score(test_y, ensemble_predictions)
ensemble_mse = metrics.mean_squared_error(test_y, ensemble_predictions)

single_r2 = metrics.r2_score(test_y, single_predictions)
single_mse = metrics.mean_squared_error(test_y, single_predictions)
```

```
# --- SECTION 4 ---
# Print the metrics
print('Bagging r-squared: %.2f' % ensemble_r2)
print('Bagging MSE: %.2f' % ensemble_mse)
print('-'*30)
print('Decision Tree r-squared: %.2f' % single_r2)
print('Decision Tree MSE: %.2f' % single_mse)
```

The ensemble can greatly outperform the single model, by producing both higher R-squared and lower **mean squared error** (**MSE**). As mentioned earlier, this is due to the fact that the base learners are allowed to create deep and unstable models. The actual results of the two models are provided in the following output:

```
Bagging r-squared: 0.52
Bagging MSE: 2679.12
------------------------------
Decision Tree r-squared: 0.15
Decision Tree MSE: 4733.35
```

Summary

In this chapter, we presented the main concept of creating bootstrap samples and estimating bootstrap statistics. Building on this foundation, we introduced bootstrap aggregating, or bagging, which uses a number of bootstrap samples to train many base learners that utilize the same machine learning algorithm. Later, we provided a custom implementation of bagging for classification, as well as the means to parallelize it. Finally, we showcased the use of scikit-learn's own implementation of bagging for regression and classification problems.

The chapter can be summarized as follows. **Bootstrap samples** are created by resampling with replacement from the original dataset. The main idea is to treat the original sample as the population, and each subsample as an original sample. If the original dataset and the bootstrap dataset have the same size, each instance has a probability of **63.2%** of being included in the bootstrap dataset (sample). Bootstrap methods are useful for calculating statistics such as confidence intervals and standard error, **without making assumptions** about the underlying distribution. **Bagging** generates a number of bootstrap samples to train each individual base learner. Bagging benefits **unstable learners**, where small variations in the train set induce great variations in the generated model. Bagging is a suitable ensemble learning method to reduce **variance**.

Bagging allows for easy **parallelization**, as each bootstrap sample and base learner can be generated, trained, and tested individually. As with all ensemble learning methods, using bagging reduces the **interpretability** and motivation behind individual predictions.

In the next chapter, we will introduce the second generative method, Boosting.

6
Boosting

The second generative method we will discuss is boosting. Boosting aims to combine a number of weak learners into a strong ensemble. It is able to reduce bias, but also variance. Here, weak learners are individual models that perform slightly better than random. For example, in a classification dataset with two classes and an equal number of instances belonging to each class, a weak learner will be able to classify the dataset with an accuracy of slightly more than 50%.

In this chapter, we will present two classic boosting algorithms, Gradient Boosting and AdaBoost. Furthermore, we will explore the use of scikit-learn implementations for classification and regression. Finally, we will experiment with a recent boosting algorithm and its implementation, XGBoost.

The main topics covered are as follows:

- The motivation behind using boosting ensembles
- The various algorithms
- Leveraging scikit-learn to create boosting ensembles in Python
- Utilizing the XGBoost library for Python

Technical requirements

You will require basic knowledge of machine learning techniques and algorithms. Furthermore, a knowledge of python conventions and syntax is required. Finally, familiarity with the NumPy library will greatly help the reader to understand some custom algorithm implementations.

The code files of this chapter can be found on GitHub:

https://github.com/PacktPublishing/Hands-On-Ensemble-Learning-with-Python/tree/master/Chapter06

Check out the following video to see the Code in Action: http://bit.ly/2ShWstT.

AdaBoost

AdaBoost is one of the most popular boosting algorithms. Similar to bagging, the main idea behind the algorithm is to create a number of uncorrelated weak learners and then combine their predictions. The main difference with bagging is that instead of creating a number of independent bootstrapped train sets, the algorithm sequentially trains each weak learner, assigns weights to all instances, samples the next train set based on the instance's weights, and repeats the whole process. As a base learner algorithm, usually decision trees consisting of a single node are used. These decision trees, with a depth of a single level, are called **decision stumps**.

Weighted sampling

Weighted sampling is the sampling process were each candidate has a corresponding weight, which determines its probability of being sampled. The weights are normalized, in order for their sum to equal one. Then, the normalized weights correspond to the probability that any individual will be sampled. For a simple example with three candidates, assuming weights of 1, 5, and 10, the following table depicts the normalized weights and the corresponding probability that any candidate will be chosen.

Candidate	Weight	Normalized weight	Probability
1	1	0.0625	6.25%
2	5	0.3125	31.25%
3	10	0.625	62.50%

Instance weights to probabilities

Creating the ensemble

Assuming a classification problem, the AdaBoost algorithm can be described on a high-level basis, from its basic steps. For regression purposes, the steps are similar:

1. Initialize all of the train set instance's weights equally, so their sum equals 1.
2. Generate a new set by sampling with replacement, according to the weights.
3. Train a weak learner on the sampled set.

4. Calculate its error on the original train set.
5. Add the weak learner to the ensemble and save its error rate.
6. Adjust the weights, increasing the weights of misclassified instances and decreasing the weights of correctly classified instances.
7. Repeat from *Step 2*.
8. The weak learners are combined by voting. Each learner's vote is weighted, according to its error rate.

The whole process is depicted in the following diagram:

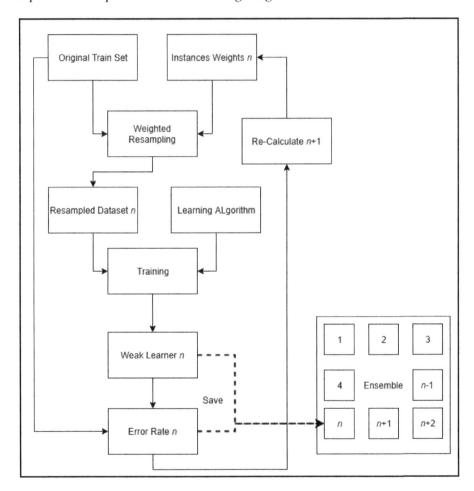

The process of creating the ensemble for the nth learner

In essence, this makes each new classifier focus on the instances that the previous learners could not handle correctly. Assuming a binary classification problem, we may start with a dataset that looks like the following diagram:

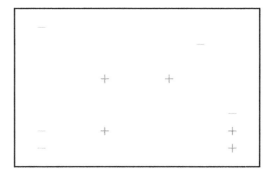

Our initial dataset

Here, all weights are equal. The first decision stump decides to partition the problem space as follows. The dotted line represents the decision boundary. The two black + and - symbols denote the sub-space that the decision stump classifies every instance as positive or negative, respectively. This leaves two misclassified instances. These instance weights will be increased, while all other weights will be decreased:

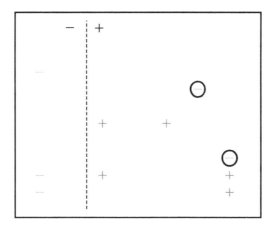

The first decision stump's space partition and errors

By creating another dataset, where the two misclassified instances are dominant (they may be included several times, as we sample with replacement and their weights are larger than the other instances), the second decision stump partitions the space, as follows:

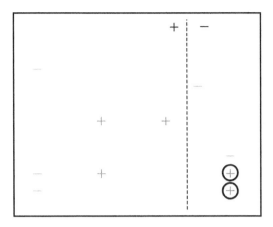

The second decision stump's space partition and errors

Finally, after repeating the process for a third decision stump, the final ensemble has partitioned the space as depicted in the following diagram:

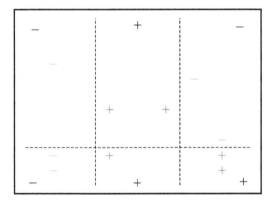

The final ensemble's partition of the problem space

Implementing AdaBoost in Python

In order to better understand how AdaBoost works, we will present a basic implementation in Python. We will use the breast cancer classification dataset for this example. As always, we first load the libraries and data:

```
# --- SECTION 1 ---
# Libraries and data loading
from copy import deepcopy
```

```
from sklearn.datasets import load_breast_cancer
from sklearn.tree import DecisionTreeClassifier
from sklearn import metrics
import numpy as np
bc = load_breast_cancer()
train_size = 400
train_x, train_y = bc.data[:train_size], bc.target[:train_size]
test_x, test_y = bc.data[train_size:], bc.target[train_size:]
np.random.seed(123456)
```

We then create the ensemble. First, we declare the ensemble's size and the base learner type. As mentioned earlier, we use decision stumps (decision trees only a single level deep).

Furthermore, we create a NumPy array for the data instance weights, the learners' weights, and the learners' errors:

```
# --- SECTION 2 ---
# Create the ensemble
ensemble_size = 3
base_classifier = DecisionTreeClassifier(max_depth=1)
# Create the initial weights
data_weights = np.zeros(train_size) + 1/train_size
# Create a list of indices for the train set
indices = [x for x in range(train_size)]
base_learners = []
learners_errors = np.zeros(ensemble_size)
learners_weights = np.zeros(ensemble_size)
```

For each base learner, we will create a deepcopy of the original classifier, train it on a sample dataset, and evaluate it. First, we create the copy and sample with replacement from the original test set, according to the instance's weights:

```
# Create each base learner
for i in range(ensemble_size):
    weak_learner = deepcopy(base_classifier)
    # Choose the samples by sampling with replacement.
    # Each instance's probability is dictated by its weight.
    data_indices = np.random.choice(indices, train_size, p=data_weights)
    sample_x, sample_y = train_x[data_indices], train_y[data_indices]
```

We then fit the learner on the sampled dataset and predict on the original train set. We use the `predictions` to see which instances are correctly classified and which instances are misclassified:

```
# Fit the weak learner and evaluate it
weak_learner.fit(sample_x, sample_y)
predictions = weak_learner.predict(train_x)
errors = predictions != train_y
corrects = predictions == train_y
```

In the following, the weighted errors are classified. Both `errors` and `corrects` are lists of Booleans (`True` or `False`), but Python handles them as 1 and 0. This allows us to multiply element-wise with `data_weights`. The learner's error is then calculated with the average weighted error:

```
# Calculate the weighted errors
weighted_errors = data_weights*errors
# The base learner's error is the average of the weighted errors
learner_error = np.mean(weighted_errors)
learners_errors[i] = learner_error
```

Finally, the learner's weight can be calculated as half the natural logarithm of the weighted accuracy over the weighted error. In turn, we can use the learner's weight to calculate the new data weights. For erroneously classified instances, the new weight equals the natural exponent of the old weight times the learner's weight. For correctly classified instances, the negative multiple is used instead. Finally, the new weights are normalized and the base learner is added to the `base_learners` list:

```
# The learner's weight
learner_weight = np.log((1-learner_error)/learner_error)/2
learners_weights[i] = learner_weight
# Update the data weights
data_weights[errors] = np.exp(data_weights[errors] * learner_weight)
data_weights[corrects] = np.exp(-data_weights[corrects] *
learner_weight)
data_weights = data_weights/sum(data_weights)
# Save the learner
base_learners.append(weak_learner)
```

In order to make predictions with the ensemble, we combine each individual prediction through a weighted majority voting. As this is a binary classification problem, if the weighted average is more than 0.5, the instance is classified as 0; otherwise, it's classified as 1:

```
# --- SECTION 3 ---
# Evaluate the ensemble
ensemble_predictions = []
for learner, weight in zip(base_learners, learners_weights):
    # Calculate the weighted predictions
    prediction = learner.predict(test_x)
    ensemble_predictions.append(prediction*weight)
    # The final prediction is the weighted mean of the individual
predictions
    ensemble_predictions = np.mean(ensemble_predictions, axis=0) >= 0.5
    ensemble_acc = metrics.accuracy_score(test_y, ensemble_predictions)

# --- SECTION 4 ---
# Print the accuracy
print('Boosting: %.2f' % ensemble_acc)
```

The final accuracy achieved by this ensemble is 95%.

Strengths and weaknesses

Boosting algorithms are able to reduce both bias and variance. For a long time, they were considered immune to overfitting, but in fact they can overfit, although they are extremely robust. One possible explanation is that the base learners, in order to classify outliers, create very strong and complicated rules that rarely fit other instances. In the following diagram, an example is depicted. The ensemble has generated a set of rules in order to correctly classify the outlier, but the rules are so strong that only an identical example (that is, with the exact same feature values) could fit into the sub-space defined by the rules:

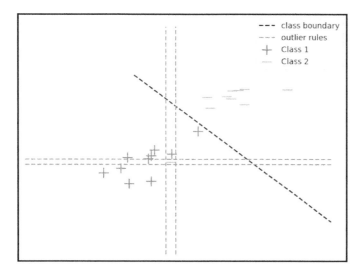

Generated rules for an outlier

One disadvantage of many boosting algorithms is that they are not easily parallelized, as the models are created in a sequential fashion. Furthermore, they pose the usual problems of ensemble learning techniques, such as reduction in interpretability and additional computational costs.

Gradient boosting

Gradient boosting is another boosting algorithm. It is a more generalized boosting framework compared to AdaBoost, which also makes it more complicated and math-intensive. Instead of trying to emphasize problematic instances by assigning weights and resampling the dataset, gradient boosting builds each base learner on the previous learner's errors. Furthermore, gradient boosting uses decision trees of varying depths. In this section, we will present gradient boosting, without delving much into the math involved. Instead, we will present the basic concepts, as well as a custom Python implementation.

Creating the ensemble

The gradient boosting algorithm (for regression purposes) starts by calculating the mean of the target variable for the train set and uses it as an initial prediction. Then, it calculates the difference of each instance's target from the prediction (mean), in order to calculate the error. These errors are also called **pseudo-residuals**.

Following that, it creates a decision tree that tries to predict the pseudo-residuals. By repeating this process, a number of times, the whole ensemble is created. Similar to AdaBoost, gradient boosting assigns a weight to each tree. Contrary to AdaBoost, this weight does not depend on the tree's performance. Instead, it is a constant term, which is called **learning rate**. Its purpose is to increase the ensemble's generalization ability, by restricting its over-fitting power. The algorithm's steps are as follows:

1. Define the learning rate (smaller than 1) and the ensemble's size.
2. Calculate the train set's target mean.
3. Using the mean as a very simple initial prediction, calculate each instance's target difference from the mean. These errors are called pseudo-residuals.
4. Build a decision tree, by using the original train set's features and the pseudo-residuals as targets.
5. Make predictions on the train set, using the decision tree (we try to predict the pseudo-residuals). Multiply the predicted values by the learning rate.
6. Add the multiplied values to the previously stored predicted values. Use the newly calculated values as predictions.
7. Calculate the new pseudo-residuals using the calculated predictions.
8. Repeat from *Step 4* until the desired ensemble size is achieved.

Note that in order to produce the final ensemble's predictions, each base learner's prediction is multiplied by the learning rate and added to the previous learner's prediction. The calculated mean can be regarded as the first base learner's prediction.

At each step s, for a learning rate lr, the prediction is calculated as follows:

$$p_s = mean + lr \cdot p_1 + lr \cdot p_2 + \cdots + lr \cdot p_s$$

The residuals are calculated as the difference from the actual target value t:

$$r_s = t - p_s$$

The whole process is depicted in the following diagram:

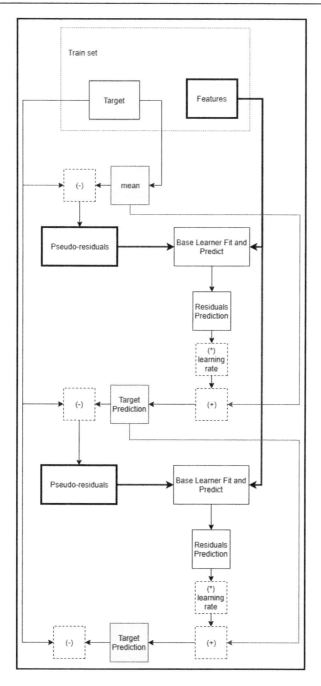

Steps to create a gradient boosting ensemble

Further reading

As this is a hands-on book, we will not go further into the mathematical aspect of the algorithm. Nonetheless, for the mathematically curious or inclined, we recommend the following papers. The first is a more regression-specific framework, while the second is more general:

- Friedman, J.H., 2001. Greedy function approximation: a gradient boosting machine. *Annals of statistics*, pp.1189-1232.
- Mason, L., Baxter, J., Bartlett, P.L. and Frean, M.R., 2000. Boosting algorithms as gradient descent. In *Advances in neural information processing systems* (pp. 512-518).

Implementing gradient boosting in Python

Although gradient boosting can be complex and mathematically intensive, if we focus on conventional regression problems, it can be quite simple. In order to demonstrate this, we present a custom implementation in Python, using standard scikit-learn decision trees. For our implementation, we will use the diabetes regression dataset. First, we load the libraries and data, and set the seed for NumPy's random number generator:

```
# --- SECTION 1 ---
# Libraries and data loading
from copy import deepcopy
from sklearn.datasets import load_diabetes
from sklearn.tree import DecisionTreeRegressor
from sklearn import metrics
import numpy as np
diabetes = load_diabetes()
train_size = 400
train_x, train_y = diabetes.data[:train_size], diabetes.target[:train_size]
test_x, test_y = diabetes.data[train_size:], diabetes.target[train_size:]
np.random.seed(123456)
```

Following this, we define the ensemble's size, learning rate, and the Decision Tree's maximum depth. Furthermore, we create a list to store the individual base learners, as well as a NumPy array to store the previous predictions.

As mentioned earlier, our initial prediction is the train set's target mean. Instead of defining a maximum depth, we could also define a maximum number of leaf nodes by passing the `max_leaf_nodes=3` argument to the constructor:

```
# --- SECTION 2 ---
# Create the ensemble
# Define the ensemble's size, learning rate and decision tree depth
ensemble_size = 50
learning_rate = 0.1
base_classifier = DecisionTreeRegressor(max_depth=3)
# Create placeholders for the base learners and each step's prediction
base_learners = []
# Note that the initial prediction is the target variable's mean
previous_predictions = np.zeros(len(train_y)) + np.mean(train_y)
```

The next step is to create and train the ensemble. We start by calculating the pseudo-residuals, using the previous predictions. We then create a deep copy of the base learner class and train it on the train set, using the pseudo-residuals as targets:

```
# Create the base learners
for _ in range(ensemble_size):
    # Start by calculating the pseudo-residuals
    errors = train_y - previous_predictions
    # Make a deep copy of the base classifier and train it on the
    # pseudo-residuals
    learner = deepcopy(base_classifier)
    learner.fit(train_x, errors)
    predictions = learner.predict(train_x)
```

Finally, we use the trained base learner in order to predict the pseudo-residuals on the train set. We multiply the predictions by the learning rate and add them to our previous predictions. Finally, we append the base learner to the `base_learners` list:

```
    # Multiply the predictions with the learning rate and add the results
    # to the previous prediction
    previous_predictions = previous_predictions + learning_rate*predictions
    # Save the base learner
    base_learners.append(learner)
```

In order to make predictions with our ensemble and evaluate it, we use the test set's features in order to predict pseudo-residuals, multiply them by the learning rate, and add them to the train set's target mean. It is important to use the original train set's mean as a starting point, because each tree predicts deviation from that original mean:

```
# --- SECTION 3 ---
# Evaluate the ensemble
# Start with the train set's mean
previous_predictions = np.zeros(len(test_y)) + np.mean(train_y)
# For each base learner predict the pseudo-residuals for the test set and
# add them to the previous prediction,
# after multiplying with the learning rate
for learner in base_learners:
    predictions = learner.predict(test_x)
    previous_predictions = previous_predictions + learning_rate*predictions


# --- SECTION 4 ---
# Print the metrics
r2 = metrics.r2_score(test_y, previous_predictions)
mse = metrics.mean_squared_error(test_y, previous_predictions)
print('Gradient Boosting:')
print('R-squared: %.2f' % r2)
print('MSE: %.2f' % mse)
```

The algorithm is able to achieve an R-squared value of 0.59 and an MSE of 2253.34 with this particular setup.

Using scikit-learn

Although for educational purposes it is useful to code our own algorithms, scikit-learn has some very good implementations for both classification and regression problems. In this section, we will go through the implementations, as well as see how we can extract information about the generated ensembles.

Using AdaBoost

Scikit-learn's Adaboost implementations exist in the `sklearn.ensemble` package, in the `AdaBoostClassifier` and `AdaBoostRegressor` classes.

Like all scikit-learn classifiers, we use the `fit` and `predict` functions in order to train the classifier and predict on the test set. The first parameter is the base classifier that the algorithm will use. The `algorithm="SAMME"` parameter forces the classifier to use a discrete boosting algorithm. For this example, we use the hand-written digits recognition problem:

```
# --- SECTION 1 ---
# Libraries and data loading
import numpy as np

from sklearn.datasets import load_digits
from sklearn.tree import DecisionTreeClassifier
from sklearn.ensemble import AdaBoostClassifier
from sklearn import metrics

digits = load_digits()
train_size = 1500
train_x, train_y = digits.data[:train_size], digits.target[:train_size]
test_x, test_y = digits.data[train_size:], digits.target[train_size:]
np.random.seed(123456)

# --- SECTION 2 ---
# Create the ensemble
ensemble_size = 200
ensemble = AdaBoostClassifier(DecisionTreeClassifier(max_depth=1),
                              algorithm="SAMME",
                              n_estimators=ensemble_size)

# --- SECTION 3 ---
# Train the ensemble
ensemble.fit(train_x, train_y)

# --- SECTION 4 ---
# Evaluate the ensemble
ensemble_predictions = ensemble.predict(test_x)
ensemble_acc = metrics.accuracy_score(test_y, ensemble_predictions)

# --- SECTION 5 ---
# Print the accuracy
print('Boosting: %.2f' % ensemble_acc)
```

This results in an ensemble with 81% accuracy on the test set. One advantage of using the provided implementation is that we can access and plot each individual base learner's errors and weights. We can access them through `ensemble.estimator_errors_` and `ensemble.estimator_weights_`, respectively. By plotting the weights, we can gauge where the ensemble stops to benefit from additional base learners. By creating an ensemble of 1,000 base learners, we see that from approximately the 200 base learners mark, the weights are stabilized. Thus, there is little point in adding more than 200. This is further confirmed by the fact that the ensemble of size 1,000 achieves an 82% accuracy, a small increase over the 81% achieved with 200 base learners:

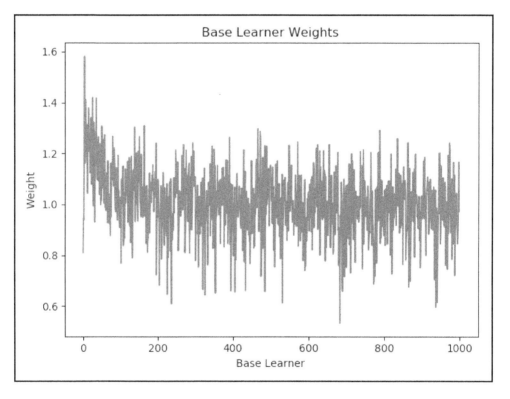

Base learner weights for an ensemble of 1,000 base learners

The regression implementation adheres to the same principles. Here, we test the algorithm on the diabetes dataset:

```
# --- SECTION 1 ---
# Libraries and data loading
from copy import deepcopy
from sklearn.datasets import load_diabetes
from sklearn.ensemble import AdaBoostRegressor
from sklearn.tree import DecisionTreeRegressor
from sklearn import metrics

import numpy as np

diabetes = load_diabetes()

train_size = 400
train_x, train_y = diabetes.data[:train_size], diabetes.target[:train_size]
test_x, test_y = diabetes.data[train_size:], diabetes.target[train_size:]

np.random.seed(123456)

# --- SECTION 2 ---
# Create the ensemble
ensemble_size = 1000
ensemble = AdaBoostRegressor(n_estimators=ensemble_size)

# --- SECTION 3 ---
# Evaluate the ensemble
ensemble.fit(train_x, train_y)
predictions = ensemble.predict(test_x)

# --- SECTION 4 ---
# Print the metrics
r2 = metrics.r2_score(test_y, predictions)
mse = metrics.mean_squared_error(test_y, predictions)

print('Gradient Boosting:')
print('R-squared: %.2f' % r2)
print('MSE: %.2f' % mse)
```

The ensemble generates an R-squared of 0.59 and an MSE of 2256.5. By plotting the weights of the base learners, we see that the algorithm has stopped early, due to negligible improvement in predictive power, after the 151st base learner. This is indicated by the zero valued weights in the plot. Furthermore, by printing the length of `ensemble.estimators_`, we observe that its length is only 151. This is the equivalent of the `base_learners` list in our implementation:

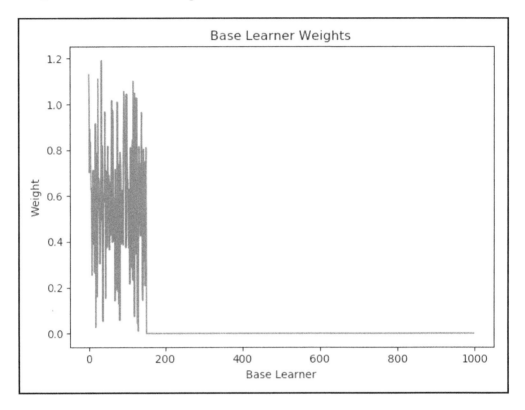

Base learner weights for the regression Adaboost

Using gradient boosting

Scikit-learn also implements gradient boosting regression and classification. They too are included in the ensemble package, under GradientBoostingRegressor and GradientBoostingClassifier, respectively. The two classes store the errors at each step, in the train_score_ attribute of the object. Here, we present an example for the diabetes regression dataset. The train and validation processes follow the scikit-learn standard, using the fit and predict functions. The only parameter that needs to be specified is the learning rate, which is passed to the GradientBoostingRegressor constructor through the learning_rate parameter:

```
# --- SECTION 1 ---
# Libraries and data loading
from sklearn.datasets import load_diabetes
from sklearn.ensemble import GradientBoostingRegressor
from sklearn import metrics
import numpy as np
diabetes = load_diabetes()
train_size = 400
train_x, train_y = diabetes.data[:train_size], diabetes.target[:train_size]
test_x, test_y = diabetes.data[train_size:], diabetes.target[train_size:]
np.random.seed(123456)

# --- SECTION 2 ---
# Create the ensemble
ensemble_size = 200
learning_rate = 0.1
ensemble = GradientBoostingRegressor(n_estimators=ensemble_size,
  learning_rate=learning_rate)

# --- SECTION 3 ---
# Evaluate the ensemble
ensemble.fit(train_x, train_y)
predictions = ensemble.predict(test_x)

# --- SECTION 4 ---
# Print the metrics
r2 = metrics.r2_score(test_y, predictions)
mse = metrics.mean_squared_error(test_y, predictions)
print('Gradient Boosting:')
print('R-squared: %.2f' % r2)
print('MSE: %.2f' % mse)
```

The ensemble achieves an R-squared of 0.44 and an MSE of 3092. Furthermore, if we use matplotlib to plot ensemble.train_score_, we can see that diminishing returns appear after around 20 base learners. If we further analyze the errors, by calculating the improvements (difference between base learners), we see that after 25 base learners there are cases where adding a base learner worsens the performance.

Although on average the performance continues to increase, after 50 base learners there is no significant improvement. Thus, we repeat the experiment, with ensemble_size = 50, yielding an R-squared of 0.61 and an MSE of 2152:

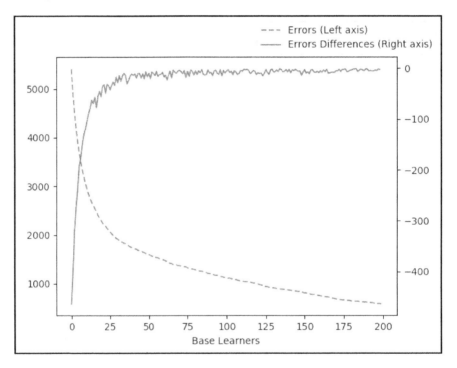

Errors and differences for gradient boost regression

For the classification example, we use the hand-written digit classification dataset. Again, we define the n_estimators and learning_rate parameters:

```
# --- SECTION 1 ---
# Libraries and data loading
import numpy as np

from sklearn.datasets import load_digits
from sklearn.tree import DecisionTreeClassifier
from sklearn.ensemble import GradientBoostingClassifier
from sklearn import metrics


digits = load_digits()

train_size = 1500
train_x, train_y = digits.data[:train_size], digits.target[:train_size]
test_x, test_y = digits.data[train_size:], digits.target[train_size:]

np.random.seed(123456)
# --- SECTION 2 ---
# Create the ensemble
ensemble_size = 200
learning_rate = 0.1
ensemble = GradientBoostingClassifier(n_estimators=ensemble_size,
 learning_rate=learning_rate)

# --- SECTION 3 ---
# Train the ensemble
ensemble.fit(train_x, train_y)

# --- SECTION 4 ---
# Evaluate the ensemble
ensemble_predictions = ensemble.predict(test_x)

ensemble_acc = metrics.accuracy_score(test_y, ensemble_predictions)

# --- SECTION 5 ---
# Print the accuracy
print('Boosting: %.2f' % ensemble_acc)
```

The accuracy achieved with the specific ensemble size is 89%. By plotting the errors and their differences, we see that there are again diminishing returns, but there are no cases where performance significantly drops. Thus, we do not expect a predictive performance improvement by reducing the ensemble size.

XGBoost

XGBoost is a boosting library with parallel, GPU, and distributed execution support. It has helped many machine learning engineers and data scientists to win Kaggle.com competitions. Furthermore, it provides an interface that resembles scikit-learn's interface. Thus, someone already familiar with the interface is able to quickly utilize the library. Additionally, it allows for very fine control over the ensemble's creation. It supports monotonic constraints (that is, the predicted value should only increase or decrease, relative to a specific feature), as well as feature interaction constraints (for example, if a decision tree creates a node that splits by age, it should not use sex as a splitting feature for all children of that specific node). Finally, it adds an additional regularization parameter, gamma, which further reduces the overfitting capabilities of the generated ensemble. The corresponding paper is Chen, T. and Guestrin, C., 2016, August. Xgboost: A scalable tree boosting system. In *Proceedings of the 22nd acm sigkdd international conference on knowledge discovery and data mining* (pp. 785-794). ACM.

Using XGBoost for regression

We will present a simple regression example with XGBoost, using the diabetes dataset. As it will be shown, its usage is quite simple and similar to the scikit-learn classifiers. XGBoost implements regression with XGBRegressor. The constructor has a respectably large number of parameters, which are very well-documented in the official documentation. In our example, we will use the n_estimators, n_jobs, max_depth, and learning_rate parameters. Following scikit-learn's conventions, they define the ensemble size, the number of parallel processes, the tree's maximum depth, and the learning rate, respectively:

```python
# --- SECTION 1 ---
# Libraries and data loading
from sklearn.datasets import load_diabetes
from xgboost import XGBRegressor
from sklearn import metrics
import numpy as np
diabetes = load_diabetes()
train_size = 400
train_x, train_y = diabetes.data[:train_size], diabetes.target[:train_size]
test_x, test_y = diabetes.data[train_size:], diabetes.target[train_size:]
```

```
np.random.seed(123456)

# --- SECTION 2 ---
# Create the ensemble
ensemble_size = 200
ensemble = XGBRegressor(n_estimators=ensemble_size, n_jobs=4,
                        max_depth=1, learning_rate=0.1,
  objective ='reg:squarederror')
```

The rest of the code evaluates the generated `ensemble`, and is similar to any of the previous examples:

```
# --- SECTION 3 ---
# Evaluate the ensemble
ensemble.fit(train_x, train_y)
predictions = ensemble.predict(test_x)

# --- SECTION 4 ---
# Print the metrics
r2 = metrics.r2_score(test_y, predictions)
mse = metrics.mean_squared_error(test_y, predictions)
print('Gradient Boosting:')
print('R-squared: %.2f' % r2)
print('MSE: %.2f' % mse)
```

XGBoost achieves an R-squared of 0.65 and an MSE of 1932.9, the best performance out of all the boosting methods we tested and implemented in this chapter. Furthermore, we did not fine-tune any of its parameters, which further displays its modeling power.

Using XGBoost for classification

For classification purposes, the corresponding class is implemented in `XGBClassifier`. The constructor's parameters are the same as the regression implementation. For our example, we use the hand-written digit classification problem. We set the `n_estimators` parameter to `100` and `n_jobs` to `4`. The rest of the code follows the usual template:

```
# --- SECTION 1 ---
# Libraries and data loading
from sklearn.datasets import load_digits
from xgboost import XGBClassifier
from sklearn import metrics
import numpy as np
digits = load_digits()
train_size = 1500
train_x, train_y = digits.data[:train_size], digits.target[:train_size]
```

```
test_x, test_y = digits.data[train_size:], digits.target[train_size:]
np.random.seed(123456)

# --- SECTION 2 ---
# Create the ensemble
ensemble_size = 100
ensemble = XGBClassifier(n_estimators=ensemble_size, n_jobs=4)

# --- SECTION 3 ---
# Train the ensemble
ensemble.fit(train_x, train_y)

# --- SECTION 4 ---
# Evaluate the ensemble
ensemble_predictions = ensemble.predict(test_x)
ensemble_acc = metrics.accuracy_score(test_y, ensemble_predictions)

# --- SECTION 5 ---
# Print the accuracy
print('Boosting: %.2f' % ensemble_acc)
```

The ensemble correctly classifies the test set with 89% accuracy, also the highest achieved for any boosting algorithm.

Other boosting libraries

Two other boosting libraries that are gaining popularity are Microsoft's LightGBM and Yandex' CatBoost. Both of these libraries can match (and even outperform) XGBoost, under certain circumstances. Nonetheless, XGBoost is the best of all three out of the box, without the need of fine-tuning and special data treatment.

Summary

In this chapter, we presented one of the most powerful ensemble learning techniques, boosting. We presented two popular boosting algorithms, AdaBoost and gradient boosting. We presented custom implementations for both algorithms, as well as usage examples for the scikit-learn implementations. Furthermore, we briefly presented XGBoost, a library dedicated to regularized, distributed boosting. XGBoost was able to outperform all other methods and implementations on both regression as well as classification problems.

AdaBoost creates a number of base learners by employing weak learners (slightly better than random guessing). Each new base learner is trained on a weighted sample from the original train set. Weighted sampling from a dataset assigns a weight to each instance and then samples from the dataset, using the weights in order to calculate the probability that each instance will be sampled.

The data weights are calculated based on the previous base learner's errors. The base learner's error is also used to calculate the learner's weight. The base learners' predictions are combined through voting, using each learner's weight. Gradient boosting builds its ensemble by training each new base learner using the previous prediction's errors as a target. The initial prediction is the train dataset's target mean. Boosting methods cannot be parallelized in the degree that bagging methods can be. Although robust to overfitting, boosting methods can overfit.

In scikit-learn, AdaBoost implementations store the individual learners' weights, which can be used to identify the point where additional base learners do not contribute to the ensemble's predictive power. Gradient Boosting implementations store the ensemble's error at each step (base learner), which can also help to identify an optimal number of base learners. XGBoost is a library dedicated to boosting, with regularization capabilities that further reduce the overfitting ability of the ensembles. XGBoost is frequently a part of winning machine learning models in many Kaggle competitions.

7
Random Forests

Bagging is generally used to reduce variance of a model. It achieves it by creating an ensemble of base learners, each one trained on a unique bootstrap sample of the original train set. This forces diversity between the base learners. Random Forests expand on bagging by inducing randomness not only on each base learner's train samples, but in the features as well. Furthermore, their performance is similar to boosting techniques, although they do not require as much fine-tuning as boosting methods.

In this chapter, we will provide the basic background of random forests, as well as discuss the strengths and weaknesses of the method. Finally, we will present usage examples, using the scikit-learn implementation. The main topics covered in this chapter are as follows:

- How Random Forests build their base learners
- How randomness can be utilized in order to build better random forest ensembles
- The strengths and weaknesses of Random Forests
- Utilizing scikit-learn's implementation for regression and classification

Technical requirements

You will require basic knowledge of machine learning techniques and algorithms. Furthermore, a knowledge of python conventions and syntax is required. Finally, familiarity with the NumPy library will greatly help the reader to understand some custom algorithm implementations.

The code files of this chapter can be found on GitHub:

https://github.com/PacktPublishing/Hands-On-Ensemble-Learning-with-Python/tree/master/Chapter07

Check out the following video to see the Code in Action: http://bit.ly/2LY5OJR.

Understanding random forest trees

In this section, we will go over the methodology of building a basic random forest tree. There are other methods that can be employed, but they all strive to achieve the same goal: diverse trees that serve as the ensemble's base learners.

Building trees

As mentioned in `Chapter 1`, *A Machine Learning Refresher*, create a tree by selecting at each node a single feature and split point, such that the train set is best split. When an ensemble is created, we wish the base learners to be as uncorrelated (diverse) as possible.

Bagging is able to produce reasonably uncorrelated trees by diversifying each tree's train set through bootstrapping. But bagging only diversifies the trees by acting on one axis: each set's instances. There is still a second axis on which we can introduce diversity, the features. By selecting a subset of the available features during training, the generated base learners can be even more diverse. In random forests, for each tree and at each node, only a subset of the available features is considered when choosing the best feature/split point combination. The number of features that will be selected can be optimized by hand, but one-third of all features for regression problems and the square root of all features are considered to be a good starting point.

The algorithm's steps are as follows:

1. Select the number of features m that will be considered at each node
2. For each base learner, do the following:
    1. Create a bootstrap train sample
    2. Select the node to split
    3. Select m features randomly
    4. Pick the best feature and split point from m
    5. Split the node into two nodes
    6. Repeat from step 2-2 until a stopping criterion is met, such as maximum tree depth

Illustrative example

In order to better illustrate the process, let's consider the following dataset, indicating whether a second shoulder dislocation has occurred after the first (recurrence):

Age	Operated	Sex	Recurrence
15	y	m	y
45	n	f	n
30	y	m	y
18	n	m	n
52	n	f	y

Shoulder dislocation recurrence dataset

In order to build a Random Forest tree, we must first decide the number of features that will be considered in each split. As we have three features, we will use the square root of 3, which is approximately 1.7. Usually, we use the floor of this number (we round it down to the closest integer), but as we want to illustrate the process, we will use two features in order to better demonstrate it. For the first tree, we generate a bootstrap sample. The second row is an instance that was chosen twice from the original dataset:

Age	Operated	Sex	Recurrence
15	y	m	y
15	y	m	y
30	y	m	y
18	n	m	n
52	n	f	y

The bootstrap sample

Next, we create the root node. First, we randomly select two features to consider. We choose **operated** and **sex**. The best split is given for **operated**, as we get a leaf with 100% accuracy and one node with 50% accuracy. The resulting tree is depicted as follows:

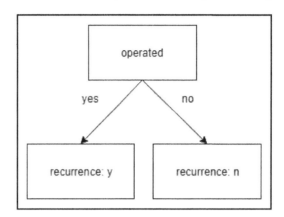

The tree after the first split

Next, we again select two features at random and the one that offers the best split. We now choose **operated** and **age**. As both misclassified instances were not operated, the best split is offered through the age feature.

Thus, the final tree is a tree with three leaves, where if someone is operated they have a recurrence, while if they are not operated and are over the age of 18 they do not:

Note that medical research indicates that young males have the highest chance for shoulder dislocation recurrence. The dataset here is a toy example that does not reflect reality.

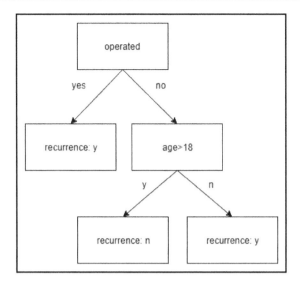

The final decision tree

Extra trees

Another method to create trees in a Random Forest ensemble is Extra Trees (extremely randomized trees). The main difference with the previous method is that the feature and split point combination does not have to be the optimal. Instead, a number of split points are randomly generated, one for each available feature. The best split point of those generated is selected. The algorithm constructs a tree as follows:

1. Select the number of features m that will be considered at each node and the minimum number of samples n in order to split a node
2. For each base learner, do the following:
    1. Create a bootstrap train sample
    2. Select the node to split (the node must have at least n samples)
    3. Select m features randomly
    4. Randomly generate m split points, with values between the minimum and maximum value of each feature
    5. Select the best of these split points
    6. Split the node into two nodes and repeat from step 2-2 until there are no available nodes

Creating forests

By creating a number of trees using any valid randomization method, we have essentially created a forest, hence the algorithm's name. After generating the ensemble's trees, their predictions must be combined in order to have a functional ensemble. This is usually achieved through majority voting for classification problems and through averaging for regression problems. There are a number of hyperparameters associated with Random Forests, such as the number of features to consider at each node split, the number of trees in the forest, and the individual tree's size. As mentioned earlier, a good starting point for the number of features to consider is as follows:

- The square root of the number of total features for classification problems
- One-third of the number of total features for regression problems

The total number of trees can be fine-tuned by hand, as the ensemble's error converges to a limit when this number increases. Out-of-bag errors can be utilized to find an optimal value. Finally, the size of each tree can be a deciding factor in overfitting. Thus, if overfitting is observed, the tree size should be reduced.

Analyzing forests

Random Forests provide information about the underlying dataset that most of other methods cannot easily provide. A prominent example is the importance of each individual feature in the dataset. One method to estimate feature importance is to use the Gini index for each node of each tree and compare each feature's cumulative value. Another method uses the out-of-bag samples. First, the out-of-bag accuracy is recorded for all base learners. Then, a single feature is chosen and its values are shuffled in the out-of-bag samples. This results in out-of-bag sample sets with the same statistical properties as the original sets, but any predictive power that the chosen feature might have is removed (as there is now zero correlation between the selected feature's values and the target). The difference in accuracy between the original and the partially random dataset is used as measure for the selected feature's importance.

Concerning bias and variance, although random forests seem to cope well with both, they are certainly not immune. Bias can appear when the available features are great in number, but only few are correlated to the target. When using the recommended number of features to consider at each split (for example, the square root of the number of total features), the probability that a relevant feature will be selected can be small. The following graph shows the probability that at least one relevant feature will be selected, as a function of relevant and irrelevant features (when the square root of the number of total features is considered at each split):

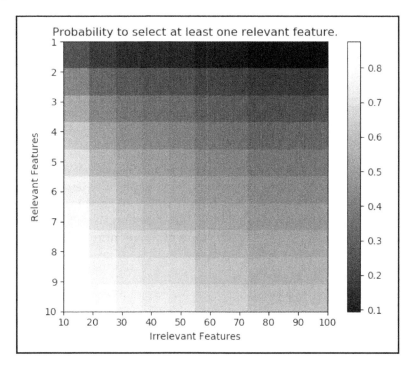

Probability to select at least one relevant feature as a function of the number of relevant and irrelevant features

 The Gini index measures the frequency of incorrect classifications, assuming that a randomly sampled instance would be classified according to the label distribution dictated by a specific node.

Variance can also appear in Random Forests, although the method is sufficiently resistant to it. Variance usually appears when the individual trees are allowed to grow fully. We have previously mentioned that as the number of trees increases, the error approximates a certain limit. Although this claim still holds true, it is possible that the limit itself overfits the data. Restricting the tree size (by increasing the minimum number of samples per leaf or reducing the maximum depth) can potentially help in such circumstances.

Strengths and weaknesses

Random Forests are a very robust ensemble learning method, able to reduce both bias and variance, similar to boosting. Furthermore, the algorithm's nature allows it to be fully parallelized, both during training, as well as during prediction. This is a considerable advantage over boosting methods, especially when large datasets are concerned. Furthermore, they require less hyperparameter fine-tuning, compared to boosting techniques, especially XGBoost.

The main weaknesses of random forests are their sensitivity to class imbalances, as well as the problem we mentioned earlier, which involves a low ratio of relevant to irrelevant features in the train set. Furthermore, when the data contains low-level non-linear patterns (such as in raw, high-resolution image recognition), Random Forests usually are outperformed by deep neural networks. Finally, Random Forests can be computationally expensive when very large datasets are used combined with unrestricted tree depth.

Using scikit-learn

scikit-learn implements both conventional Random Forest trees, as well as Extra Trees. In this section, we will provide basic regression and classification examples with both algorithms, using the scikit-learn implementations.

Random forests for classification

The Random Forests classification class is implemented in `RandomForestClassifier`, under the `sklearn.ensemble` package. It has a number of parameters, such as the ensemble's size, the maximum tree depth, the number of samples required to make or split a node, and many more.

In this example, we will try to classify the hand-written digits dataset, using the Random Forest classification ensemble. As usual, we load the required classes and data and set the seed for our random number generator:

```
# --- SECTION 1 ---
# Libraries and data loading
from sklearn.datasets import load_digits
from sklearn.ensemble import RandomForestClassifier
from sklearn import metrics
import numpy as np

digits = load_digits()

train_size = 1500
train_x, train_y = digits.data[:train_size], digits.target[:train_size]
test_x, test_y = digits.data[train_size:], digits.target[train_size:]

np.random.seed(123456)
```

Following this, we create the ensemble, by setting
the n_estimators and n_jobs parameters. These parameters dictate the number of trees that will be generated and the number of parallel jobs that will be run. We train the ensemble using the fit function and evaluate it on the test set by measuring its achieved accuracy:

```
# --- SECTION 2 ---
# Create the ensemble
ensemble_size = 500
ensemble = RandomForestClassifier(n_estimators=ensemble_size, n_jobs=4)

# --- SECTION 3 ---
# Train the ensemble
ensemble.fit(train_x, train_y)

# --- SECTION 4 ---
# Evaluate the ensemble
ensemble_predictions = ensemble.predict(test_x)

ensemble_acc = metrics.accuracy_score(test_y, ensemble_predictions)

# --- SECTION 5 ---
# Print the accuracy
print('Random Forest: %.2f' % ensemble_acc)
```

The classifier is able to achieve an accuracy of 93%, which is even higher than the previously best-performing method, XGBoost (`Chapter 6`, *Boosting*). We can visualize the approximation of the error limit we mentioned earlier, by plotting validation curves (from `Chapter 2`, *Getting Started with Ensemble Learning*) for a number of ensemble sizes. We test for sizes of 10, 50, 100, 150, 200, 250, 300, 350, and 400 trees. The curves are depicted in the following graph. We can see that the ensemble approaches a 10-fold cross-validation error of 96%:

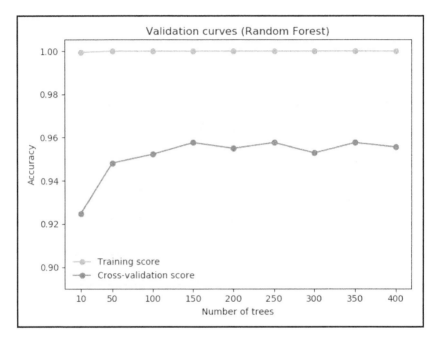

Validation curves for a number of ensemble sizes

Random forests for regression

Scikit-learn also implements random forests for regression purposes in the `RandomForestRegressor` class. It is also highly parameterizable, with hyper-parameters concerning both the ensemble as a whole, as well as the individual trees. Here, we will generate an ensemble in order to model the diabetes regression dataset. The code follows the standard procedure of loading libraries and data, creating the ensemble and calling the `fit` and predict methods, along with calculating the MSE and R-squared values:

```
# --- SECTION 1 ---
# Libraries and data loading
```

```
from copy import deepcopy
from sklearn.datasets import load_diabetes
from sklearn.ensemble import RandomForestRegressor
from sklearn import metrics

import numpy as np

diabetes = load_diabetes()

train_size = 400
train_x, train_y = diabetes.data[:train_size], diabetes.target[:train_size]
test_x, test_y = diabetes.data[train_size:], diabetes.target[train_size:]

np.random.seed(123456)

# --- SECTION 2 ---
# Create the ensemble
ensemble_size = 100
ensemble = RandomForestRegressor(n_estimators=ensemble_size, n_jobs=4)

# --- SECTION 3 ---
# Evaluate the ensemble
ensemble.fit(train_x, train_y)
predictions = ensemble.predict(test_x)

# --- SECTION 4 ---
# Print the metrics
r2 = metrics.r2_score(test_y, predictions)
mse = metrics.mean_squared_error(test_y, predictions)

print('Random Forest:')
print('R-squared: %.2f' % r2)
print('MSE: %.2f' % mse)
```

The ensemble is able to produce an R-squared of 0.51 and an MSE of 2722.67 on the test set. As the R-squared and MSE on the train set are 0.92 and 468.13 respectively, it is safe to assume that the ensemble overfits. This is a case where the error limit overfits, and thus we need to regulate the individual trees in order to achieve better results. By reducing the minimum number of samples required to be at each leaf node (increased to 20, from the default value of 2) through `min_samples_leaf=20`, we are able to increase R-squared to 0.6 and reduce MSE to 2206.6. Furthermore, by increasing the ensemble size to 1000, R-squared is further increased to 0.61 and MSE is further decreased to 2158.73.

Extra trees for classification

Apart from conventional Random Forests, scikit-learn also implements Extra Trees. The classification implementation lies in the `ExtraTreesClassifier`, in the `sklearn.ensemble` package. Here, we repeat the hand-written digit recognition example, using the Extra Trees classifier:

```
# --- SECTION 1 ---
# Libraries and data loading
from sklearn.datasets import load_digits
from sklearn.ensemble import ExtraTreesClassifier
from sklearn import metrics
import numpy as np

digits = load_digits()

train_size = 1500
train_x, train_y = digits.data[:train_size], digits.target[:train_size]
test_x, test_y = digits.data[train_size:], digits.target[train_size:]

np.random.seed(123456)
# --- SECTION 2 ---
# Create the ensemble
ensemble_size = 500
ensemble = ExtraTreesClassifier(n_estimators=ensemble_size, n_jobs=4)

# --- SECTION 3 ---
# Train the ensemble
ensemble.fit(train_x, train_y)

# --- SECTION 4 ---
# Evaluate the ensemble
ensemble_predictions = ensemble.predict(test_x)

ensemble_acc = metrics.accuracy_score(test_y, ensemble_predictions)

# --- SECTION 5 ---
# Print the accuracy
print('Extra Tree Forest: %.2f' % ensemble_acc)
```

As you may notice, the only difference with the previous example is the switch from `RandomForestClassifier` to `ExtraTreesClassifier`. Nonetheless, the ensemble achieves an even higher test accuracy score of 94%. Once again, we create validation curves for a number of ensemble sizes, depicted as follows. The 10-fold cross validation error limit for this ensemble is approximately at 97%, which further confirms that it outperforms the conventional Random Forest approach:

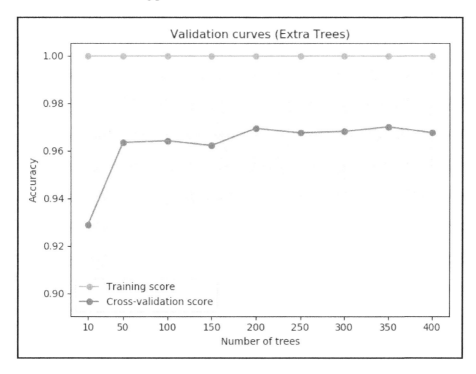

Extra Trees validation curves for a number of ensemble sizes

Extra trees regression

Finally, we present the regression implementation of Extra Trees, implemented in `ExtraTreesRegressor`. In the following code, we repeat the previously presented example of modeling the diabetes dataset, using the regression version of Extra Trees:

```
# --- SECTION 1 ---
# Libraries and data loading
from copy import deepcopy
from sklearn.datasets import load_diabetes
from sklearn.ensemble import ExtraTreesRegressor
```

```
from sklearn import metrics

import numpy as np

diabetes = load_diabetes()

train_size = 400
train_x, train_y = diabetes.data[:train_size], diabetes.target[:train_size]
test_x, test_y = diabetes.data[train_size:], diabetes.target[train_size:]

np.random.seed(123456)

# --- SECTION 2 ---
# Create the ensemble
ensemble_size = 100
ensemble = ExtraTreesRegressor(n_estimators=ensemble_size, n_jobs=4)

# --- SECTION 3 ---
# Evaluate the ensemble
ensemble.fit(train_x, train_y)
predictions = ensemble.predict(test_x)

# --- SECTION 4 ---
# Print the metrics
r2 = metrics.r2_score(test_y, predictions)
mse = metrics.mean_squared_error(test_y, predictions)

print('Extra Trees:')
print('R-squared: %.2f' % r2)
print('MSE: %.2f' % mse)
```

Similar to the classification examples, Extra Trees outperform conventional random forests by achieving a test R-squared of 0.55 (0.04 better than Random Forests) and an MSE of 2479.18 (a difference of 243.49). Still, the ensemble seems to overfit, as it perfectly predicts in-sample data. By setting `min_samples_leaf=10` and the ensemble size to 1000, we are able to produce an R-squared of 0.62 and an MSE of 2114.

Summary

In this chapter, we discussed Random Forests, an ensemble method utilizing decision trees as its base learners. We presented two basic methods of constructing the trees: the conventional Random Forests approach, where a subset of features is considered at each split, as well as Extra Trees, where the split points are chosen almost randomly. We discussed the basic characteristics of the ensemble method. Furthermore, we presented regression and classification examples using the scikit-learn implementations of Random Forests and Extra Trees. The key points of this chapter that summarize its contents are provided below.

Random Forests use bagging in order to create train sets for their base learners. At each node, each tree considers only a subset of the available features and computes the optimal feature/split point combination. The number of features to consider at each point is a hyper-parameter that must be tuned. Good starting points are as follows:

- The square root of the total number of parameters for classification problems
- One-third of the total number of parameters for regression problems

Extra trees and random forests use the **whole dataset** for each base learner. In extra trees and random forests, instead of calculating the optimal feature/split-point combination of the feature subset at each node, a random split point is generated for each feature in the subset and the best is selected. Random forests can give information regarding the importance of each feature. Although relatively resistant to overfitting, random forests are not immune to it. Random forests can exhibit high bias when the ratio of relevant to irrelevant features is low. Random forests can exhibit high variance, although the ensemble size does not contribute to the problem. In the next chapter, we will present ensemble learning techniques that can be applied to unsupervised learning methods (clustering).

Section 4: Clustering

In this section, we will cover the use of ensembles for clustering applications.

This section comprises the following chapters:

- Chapter 8, *Clustering*

8
Clustering

One of the most widely used unsupervised learning methods is clustering. Clustering aims to uncover structure in unlabeled data. The aim is to group together data instances, such that there is great similarity between instances of the same cluster, and little similarity between instances of different clusters. As with supervised learning methods, clustering can benefit from combining many base learners. In this chapter, we present k-means; a simple and widely used clustering algorithm. Furthermore, we discuss how ensembles can be used to improve the algorithm's performance. Finally, we use OpenEnsembles, a scikit-learn compatible Python library that implements ensemble clustering. The main topics covered in this chapter are as follows:

- How the K-means algorithm works
- Its strengths and weaknesses
- How ensembles can improve its performance
- Utilizing OpenEnsembles to create clustering ensembles

Technical requirements

You will require basic knowledge of machine learning techniques and algorithms. Furthermore, a knowledge of python conventions and syntax is required. Finally, familiarity with the NumPy library will greatly help the reader to understand some custom algorithm implementations.

The code files of this chapter can be found on GitHub:

`https://github.com/PacktPublishing/Hands-On-Ensemble-Learning-with-Python/tree/master/Chapter08`

Check out the following video to see the Code in Action: `http://bit.ly/2YYzniq`.

Consensus clustering

Consensus clustering is an alias for ensemble learning when it is applied to clustering methods. In clustering, each base learner assigns a label to each instance, although it is not conditioned on a specific target. Instead, the base learner generates a number of clusters and assigns each instance to a cluster. The label is the cluster itself. As will be demonstrated later, two base learners, produced by the same algorithm, can generate different clusters. Thus, it is not as straightforward to combine their cluster predictions as it is to combine regression or classification predictions.

Hierarchical clustering

Hierarchical clustering initially creates as many clusters as there are instances in the dataset. Each cluster contains only a single instance. Following this, it repeatedly finds the two clusters with the minimum distance between them (for example, the Euclidean distance), and merges them together into a new cluster. The process ends when there is only a single cluster. The method's output is a dendrogram, which indicates how instances are hierarchically organized. An example is depicted in the following figure:

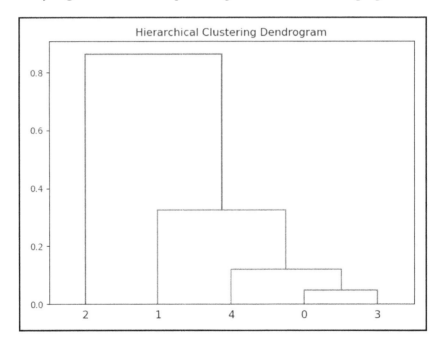

Dendrogram example

K-means clustering

K-means is a relatively simple and effective way to cluster data. The main idea is that by starting with a number of *K* points as the initial cluster centers, each instance is assigned to the nearest cluster center. Then, the centers are re-calculated as the mean point of their respective members. This process repeats until the cluster centers no longer change. The main steps are as follows:

1. Select the number of clusters, *K*
2. Select *K* random instances as the initial cluster centers
3. Assign each instance to the closest cluster center
4. Re-calculate the cluster centers as the mean of each cluster's members
5. If the new centers differ from the previous, go back to *Step 3*

A graphical example is depicted as follows. After four iterations, the algorithm converges:

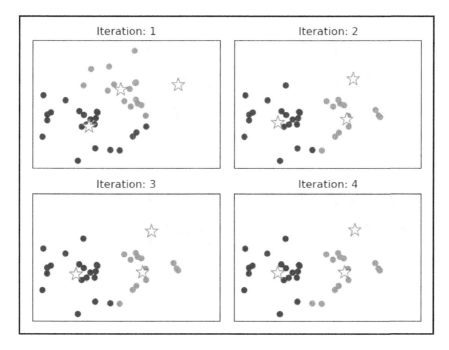

The first four iterations on a toy dataset. Stars represent the cluster centers

Strengths and weaknesses

K-means is a simple algorithm, both to understand, as well as to implement. Furthermore, it usually converges relatively fast, requiring small computing power. Nonetheless, it has some disadvantages. The first one is its sensitivity to the initial conditions. Depending on the examples chosen as the first cluster centers, it can require more iterations in order to converge. For example, in the following diagram we present three initial points that put the algorithm at a disadvantage. In fact, in the third iteration, two cluster centers happen to coincide:

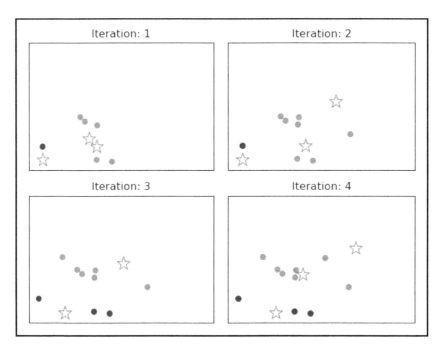

An example of unfortunate initial cluster centers

Thus, the algorithm does not produce clusters deterministically. Another major problem is the number of clusters. This is a parameter that the data analyst must choose. There are usually three different solutions to this problem. The first concerns problems where some prior knowledge about the problem exists. Such examples are datasets where there is a need to uncover the structure of something that is known, for example, what is the driving factor behind athletes who improve their performance during a season, given their statistics? In this example, a sports coach could advise that athletes actually either improve drastically, stay the same, or deteriorate. Thus, the analyst could choose 3 as the number of clusters. Another possible solution is to experiment with different values of *K*, and measure the appropriateness of each value. This approach does not require any prior knowledge about the problem domain, but introduces the problem of measuring the appropriateness of each solution. We will see how we can solve these problems in the rest of this chapter.

Using scikit-learn

The scikit-learn has a number of clustering techniques available for use. Here, we briefly present how to use K-means. The algorithm is implemented in the `KMeans` class, which is contained in the `sklearn.cluster` package. This package contains all the clustering algorithms that are available in scikit-learn. In this chapter, we will use mainly K-means, as it is one of the most intuitive algorithms. Furthermore, the techniques used in this chapter can be applied to almost any clustering algorithm. For this experiment, we will try to cluster breast cancer data, in order to explore the possibility of distinguishing malignant cases from benign cases. In order to better visualize the results, we will first perform a **t-Distributed Stochastic Neighbor Embedding (t-SNE)** decomposition, and use the two-dimensional embeddings as features. In order to proceed, we first load the required data and libraries, as well as set the seed for the NumPy random number generator:

You can read more about t-SNE at `https://lvdmaaten.github.io/tsne/`.

```
import matplotlib.pyplot as plt
import numpy as np

from sklearn.cluster import KMeans
from sklearn.datasets import load_breast_cancer
from sklearn.manifold import TSNE

np.random.seed(123456)

bc = load_breast_cancer()
```

Following this, we instantiate t-SNE, and transform our data. We plot the data in order to visually inspect and examine the data structure:

```
data = tsne.fit_transform(bc.dataa)
reds = bc.target == 0
blues = bc.target == 1
plt.scatter(data[reds, 0], data[reds, 1], label='malignant')
plt.scatter(data[blues, 0], data[blues, 1], label='benign')
plt.xlabel('1st Component')
plt.ylabel('2nd Component')
plt.title('Breast Cancer dataa')
plt.legend()
```

The preceding code generates the following plot. We observe two distinct areas. The area populated by the blue points denotes embedding values that imply a high risk that the tumor is malignant:

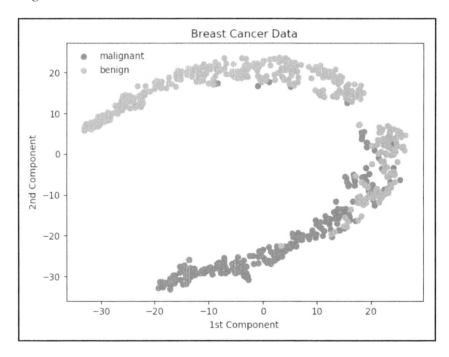

Plot of the two embeddings (components) of the breast cancer data

As we have identified that there exists some structure in the data, we will try to use K-means clustering in order to model it. By intuition, we assume that two clusters would suffice, as we try to separate two distinct regions, and we know that there are two classes in the dataset. Nonetheless, we will also experiment with four and six clusters, as they might provide more insight on the data. We will measure the percentage of each class assigned to each cluster, in order to gauge their quality. We do this by populating the classified dictionary. Each key corresponds to a cluster. Each key also points to a second dictionary, where the number of malignant and benign cases are recorded for the specific cluster. Furthermore, we plot the cluster assignments, as we want to see how the data is distributed among the clusters:

```
plt.figure()
plt.title('2, 4, and 6 clusters.')
for clusters in [2, 4, 6]:
 km = KMeans(n_clusters=clusters)
 preds = km.fit_predict(data)
 plt.subplot(1, 3, clusters/2)
 plt.scatter(*zip(*data), c=preds)

classified = {x: {'m': 0, 'b': 0} for x in range(clusters)}

for i in range(len(data)):
 cluster = preds[i]
 label = bc.target[i]
 label = 'm' if label == 0 else 'b'
 classified[cluster][label] = classified[cluster][label]+1

print('-'*40)
for c in classified:
 print('Cluster %d. Malignant percentage: ' % c, end=' ')
 print(classified[c], end=' ')
 print('%.3f' % (classified[c]['m'] /
 (classified[c]['m'] + classified[c]['b'])))
```

The results are depicted on the following table and figure:

Cluster	Malignant	Benign	Malignant percentage
2 clusters			
0	206	97	0.68
1	6	260	0.023
4 clsuters			
0	2	124	0.016
1	134	1	0.993
2	72	96	0.429
3	4	136	0.029
6 clusters			
0	2	94	0.021
1	81	10	0.89
2	4	88	0.043
3	36	87	0.0293
4	0	78	0
5	89	0	1

Distribution of malignant and benign cases among the clusters

We observe that the algorithm is able to separate the instances belonging to each class quite effectively, even though it has no information about the labels:

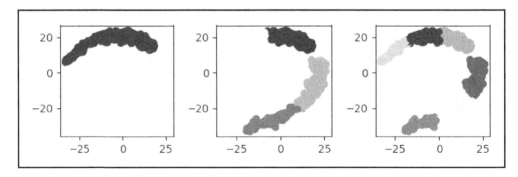

Cluster assignment of each instance: 2, 4, and 6 clusters

Furthermore, we see that as we increase the number of clusters, the instances assigned to dominantly malignant or benign clusters does not increase, but the regions are better separated. This enables greater granularity and a more accurate prediction of probability that a selected instance belongs to either class. If we repeat the experiment without transforming the data, we get the following results:

Cluster	Malignant	Benign	Malignant percentage
2 clusters			
0	82	356	0.187
1	130	1	0.992
4 clusters			
0	6	262	0.022
1	100	1	0.99
2	19	0	1
3	87	94	0.481
6 clusters			
0	37	145	0.203
1	37	0	1
2	11	0	1
3	62	9	0.873
4	5	203	0.024
5	60	0	1

Clustering results on the data without t-sne transform

There are also two metrics that can be used in order to determine cluster quality. For data where the ground truth is known (essentially, labeled data), homogeneity measures the rate by which each cluster is dominated by a single class. For data where the ground truth is not known, the silhouette coefficient measures the intra-cluster cohesiveness and the inter-cluster separability. These metrics are implemented in scikit-learn under the `metrics` package, by the `silhouette_score` and `homogeneity_score` functions. The two metrics for each method are depicted in the following table. Homogeneity is higher for the transformed data, but the silhouette score is lower.

This is expected, as the transformed data has only two dimensions, thus making the possible distance between the instances themselves smaller:

Metric	Clusters	Raw data	Transformed data
Homogeneity	2	0.422	0.418
	4	0.575	0.603
	6	0.620	0.648
Silhouette	2	0.697	0.500
	4	0.533	0.577
	6	0.481	0.555

Homogeneity and silhouette scores for clusterings of the raw and transformed data

Using voting

Voting can be utilized in order to combine different clusterings of the same dataset. It is similar to voting for supervised learning, as each model (base learner) contributes to the final result with a vote. Here arises a problem of linking two clusters originating from two different clusterings. As each model will produce different clusters with different centers, we have to link similar clusters originating from different models. This is accomplished by linking together clusters that share the greatest number of instances. For example, assume that the following table and figure clusterings have occurred for a particular dataset:

Three distinct clustering results

The following table depicts each instance's cluster assignments for the three different clusterings.

Instance	1	2	3	4	5	6	7	8	9	10
Clustering 1	0	0	2	2	2	0	0	1	0	2
Clustering 2	1	1	2	2	2	1	0	1	1	2
Clustering 3	0	0	2	2	2	1	0	1	1	2

Cluster membership of each instance

Using the preceding mapping, we can calculate the co-association matrix for each instance. This matrix indicates how many times a pair of instances has been assigned to the same cluster:

Instances	1	2	3	4	5	6	7	8	9	10
1	3	3	0	0	0	2	2	1	2	0
2	3	3	0	0	0	2	2	1	2	0
3	0	0	3	3	3	0	0	0	0	3
4	0	0	3	3	3	0	0	0	0	3
5	0	0	3	3	3	0	0	0	0	3
6	2	2	0	0	0	3	1	0	3	0
7	2	2	0	0	0	1	3	0	1	0
8	1	1	0	0	0	0	0	3	2	0
9	2	2	0	0	0	3	1	2	3	0
10	0	0	3	3	3	0	0	0	0	3

Co-association matrix for the previous example

By dividing each element with the number of base learners in the ensemble, and clustering together samples that have a value greater than 0.5, we get the following cluster assignments:

Instance	1	2	3	4	5	6	7	8	9	10
Voting clustering	0	0	1	1	1	0	0	0	0	1

The voting cluster memberships

As it is evident, the clustering is more stable. Furthermore, it is apparent that two clusters are sufficient for this dataset. By plotting the data and their cluster membership, we can see that there are two distinct groups, which is exactly what the voting ensemble was able to model, although each base learner generated three distinct cluster centers:

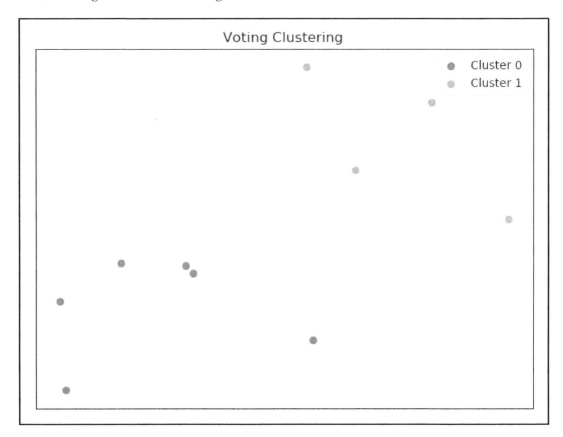

Final cluster memberships for the voting ensemble

Using OpenEnsembles

OpenEnsembles is a Python library that is dedicated to ensemble methods for clustering. In this section, we will present its usage and utilize it in order to cluster some of our example datasets. In order to install the library, the `pip install openensembles` command must be executed in the Terminal. Although it leverages scikit-learn, its interface is different. One major difference is that data must be passed as a `data` class, implemented by OpenEnsembles. The constructor has two input parameters: a pandas `DataFrame` which contains the data, and a list which contains the feature names:

```
# --- SECTION 1 ---
# Libraries and data loading
import openensembles as oe
import pandas as pd
import sklearn.metrics

from sklearn.datasets import load_breast_cancer

bc = load_breast_cancer()

# --- SECTION 2 ---
# Create the data object
cluster_data = oe.data(pd.DataFrame(bc.data), bc.feature_names)
```

In order to create a `cluster` ensemble, a `cluster` class object is created, passing the data as the parameter:

```
ensemble = oe.cluster(cluster_data)
```

In this example, we will calculate the homogeneity score for a number of *K* values and ensemble sizes. In order to add a base learner to the ensemble, the `cluster` method of the `cluster` class must be called. The method accepts as arguments, `source_name`, which denotes the source data matrix name, `algorithm`. This dictates what algorithm the base learners will utilize, `output_name`, which will be the dictionary key for accessing the results of the specific base learner and `K`, the number of clusters for the specific base learner. Finally, in order to compute the final cluster memberships through majority voting, the `finish_majority_vote` method must be called. The only parameter that must be specified is the `threshold` value:

```
# --- SECTION 3 ---
# Create the ensembles and calculate the homogeneity score
for K in [2, 3, 4, 5, 6, 7]:
 for ensemble_size in [3, 4, 5]:
 ensemble = oe.cluster(cluster_data)
 for i in range(ensemble_size):
```

```
name = f'kmeans_{ensemble_size}_{i}'
ensemble.cluster('parent', 'kmeans', name, K)

preds = ensemble.finish_majority_vote(threshold=0.5)
print(f'K: {K}, size {ensemble_size}:', end=' ')
print('%.2f' % sklearn.metrics.homogeneity_score(
    bc.target, preds.labels['majority_vote']))
```

It is evident that five clusters produce the best results for all three ensemble sizes. The results are summarized in the following table:

K	Size	Homogeneity
2	3	0.42
2	4	0.42
2	5	0.42
3	3	0.45
3	4	0.47
3	5	0.47
4	3	0.58
4	4	0.58
4	5	0.58
5	3	0.6
5	4	0.61
5	5	0.6
6	3	0.35
6	4	0.47
6	5	0.35
7	3	0.27
7	4	0.63
7	5	0.37

OpenEnsembles majority vote cluster homogeneity for the breast cancer dataset

If we transform the data into two embeddings with t-SNE, and repeat the experiment, we get the following homogeneity scores:

K	Size	Homogeneity
2	3	0.42
2	4	0.42
2	5	0.42
3	3	0.59
3	4	0.59
3	5	0.59
4	3	0.61
4	4	0.61
4	5	0.61
5	3	0.61
5	4	0.61
5	5	0.61
6	3	0.65
6	4	0.65
6	5	0.65
7	3	0.66
7	4	0.66
7	5	0.66

Majority vote cluster homogeneity for the transformed breast cancer dataset

Using graph closure and co-occurrence linkage

Two other methods that can be used to combine cluster results are graph closure and co-occurrence linkage. Here, we demonstrate how to use OpenEnsembles to create both types of ensembles.

Graph closure

Graph closure creates a graph from the co-occurrence matrix. Every element (instance pair) is treated as a node. Pairs that have a higher value than the threshold are connected by an edge. Following this, a clique formation occurs, according to a specified size (specified by the number of nodes in the clique). Cliques are subsets of the graph's nodes, such that every two nodes of the clique are neighbors. Finally, the cliques are combined to form unique clusters. In OpenEnsembles, it is implemented by the `finish_graph_closure` function, in the `cluster` class. The `clique_size` parameter determines the number of nodes in each clique. The `threshold` parameter determines the minimum co-occurrence that a pair must have in order to be connected by an edge in the graph. Similar to the previous example, we will use graph closure in order to cluster the breast cancer dataset. Notice that the only change in the code will be the usage of `finish_graph_closure`, instead of `finish_majority_vote`. First, we load the libraries and the dataset, and create the OpenEnsembles data object:

```
# --- SECTION 1 ---
# Libraries and data loading
import openensembles as oe
import pandas as pd
import sklearn.metrics

from sklearn.datasets import load_breast_cancer

bc = load_breast_cancer()

# --- SECTION 2 ---
# Create the data object
cluster_data = oe.data(pd.DataFrame(bc.data), bc.feature_names)
```

Then, we create the ensemble and use `graph_closure` in order to combine the cluster results. Notice that the dictionary key also changes to `'graph_closure'`:

```
# --- SECTION 3 ---
# Create the ensembles and calculate the homogeneity score
for K in [2, 3, 4, 5, 6, 7]:
  for ensemble_size in [3, 4, 5]:
   ensemble = oe.cluster(cluster_data)
   for i in range(ensemble_size):
   name = f'kmeans_{ensemble_size}_{i}'
   ensemble.cluster('parent', 'kmeans', name, K)

  preds = ensemble.finish_majority_vote(threshold=0.5)
  print(f'K: {K}, size {ensemble_size}:', end=' ')
  print('%.2f' % sklearn.metrics.homogeneity_score(
   bc.target, preds.labels['majority_vote']))
```

The effect of K and the ensemble size on the clustering quality is similar to majority voting, although it does not achieve the same level of performance. The results are depicted in the following table:

K	Size	Homogeneity
2	3	0.42
2	4	0.42
2	5	0.42
3	3	0.47
3	4	0
3	5	0.47
4	3	0.58
4	4	0.58
4	5	0.58
5	3	0.6
5	4	0.5
5	5	0.5
6	3	0.6
6	4	0.03
6	5	0.62
7	3	0.63
7	4	0.27
7	5	0.27

Homogeneity for graph closure clustering on the raw breast cancer data

Co-occurrence matrix linkage

Co-occurrence matrix linkage treats the co-occurrence matrix as a distance matrix between instances, and utilizes the distances in order to perform hierarchical clustering. The clustering stops when there is no element on the matrix with a value greater than the threshold. Again, we repeat the example. We use the `finish_co_occ_linkage` function to utilize co-occurrence matrix linkage with `threshold=0.5`, and use the `'co_occ_linkage'` key to access the results:

```
# --- SECTION 1 ---
# Libraries and data loading
import openensembles as oe
import pandas as pd
import sklearn.metrics

from sklearn.datasets import load_breast_cancer

bc = load_breast_cancer()

# --- SECTION 2 ---
# Create the data object
cluster_data = oe.data(pd.DataFrame(bc.data), bc.feature_names)

# --- SECTION 3 ---
# Create the ensembles and calculate the homogeneity score
for K in [2, 3, 4, 5, 6, 7]:
 for ensemble_size in [3, 4, 5]:
  ensemble = oe.cluster(cluster_data)
  for i in range(ensemble_size):
  name = f'kmeans_{ensemble_size}_{i}'
  ensemble.cluster('parent', 'kmeans', name, K)
  preds = ensemble.finish_co_occ_linkage(threshold=0.5)
  print(f'K: {K}, size {ensemble_size}:', end=' ')
  print('%.2f' % sklearn.metrics.homogeneity_score(
        bc.target, preds.labels['co_occ_linkage']))
```

The following table summarizes the results. Notice that it outperforms the other two methods. Furthermore, the results are more stable, and less time is required to execute it than either of the other two methods:

K	Size	Homogeneity
2	3	0.42
2	4	0.42
2	5	0.42
3	3	0.47
3	4	0.47
3	5	0.45
4	3	0.58
4	4	0.58
4	5	0.58
5	3	0.6
5	4	0.6
5	5	0.6
6	3	0.59
6	4	0.62
6	5	0.62
7	3	0.62
7	4	0.63
7	5	0.63

Homogeneity results for co-occurrence cluster linkage on the raw breast cancer dataset

Summary

In this chapter, we presented the K-means clustering algorithm and clustering ensemble methods. We explained how majority voting can be used in order to combine cluster assignments from an ensemble, and how it can outperform the individual base learners. Furthermore, we presented the OpenEnsembles Python library, which is dedicated to clustering ensembles. The chapter can be summarized as follows.

K-means creates K clusters, and assigns instances to each cluster by iteratively considering the cluster center to be the mean of its members. It can be sensitive to the initial conditions, and the selected number of clusters. Majority voting can help to overcome the algorithm's disadvantages. **Majority voting** clusters together instances that have a high co-occurrence. **Co-occurrence matrices** show how frequently a pair of instances has been assigned to the same cluster by the same base learner. **Graph closure** uses co-occurrence matrices in order to create graphs, and clusters the data based on cliques. **Co-occurrence linkage** uses a specific clustering algorithm, hierarchical (agglomerative) clustering, by treating the co-occurrence matrix as a pairwise distance matrix. In the next chapter, we will try to utilize all the ensemble learning techniques that we have covered in this book, in order to classify fraudulent credit card transactions.

5
Section 5: Real World Applications

In this section, we will cover the use of ensemble learning for a wide array of real-world machine learning tasks.

This section comprises the following chapters:

- Chapter 9, *Classifying Fraudulent Transactions*
- Chapter 10, *Predicting Bitcoin Prices*
- Chapter 11, *Evaluating Sentiment on Twitter*
- Chapter 12, *Recommending Movies with Keras*
- Chapter 13, *Clustering World Happiness*

9
Classifying Fraudulent Transactions

In this chapter, we will attempt to classify fraudulent transactions in a dataset concerning credit card transactions from European card holders that occurred during September 2013. The main problem in this dataset is the extremely small number of fraudulent transactions, compared to the dataset's size. These types of datasets are called unbalanced, as there are unequal percentages of each label. We will try to create ensembles that can classify our particular dataset, which contains a small number of fraudulent transactions.

In this chapter we will cover the following topics:

- Getting familiar with the dataset
- Exploratory analysis
- Voting
- Stacking
- Bagging
- Boosting
- Using random forests
- Comparative analysis of ensembles

Technical requirements

You will require basic knowledge of machine learning techniques and algorithms. Furthermore, a knowledge of python conventions and syntax is required. Finally, familiarity with the NumPy library will greatly help the reader to understand some custom algorithm implementations.

The code files of this chapter can be found on GitHub:

`https://github.com/PacktPublishing/Hands-On-Ensemble-Learning-with-Python/tree/master/Chapter09`

Check out the following video to see the Code in Action: `http://bit.ly/2ShwarF`.

Getting familiar with the dataset

The dataset was originally utilized in the PhD thesis of Andrea Dal Pozzolo, `Adaptive Machine learning for credit card fraud detection` ULB MLG, and has since been released by its authors for public use (`www.ulb.ac.be/di/map/adalpozz/data/creditcard.Rdata`). The dataset contains more than 284,000 instances, but only 492 instances of fraud (almost 0.17%).

Its target class value is 0 if the transaction was not a fraud, and 1 if it was. The dataset's features are a number of principal components, as the dataset has been transformed using **Principle Components Analysis (PCA)**, in order to retain the confidentiality of the data. The dataset's features are comprised of 28 PCA components, as well as the transaction's amount and the time elapsed from the first transaction in the dataset. Descriptive statistics about the dataset are provided as follows:

Feature	Time	V1	V2	V3	V4
count	284,807	284,807	284,807	284,807	284,807
mean	94,813.86	1.17E-15	3.42E-16	-1.37E-15	2.09E-15
std	47,488.15	1.96	1.65	1.52	1.42
min	0.00	-56.41	-72.72	-48.33	-5.68
max	172,792.00	2.45	22.06	9.38	16.88
Feature	V5	V6	V7	V8	V9
count	284,807	284,807	284,807	284,807	284,807
mean	9.60E-16	1.49E-15	-5.56E-16	1.18E-16	-2.41E-15
std	1.38	1.33	1.24	1.19	1.10

min	-113.74	-26.16	-43.56	-73.22	-13.43
max	34.80	73.30	120.59	20.01	15.59
Feature	**V10**	**V11**	**V12**	**V13**	**V14**
count	284,807	284,807	284,807	284,807	284,807
mean	2.24E-15	1.67E-15	-1.25E-15	8.18E-16	1.21E-15
std	1.09	1.02	1.00	1.00	0.96
min	-24.59	-4.80	-18.68	-5.79	-19.21
max	23.75	12.02	7.85	7.13	10.53
Feature	**V15**	**V16**	**V17**	**V18**	**V19**
count	284,807	284,807	284,807	284,807	284,807
mean	4.91E-15	1.44E-15	-3.80E-16	9.57E-16	1.04E-15
std	0.92	0.88	0.85	0.84	0.81
min	-4.50	-14.13	-25.16	-9.50	-7.21
max	8.88	17.32	9.25	5.04	5.59
Feature	**V20**	**V21**	**V22**	**V23**	**V24**
count	284,807	284,807	284,807	284,807	284,807
mean	6.41E-16	1.66E-16	-3.44E-16	2.58E-16	4.47E-15
std	0.77	0.73	0.73	0.62	0.61
min	-54.50	-34.83	-10.93	-44.81	-2.84
max	39.42	27.20	10.50	22.53	4.58
Feature	**V25**	**V26**	**V27**	**V28**	**Amount**
count	284,807	284,807	284,807	284,807	284,807
mean	5.34E-16	1.69E-15	-3.67E-16	-1.22E-16	88.34962
std	0.52	0.48	0.40	0.33	250.12
min	-10.30	-2.60	-22.57	-15.43	0.00
max	7.52	3.52	31.61	33.85	25,691.16

Descriptive statistics of the credit card transaction dataset

Exploratory analysis

One important characteristic of the dataset is that there are no missing values, as it is indicated by the count statistic. All features have the same number of values. Another important aspect is that most features are normalized. This is due to the PCA applied to the data. PCA normalizes the data before decomposing it into principal components. The only two features not normalized are the **Time** and **Amount** features. The following histogram for each feature is depicted:

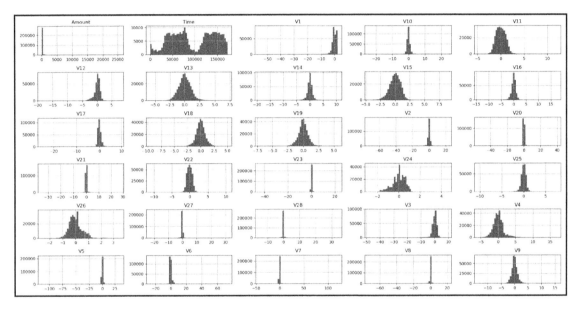

Histograms for the dataset's features

It is interesting to examine more closely the **Time** and **Amount** of each transaction. In the **Time** histogram, we notice a sudden drop in transaction frequency between 75,000 and 125,000 seconds after the first transaction (around 13 hours). This is probably due to daily time cycles (for example, during the night, when most stores are closed). The histogram for each transaction's amount is provided as follows in the logarithmic scale. It is evident that most transactions concern small amounts, with the average being almost €88.00:

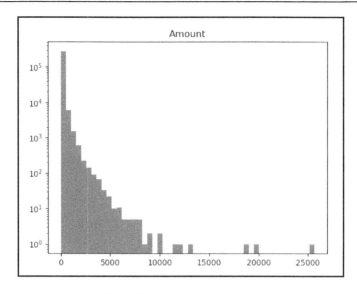

Histogram for amount. logarithmic scale for *y*-axis

In order to avoid problems with uneven distribution of weights between features, we will standardize the features **Amount** and **Time**. Algorithms that employ distance metrics for example (such as K-Nearest Neighbors), can under perform when features are not scaled correctly. The standardized features' histograms are provided as follows. Note that standardization transforms the variables in order to have a mean value close to 0 and standard deviation of 1:

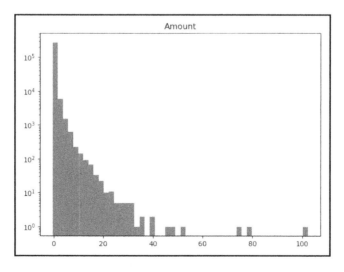

Standardized amount histogram

The following plot depicts the histogram for standardized time. We can see that it does not affect the drop in transactions during the night time:

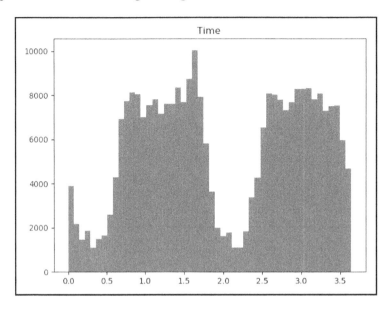

Standardized time histogram

Evaluation methods

As our dataset is highly skewed (that is, it has a high degree of class imbalance), we cannot utilize accuracy in order to evaluate our models. This is due to the fact that by classifying all instances as non-frauds, we can achieve an accuracy of 99.82%. Certainly, this number does not represent an acceptable performance, as we are unable to detect any fraudulent transactions. Thus, in order to evaluate our models, we will use recall (the percentage of frauds we detected) and F1 score, a weighted average between recall and precision (a measure of how many of the transactions predicted as fraudulent were indeed fraudulent).

Voting

In this section, we will try to classify the dataset by using voting ensembles. For our initial ensemble, we will utilize a Naive Bayes classifier, a logistic regression, and a decision tree. This will be implemented in two parts, first by testing each base learner itself and then combining the base learners into an ensemble.

Testing the base learners

To test the base learners, we will benchmark the base learners by themselves, which will help us gauge how well they perform on their own. In order to do so, first, we load the libraries and dataset and then split the data with 70% in the train set and 30% in the test set. We use `pandas` in order to easily import the CSV. Our goal is to train and evaluate each individual base learner before we train and evaluate the ensemble as a whole:

```
# --- SECTION 1 ---
# Libraries and data loading
import numpy as np
import pandas as pd

from sklearn.tree import DecisionTreeClassifier
from sklearn.linear_model import LogisticRegression
from sklearn.naive_bayes import GaussianNB
from sklearn.model_selection import train_test_split
from sklearn import metrics

np.random.seed(123456)
data = pd.read_csv('creditcard.csv')
data.Time = (data.Time-data.Time.min())/data.Time.std()
data.Amount = (data.Amount-data.Amount.mean())/data.Amount.std()

# Train-Test slpit of 70%-30%
x_train, x_test, y_train, y_test = train_test_split(
data.drop('Class', axis=1).values, data.Class.values, test_size=0.3)
```

After loading the libraries and data, we train each classifier and print the required metrics from the `sklearn.metrics` package. F1 score is implemented by the `f1_score` function and recall is implemented by the `recall_score` function. The decision tree is restricted to a maximum depth of three (`max_depth=3`), in order to avoid overfitting:

```
# --- SECTION 2 ---
# Base learners evaluation
base_classifiers = [('DT', DecisionTreeClassifier(max_depth=3)),
                    ('NB', GaussianNB()),
                    ('LR', LogisticRegression())]

for bc in base_classifiers:
 lr = bc[1]
 lr.fit(x_train, y_train)

 predictions = lr.predict(x_test)
 print(bc[0]+' f1', metrics.f1_score(y_test, predictions))
 print(bc[0]+' recall', metrics.recall_score(y_test, predictions))
```

The results are depicted in the following table. As is evident, the decision tree outperforms the other three learners. Naive Bayes has a higher recall score, but its F1 score is considerably worse, compared to the decision tree:

Learner	Metric	Value
Decision Tree	F1	0.770
	Recall	0.713
Naive Bayes	F1	0.107
	Recall	0.824
Logistic Regression	F1	0.751
	Recall	0.632

We can also experiment with the number of features present in the dataset. By plotting their correlation to the target, we can filter out features that present low correlation to the target. This table depicts each feature's correlation to the target:

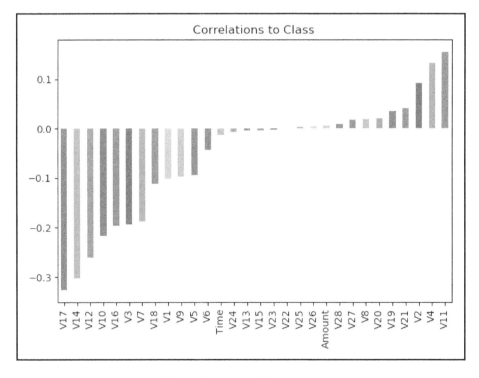

Correlation between each variable and the target

By filtering any feature with a lower absolute value than 0.1, we hope that the base learners will be able to better detect the fraudulent transactions, as the dataset's noise will be reduced.

In order to test our theory, we repeat the experiment, but remove any columns from the DataFrame where the absolute correlation is lower than 0.1, as indicated by `fs = list(correlations[(abs(correlations)>threshold)].index.values)`.

Here, `fs` holds all column names with a correlation greater than the indicated threshold:

```
# --- SECTION 3 ---
# Filter features according to their correlation to the target
np.random.seed(123456)
threshold = 0.1

correlations = data.corr()['Class'].drop('Class')
fs = list(correlations[(abs(correlations)>threshold)].index.values)
fs.append('Class')
data = data[fs]

x_train, x_test, y_train, y_test = train_test_split(data.drop('Class',
axis=1).values, data.Class.values, test_size=0.3)

for bc in base_classifiers:
  lr = bc[1]
  lr.fit(x_train, y_train)

  predictions = lr.predict(x_test)
  print(bc[0]+' f1', metrics.f1_score(y_test, predictions))
  print(bc[0]+' recall', metrics.recall_score(y_test, predictions))
```

Again, we present the results in the following table. As we can see, the decision tree has increased its F1 score, while reducing its recall. Naive Bayes has improved on both metrics, while the logistic regression model has become considerably worse:

Learner	Metric	Value
Decision Tree	F1	0.785
	Recall	0.699
Naive Bayes	F1	0.208
	Recall	0.846
Logistic Regression	F1	0.735
	Recall	0.610

Performance metrics for the three base learners for the filtered dataset

Optimizing the decision tree

We can try to optimize the tree's depth in order to maximize F1 or recall. In order to do so, we will experiment with depths in the range of *[3, 11]* on the train set.

The following graph depicts the F1 score and recall for the various maximum depths, both for the original and filtered datasets:

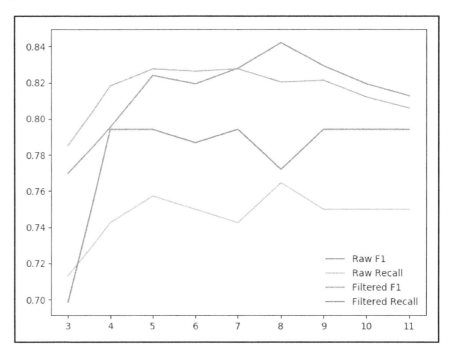

Test metrics for various tree depths

Here, we observe that for a maximum depth of 5, F1 and recall are optimized for the filtered dataset. Furthermore, recall is optimized for the original dataset as well. We will continue with a maximum depth of 5 as trying to further optimize the metrics can lead to overfitting, especially since the number of instances relevant to the metrics is extremely small. Furthermore, with a maximum depth of 5, there is an improvement both in F1, as well as in recall, when the filtered dataset is used.

Creating the ensemble

We can now proceed and create the ensemble. Again, we will first evaluate the ensemble on the original dataset, and then proceed to test it on the filtered dataset. The code is similar to the previous example. First, we load the libraries and data, and create train and test splits as follows:

```python
# --- SECTION 1 ---
# Libraries and data loading
import numpy as np
import pandas as pd

from sklearn.ensemble import VotingClassifier
from sklearn.tree import DecisionTreeClassifier
from sklearn.linear_model import LogisticRegression
from sklearn.naive_bayes import GaussianNB
from sklearn.model_selection import train_test_split
from sklearn import metrics

np.random.seed(123456)
data = pd.read_csv('creditcard.csv')
data.Time = (data.Time-data.Time.min())/data.Time.std()
data.Amount = (data.Amount-data.Amount.mean())/data.Amount.std()

# Train-Test slpit of 70%-30%
x_train, x_test, y_train, y_test = train_test_split(
  data.drop('Class', axis=1).values, data.Class.values, test_size=0.3)
```

After loading the required libraries and data, we create our ensemble, and then train and evaluate it. Finally, we repeat the experiment as follows with reduced features by filtering out features with low correlations to the target variable:

```python
# --- SECTION 2 ---
# Ensemble evaluation
base_classifiers = [('DT', DecisionTreeClassifier(max_depth=5)),
  ('NB', GaussianNB()),
  ('ensemble', LogisticRegression())]

ensemble = VotingClassifier(base_classifiers)
ensemble.fit(x_train, y_train)

print('Voting f1', metrics.f1_score(y_test, ensemble.predict(x_test)))
print('Voting recall', metrics.recall_score(y_test,
ensemble.predict(x_test)))

# --- SECTION 3 ---
```

```
# Filter features according to their correlation to the target
np.random.seed(123456)
threshold = 0.1

correlations = data.corr()['Class'].drop('Class')
fs = list(correlations[(abs(correlations)>threshold)].index.values)
fs.append('Class')
data = data[fs]

x_train, x_test, y_train, y_test = train_test_split(
  data.drop('Class', axis=1).values, data.Class.values, test_size=0.3)

ensemble = VotingClassifier(base_classifiers)
ensemble.fit(x_train, y_train)

print('Voting f1', metrics.f1_score(y_test, ensemble.predict(x_test)))
print('Voting recall', metrics.recall_score(y_test,
  ensemble.predict(x_test)))
```

The following table summarizes the results. For the original dataset, voting provides a model with a better combination of F1 and recall, compared to any single classifier.

Still, the decision tree with a maximum depth of 5 slightly outperforms it in F1 score, while Naive Bayes is able to recall a greater percentage of fraudulent transactions:

Dataset	Metric	Value
Original	F1	0.822
	Recall	0.779
Filtered	F1	0.828
	Recall	0.794

Voting results for both datasets

We can try to further diversify our ensemble by also including two additional Decision Trees, with maximum depth of three and eight, respectively. This boosts the ensemble's performance to the following numbers.

Although the performance remains the same for the filtered dataset, the ensemble is able to perform better in the original dataset. Especially for the F1 metric, it is able to outperform all other dataset/model combinations:

Dataset	Metric	Value
Original	F1	0.829
	Recall	0.787
Filtered	F1	0.828
	Recall	0.794

Voting results for both datasets with two additional decision trees

Stacking

We can also try to stack the base learners, instead of using Voting. First, we will try to stack a single decision tree with depth five, a Naive Bayes classifier, and a logistic regression. As a meta-learner, we will use a logistic regression.

The following code is responsible for loading the required libraries and data, training, and evaluating the ensemble on the original and filtered datasets. We first load the required libraries and data, while creating train and test splits:

```
# --- SECTION 1 ---
# Libraries and data loading
import numpy as np
import pandas as pd

from stacking_classifier import Stacking
from sklearn.tree import DecisionTreeClassifier
from sklearn.linear_model import LogisticRegression
from sklearn.naive_bayes import GaussianNB
from sklearn.svm import LinearSVC
from sklearn.model_selection import train_test_split
from sklearn import metrics

np.random.seed(123456)
data = pd.read_csv('creditcard.csv')
data.Time = (data.Time-data.Time.min())/data.Time.std()
data.Amount = (data.Amount-data.Amount.mean())/data.Amount.std()

# Train-Test slpit of 70%-30%
x_train, x_test, y_train, y_test = train_test_split(
  data.drop('Class', axis=1).values, data.Class.values, test_size=0.3)
```

After creating our train and test splits, we train and evaluate our ensemble on the original dataset, as well as a reduced-features dataset as follows:

```
# --- SECTION 2 ---
# Ensemble evaluation
base_classifiers = [DecisionTreeClassifier(max_depth=5),
                    GaussianNB(),
                    LogisticRegression()]
ensemble = Stacking(learner_levels=[base_classifiers,
                                    [LogisticRegression()]])

ensemble.fit(x_train, y_train)
print('Stacking f1', metrics.f1_score(y_test, ensemble.predict(x_test)))
print('Stacking recall', metrics.recall_score(y_test,
ensemble.predict(x_test)))

# --- SECTION 3 ---
# Filter features according to their correlation to the target
np.random.seed(123456)
threshold = 0.1
correlations = data.corr()['Class'].drop('Class')
fs = list(correlations[(abs(correlations) > threshold)].index.values)
fs.append('Class')
data = data[fs]
x_train, x_test, y_train, y_test = train_test_split(data.drop('Class',
axis=1).values,
                                                    data.Class.values,
test_size=0.3)
ensemble = Stacking(learner_levels=[base_classifiers,
                                    [LogisticRegression()]])
ensemble.fit(x_train, y_train)
print('Stacking f1', metrics.f1_score(y_test, ensemble.predict(x_test)))
print('Stacking recall', metrics.recall_score(y_test,
ensemble.predict(x_test)))
```

As it is seen in the following resultant table, the ensemble achieves a slightly better F1 score on the original dataset, but worse recall score, compared to the voting ensemble with the same base learners:

Dataset	Metric	Value
Original	F1	0.823
	Recall	0.750
Filtered	F1	0.828
	Recall	0.794

Stacking ensemble performance with three base learners

We can further experiment with different base learners. By adding two decision trees with maximum depths of three and eight, respectively (same with the second Voting setup), observe how stacking exhibits the same behavior. It outperforms on the F1 score and underperforms on the recall score for the original dataset.

On the filtered dataset, the performance remains on par with Voting. Finally, we experiment with second level of base learners, consisting of a Decision Tree with depth two and a linear support vector machine, which performs worse than the five base learners' setup:

Dataset	Metric	Value
Original	F1	0.844
	Recall	0.757
Filtered	F1	0.828
	Recall	0.794

Performance with five base learners

The following table depicts the results for the stacking ensemble with an additional level of base learners. As it is evident, it performs worse than the original ensemble.

Dataset	Metric	Value
Original	F1	0.827
	Recall	0.757
Filtered	F1	0.827
	Recall	0.772

Performance with five base learners on level 0 and two on level 1

Bagging

In this section, we will classify the dataset using bagging. As we have previously shown, decision trees with maximum depth of five are optimal thus, we will use these trees for our bagging example.

We would like to optimize the ensemble's size. We will generate validation curves for the original train set by testing sizes in the range of *[5, 30]*. The actual curves are depicted here in the following graph:

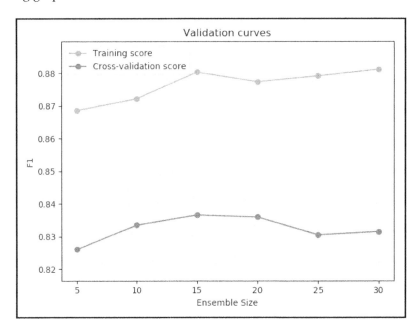

Validation curves for the original train set. for various ensemble sizes

We observe that variance is minimized for an ensemble size of 10, thus we will utilize ensembles of size 10.

The following code loads the data and libraries (*Section 1*), splits the data into train and test sets, and fits and evaluates the ensemble on the original dataset (*Section 2*) and the reduced-features dataset (*Section 3*):

```
# --- SECTION 1 ---
# Libraries and data loading
import numpy as np
import pandas as pd

from sklearn.ensemble import BaggingClassifier
from sklearn.tree import DecisionTreeClassifier
from sklearn.model_selection import train_test_split
from sklearn import metrics

np.random.seed(123456)
data = pd.read_csv('creditcard.csv')
```

```
data.Time = (data.Time-data.Time.min())/data.Time.std()
data.Amount = (data.Amount-data.Amount.mean())/data.Amount.std()
# Train-Test slpit of 70%-30%
x_train, x_test, y_train, y_test = train_test_split(
                                   data.drop('Class', axis=1).values,
data.Class.values, test_size=0.3)
```

After creating our train and test splits, we train and evaluate our ensemble on the original dataset, as well as a reduced-features dataset as follows:

```
# --- SECTION 2 ---
# Ensemble evaluation
ensemble = BaggingClassifier(n_estimators=10,
base_estimator=DecisionTreeClassifier(max_depth=5))
ensemble.fit(x_train, y_train)
print('Bagging f1', metrics.f1_score(y_test, ensemble.predict(x_test)))
print('Bagging recall', metrics.recall_score(y_test,
ensemble.predict(x_test)))
# --- SECTION 3 ---
# Filter features according to their correlation to the target
np.random.seed(123456)
threshold = 0.1
correlations = data.corr()['Class'].drop('Class')
fs = list(correlations[(abs(correlations)>threshold)].index.values)
fs.append('Class')
data = data[fs]
x_train, x_test, y_train, y_test = train_test_split(
                                   data.drop('Class', axis=1).values,
data.Class.values, test_size=0.3)
ensemble = BaggingClassifier(n_estimators=10,
base_estimator=DecisionTreeClassifier(max_depth=5))
ensemble.fit(x_train, y_train)

print('Bagging f1', metrics.f1_score(y_test, ensemble.predict(x_test)))
print('Bagging recall', metrics.recall_score(y_test,
ensemble.predict(x_test)))
```

Using bagging ensembles with trees of a maximum depth of 5 and 10 trees per ensemble, we are able to achieve the following F1 and recall scores. It outperforms both stacking and voting in both datasets on all metrics, with one exception. The F1 score for the original dataset is slightly worse than stacking (0.843 compared to 0.844):

Dataset	Metric	Value
Original	F1	0.843
	Recall	0.787
Filtered	F1	0.831
	Recall	0.794

Bagging performance for the original and filtered datasets

Although we have concluded that a maximum depth of 5 is optimal for a single decision tree, it does restrict the diversity of each tree. By increasing the maximum depth to 8, we are able to achieve an F1 score of 0.864 and a recall score of 0.816 on the filtered dataset, the best performance up to now.

Nonetheless, performance on the original dataset suffers, confirming that the features that we removed were, indeed, noise, as the trees are now able to model in-sample noise, and thus, their out-of-sample performance suffers:

Dataset	Metric	Value
Original	F1	0.840
	Recall	0.772
Filtered	F1	0.864
	Recall	0.816

Boosting

As we move on, we will start to utilize generative methods. The first generative method we will experiment with is boosting. We will first try to classify the datasets using AdaBoost. As AdaBoost resamples the dataset based on misclassifications, we expect that it will be able to handle our imbalanced dataset relatively well.

First, we must decide on the ensemble's size. We generate validation curves for a number of ensemble sizes depicted as follows:

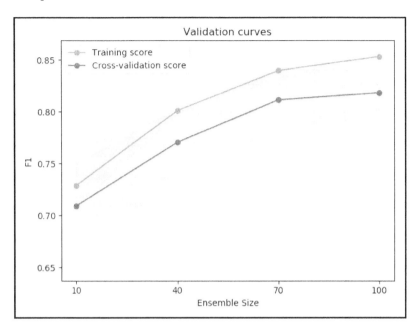

Validation curves of various ensemble sizes for AdaBoost

As we can observe, 70 base learners provide the best trade-off between bias and variance. As such, we will proceed with ensembles of size 70.

The following code implements the training and evaluation for AdaBoost:

```
# --- SECTION 1 ---
# Libraries and data loading
import numpy as np
import pandas as pd
from sklearn.ensemble import AdaBoostClassifier
from sklearn.model_selection import train_test_split
from sklearn.utils import shuffle
from sklearn import metrics

np.random.seed(123456)
data = pd.read_csv('creditcard.csv')
data.Time = (data.Time-data.Time.min())/data.Time.std()
data.Amount = (data.Amount-data.Amount.mean())/data.Amount.std()
# Train-Test slpit of 70%-30%
x_train, x_test, y_train, y_test = train_test_split(
  data.drop('Class', axis=1).values, data.Class.values, test_size=0.3)
```

We then train and evaluate our ensemble, using 70 estimators and a learning rate of 1.0:

```
# --- SECTION 2 ---
# Ensemble evaluation
ensemble = AdaBoostClassifier(n_estimators=70, learning_rate=1.0)
ensemble.fit(x_train, y_train)
print('AdaBoost f1', metrics.f1_score(y_test, ensemble.predict(x_test)))
print('AdaBoost recall', metrics.recall_score(y_test,
ensemble.predict(x_test)))
```

We reduce the number of features, by selecting only features with high correlation with respect to the target. Finally, we repeat the procedure of training and evaluating the ensemble:

```
# --- SECTION 3 ---
# Filter features according to their correlation to the target
np.random.seed(123456)
threshold = 0.1
correlations = data.corr()['Class'].drop('Class')
fs = list(correlations[(abs(correlations)>threshold)].index.values)
fs.append('Class')
data = data[fs]
x_train, x_test, y_train, y_test = train_test_split(
  data.drop('Class', axis=1).values, data.Class.values, test_size=0.3)
ensemble = AdaBoostClassifier(n_estimators=70, learning_rate=1.0)
ensemble.fit(x_train, y_train)
print('AdaBoost f1', metrics.f1_score(y_test, ensemble.predict(x_test)))
print('AdaBoost recall', metrics.recall_score(y_test,
ensemble.predict(x_test)))
```

The results are depicted in the following table. As it is evident, it does not perform as well as our previous models:

Dataset	Metric	Value
Original	F1	0.778
	Recall	0.721
Filtered	F1	0.794
	Recall	0.721

Performance of AdaBoost

We can try to increase the learning rate to 1.3, which seems to improve overall performance. If we further increase it to 1.4, we notice a drop in performance. If we increase the number of base learners to 80, we notice an increase in performance for the filtered dataset, while the original dataset seems to trade recall for F1 performance:

Dataset	Metric	Value
Original	F1	0.788
	Recall	0.765
Filtered	F1	0.815
	Recall	0.743

Performance of AdaBoost, learning_rate=1.3

Dataset	Metric	Value
Original	F1	0.800
	Recall	0.765
Filtered	F1	0.800
	Recall	0.735

Performance of AdaBoost, learning_rate=1.4

Dataset	Metric	Value
Original	F1	0.805
	Recall	0.757
Filtered	F1	0.805
	Recall	0.743

Performance of AdaBoost, learning_rate=1.4, ensemble_size=80

We can, in fact, observe a Pareto front of F1 and Recall, which is directly linked to the learning rate and number of base learners present in the ensemble. The front is depicted in the following graph:

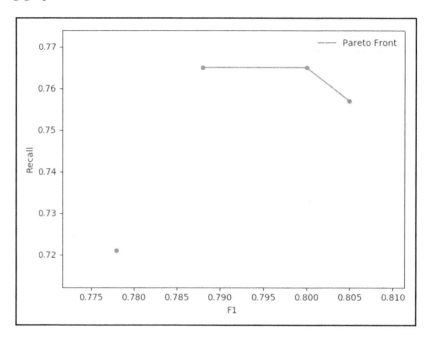

Pareto front of F1 and Recall for AdaBoost

XGBoost

We will also try to classify the dataset using XGBoost. As XGBoost uses trees of a maximum depth of three, we expect that it will outperform AdaBoost without any fine-tuning. Indeed, XGBoost is able to achieve better performance in both datasets and for all metrics (as shown in the following table), compared to most previous ensembles:

Dataset	Metric	Value
Original	F1	0.846
	Recall	0.787
Filtered	F1	0.849
	Recall	0.809

XGBoost out-of-the-box performance

By increasing the maximum depth of each tree to five, the ensemble is able to perform even better, yielding the following results:

Dataset	Metric	Value
Original	F1	0.862
	Recall	0.801
Filtered	F1	0.862
	Recall	0.824

Performance with max_depth=5

Using random forests

Finally, we will employ a random forest ensemble. Once again, using validation curves, we will determine the optimal ensemble size. From the following graph, we conclude that 50 trees provide the least possible variance in our model, thus we proceed with ensemble size 50:

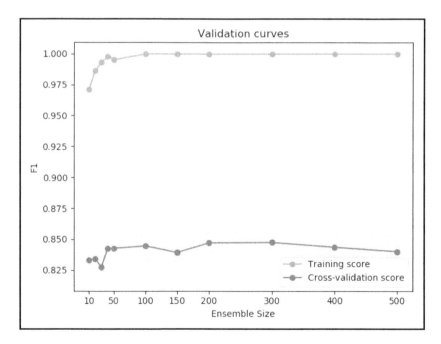

Validation curves for random forest

We provide the training and validation code as follows, as well as the achieved performance for both datasets. The following code is responsible for loading the required libraries and data, and training and evaluating the ensemble on the original and filtered datasets. We first load the required libraries and data, while creating train and test splits:

```
# --- SECTION 1 ---
# Libraries and data loading
import numpy as np
import pandas as pd

from sklearn.ensemble import RandomForestClassifier
from sklearn.model_selection import train_test_split
from sklearn.utils import shuffle
from sklearn import metrics

np.random.seed(123456)
data = pd.read_csv('creditcard.csv')
data.Time = (data.Time-data.Time.min())/data.Time.std()
data.Amount = (data.Amount-data.Amount.mean())/data.Amount.std()
np.random.seed(123456)
data = pd.read_csv('creditcard.csv')
data.Time = (data.Time-data.Time.min())/data.Time.std()
data.Amount = (data.Amount-data.Amount.mean())/data.Amount.std()
# Train-Test slpit of 70%-30%
x_train, x_test, y_train, y_test = train_test_split(
  data.drop('Class', axis=1).values, data.Class.values, test_size=0.3)
```

We then train and evaluate the ensemble, both on the original dataset, as well as on the filtered dataset:

```
# --- SECTION 2 ---
# Ensemble evaluation
ensemble = RandomForestClassifier(n_jobs=4)
ensemble.fit(x_train, y_train)
print('RF f1', metrics.f1_score(y_test, ensemble.predict(x_test)))
print('RF recall', metrics.recall_score(y_test, ensemble.predict(x_test)))

# --- SECTION 3 ---
# Filter features according to their correlation to the target
np.random.seed(123456)
threshold = 0.1
correlations = data.corr()['Class'].drop('Class')
fs = list(correlations[(abs(correlations)>threshold)].index.values)
fs.append('Class')
data = data[fs]
x_train, x_test, y_train, y_test = train_test_split(
  data.drop('Class', axis=1).values, data.Class.values, test_size=0.3)
ensemble = RandomForestClassifier(n_jobs=4)
```

```
ensemble.fit(x_train, y_train)
print('RF f1', metrics.f1_score(y_test, ensemble.predict(x_test)))
print('RF recall', metrics.recall_score(y_test, ensemble.predict(x_test)))
```

Dataset	Metric	Value
Original	F1	0.845
	Recall	0.743
Filtered	F1	0.867
	Recall	0.794

Random forest performance

As our dataset is highly skewed, we can speculate that changing the criterion for a tree's split to entropy would benefit our model. Indeed, by specifying `criterion='entropy'` in the constructor (`ensemble = RandomForestClassifier(n_jobs=4)`), we are able to increase the performance on the original dataset to an **F1** score of **0.859** and a **Recall** score of **0.786**, two of the highest scores for the original dataset:

Dataset	Metric	Value
Original	F1	0.859
	Recall	0.787
Filtered	F1	0.856
	Recall	0.787

Performance with entropy as the splitting criterion

Comparative analysis of ensembles

As we experimented with a reduced feature dataset, where we removed features without a strong correlation to the target variable, we would like to provide the final scores for the best parameters of each method. In the following graph, the results are depicted, sorted in ascending order. Bagging seems to be the most robust method when applied to the filtered dataset. XGBoost is the second best alternative, providing decent F1 and Recall scores when applied to the filtered dataset as well:

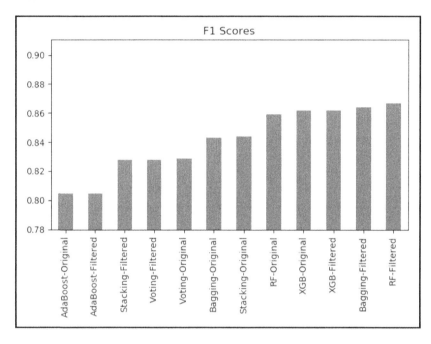

F1 scores

Recall scores, depicted in the following plot, show the clear advantage XGBoost has on this metric over the other methods, as it is able to outperform all others for both the original and filtered datasets:

Recall scores

Summary

In this chapter, we explored the possibility of detecting fraudulent transactions using various ensemble learning methods. While some performed better than others, due to the dataset's nature, it is difficult to produce good results without resampling the dataset in some way (either over-sampling or under-sampling).

We were able to show how to use each ensemble learning method and how to explore the possibility of fine-tuning its respective parameters in order to achieve better performance. In the next chapter, we will try to leverage ensemble learning techniques in order to predict Bitcoin prices.

10
Predicting Bitcoin Prices

Bitcoin and other cryptocurrencies have attracted the attention of many parties over the years, mainly due to their explosion in price levels, as well as the business opportunities that blockchain technologies offer. In this chapter, we will attempt to predict the next day's Bitcoin (BTC) price using historical data. There are many sources that offer cryptocurrency's historical price data. We will use Yahoo finance data, available at `https://finance.yahoo.com/quote/BTC-USD/history/`. In this chapter, we will focus on predicting future prices and leveraging that knowledge to invest in bitcoin.

The following topics will be covered in this chapter:

- Time series data
- Voting
- Stacking
- Bagging
- Boosting
- Random forests

Technical requirements

You will require basic knowledge of machine learning techniques and algorithms. Furthermore, a knowledge of python conventions and syntax is required. Finally, familiarity with the NumPy library will greatly help the reader to understand some custom algorithm implementations.

The code files of this chapter can be found on GitHub:

`https://github.com/PacktPublishing/Hands-On-Ensemble-Learning-with-Python/tree/master/Chapter10`

Check out the following video to see the Code in Action: `http://bit.ly/2JOsR7d`.

Time series data

Time series data is concerned with data instances in which each instance relates to a specific point in time or interval. How often we measure the variable of choice defines the time series' sampling frequency. For example, atmospheric temperature differs throughout the day and throughout the year. We can choose to measure the temperature every hour, so we have an hourly frequency, or we can choose to measure it each day, so we have a daily frequency. In finance, it is not unusual to have frequencies that are between major time intervals; this could be every 10 minutes (10m frequency) or every 4 hours (4h frequency). Another interesting characteristic of time series is that there is usually a correlation between instances that refer to proximal time points.

This is called **autocorrelation**. For example, the atmospheric temperature cannot vary by a great magnitude between consecutive minutes. Furthermore, this enables us to utilize earlier data points to predict future data points. An example of temperatures (an average of 3 hours) for Athens and Greece for the years 2016–2019 is provided in figure. Notice how most temperatures are relatively close to the previous day's temperature, even though there are variations. Furthermore, we see a repeating pattern of hot and cold months (seasons), which is called seasonality:

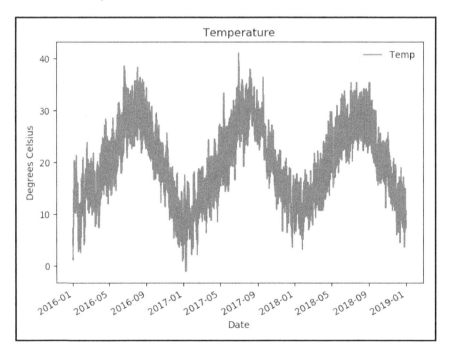

Temperatures for Athens, Greece 2016–2019

To examine the level of correlation between different points in time, we utilize the **autocorrelation function (ACF)**. ACF measures the linear correlation between a data point and previous points (called **lags**). In the following figure, the ACF for the temperature data (resampled as the month's average) is provided. It indicates a strong positive correlation with the first lag. This means that a month's temperature cannot deviate much from the previous month, which is logical. For example, December and January are cold months, and usually, their average temperatures are closer than December and March, for example. Furthermore, there is a strong negative correlation between lags 5 and 6, indicating that a cold winter results in a hot summer and vice versa:

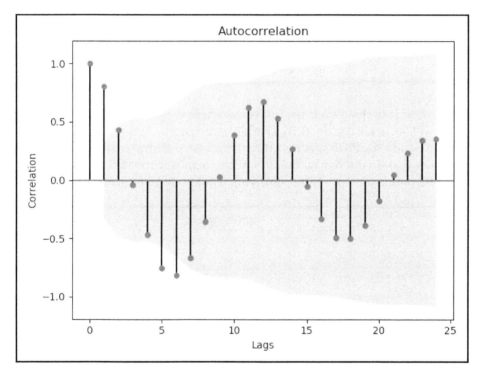

ACF for the temperature data

Bitcoin data analysis

Bitcoin data is very different from temperature data. Temperatures have more or less the same value for the same month of each year. This indicates that the distribution of temperatures does not change over time. Time series that exhibit this behavior are called **stationary**. This allows for relatively easy modeling with time series analysis tools, such as **auto regressive** (**AR**), **moving average** (**MA**), and **auto regressive integrated moving average** (**ARIMA**) models. Financial data is usually non-stationary, as seen in the daily Bitcoin close data, depicted in figure. This means that the data does not exhibit the same behavior throughout its entire history, but instead its behavior varies.

 Financial data usually provides open (the first price for the day), high (the highest price for the day), low (the lowest price for the day), and close (the last price for the day) values.

There are clear trends in the data (time intervals where the price, on average, increases or decreases), as well as heteroskedasticity (variable variance over time). One way to identify stationarity is to study the ACF function.If there is a very strong correlation between lags of a very high order that do not decay, the time series is most probably non-stationary. The ACF for the BTC data is also provided, showing weakly decaying correlations:

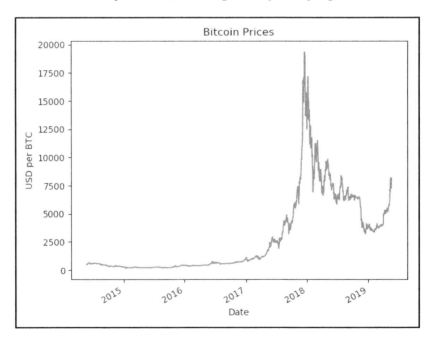

BTC/USD prices for mid-2014 to present

The following figure depicts the ACF for BTC. We can clearly see that the correlations do not drop for very high lag values:

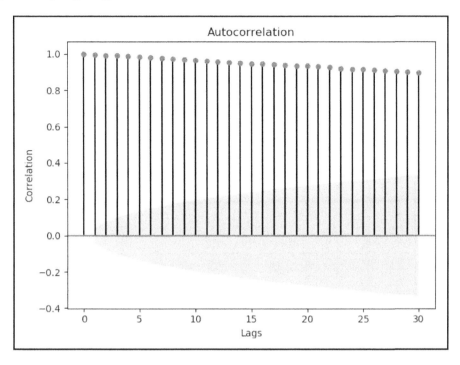

ACF for BTC data

Take a look at the following formula:

$$p = \frac{t_n - t_{n-1}}{t_{n-1}}$$

Where *p* is the percentage change, t_n is the price at time *n*, and *tn-1* is the price at time *n-1*. By applying the transformation to the data, we get a time series that is stationary, but less correlated.

The following figure shows the plots for the data, and the ACF and the average 30-day standard deviation are provided:

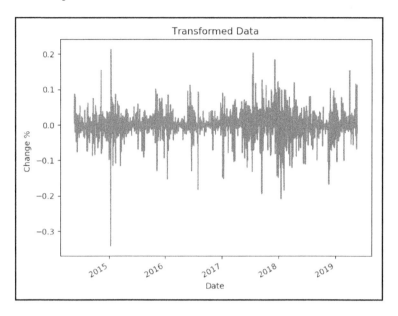

Transformed data

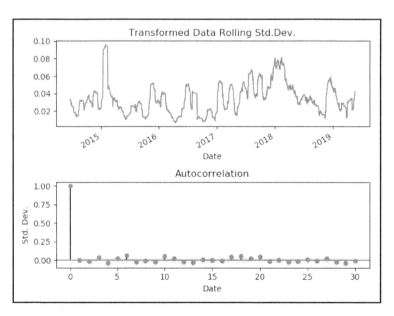

Rolling 30-day standard deviation and ACF for transformed data

Establishing a baseline

In order to establish a baseline, we will try to model the data using linear regression. Although it is a time series, we will not directly take time into account. Instead, we will utilize sliding windows of size S to generate features at each time point and use those features to predict the next point. Next, we will move the window one step forward in time to include the true value of the data point we predicted and discard the oldest data point inside the window. We will continue this process until all data points have been predicted. This is called walk-forward validation. One drawback is that we cannot predict the first S data points, as we do not have enough data to generate features for them. Another point of concern is that we need to re-train the model L-S times, in which L is the total number of points in the time series. A graphical representation of the first two steps is provided in the following figure:

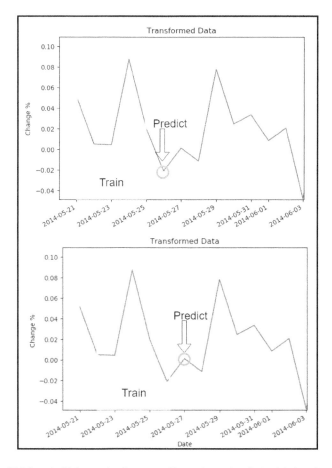

Walk-forward validation procedure, first two steps. The procedure continues for the whole time series.

First, we load the required libraries and data from the `BTC-USD.csv` file. We also set the seed for a NumPy random number generator:

```
import numpy as np
import pandas as pd
from simulator import simulate
from sklearn import metrics
from sklearn.linear_model import LinearRegression
from sklearn.model_selection import train_test_split
np.random.seed(123456)
lr = LinearRegression()
data = pd.read_csv('BTC-USD.csv')
```

We then clean the data by removing entries that contain NaN values, using `data.dropna()`, parse the dates using `pd.to_datetime`, and set the dates as an index. Finally, we calculate the percentage differences of `Close` values (and discard the first value, as it is a NaN) and save the Pandas series' length:

```
data = data.dropna()
data.Date = pd.to_datetime(data.Date)
data.set_index('Date', drop=True, inplace=True)
diffs = (data.Close.diff()/data.Close).values[1:]

diff_len = len(diffs)
```

We have created a function that generates the features at each data point. Features are essentially the different percentages at previous lags. Thus, to fill a dataset's feature with values, we only have to shift the data forward by as many points as the lags indicate. Any features that do not have available data to calculate lags, will have a value of zero. The following figure shows a toy example of a time series containing the numbers 1, 2, 3, and 4:

Features		Target
Lag 1	Lag 2	Time Series
0	0	1
1	0	2
2	1	3
3	2	4

How lag features are filled

The actual function, to fill lag *t*, selects all of the data from the time series except for the last *t* and places it in the corresponding feature, starting from index *t*. We chose to use the past 20 days as there does not seem to be any significant linear correlations after that point. Furthermore, we scale the features and targets by a factor of 100 and round them to 8 decimal points. This is important, as it allows the reproducibility of results. If the data is not rounded, overflow errors introduce stochasticity to the results, as shown in the following:

```
def create_x_data(lags=1):
 diff_data = np.zeros((diff_len, lags))

 for lag in range(1, lags+1):
  this_data = diffs[:-lag]
  diff_data[lag:, lag-1] = this_data

 return diff_data

# REPRODUCIBILITY
x_data = create_x_data(lags=20)*100
y_data = diffs*100
```

Finally, we execute the walk-forward validation. We chose a training window of 150 points, which equates to roughly 5 months. Given the data's nature and volatility, it provides a good trade-off between having a large enough train set and capturing recent market behaviors. A larger window would include market conditions that no longer reflect reality. A shorter window would provide too little data and would be prone to overfitting. We measure our model's predictive quality by utilizing the mean squared error between our predictions and the original percentage differences:

```
window = 150
preds = np.zeros(diff_len-window)
for i in range(diff_len-window-1):
 x_train = x_data[i:i+window, :]
 y_train = y_data[i:i+window]
 lr.fit(x_train, y_train)
 preds[i] = lr.predict(x_data[i+window+1, :].reshape(1, -1))

print('Percentages MSE: %.2f'%metrics.mean_absolute_error(y_data[window:],
preds))
```

Simple linear regression might produce an MSE of 18.41. We could also attempt to reconstruct the time series by multiplying each data point by (1 + prediction) to get the next predicted point. Furthermore, we could attempt to take advantage of the dataset's nature and simulate trading activity. Each time the prediction is greater than +0.5% change, we invest 100 USD in buying Bitcoins. If we have Bitcoins in our possession and the prediction is lower than -0.5%, we sell the Bitcoins at the current market close. To assess the quality of our model as a trading strategy, we utilize a simplified **Sharpe** ratio, which is calculated as the ratio of mean returns (percentage profits) over the standard deviation of the returns. Higher Sharpe values indicate a better trading strategy. The formula utilized here is calculated as follows. Usually, an alternative **safe** return percentage is subtracted from the expected return, but as we only want to compare the models we will generate with each other, we'll omit it:

$$Sharpe = \frac{E(returns)}{\sigma(returns)}$$

When utilized as a trading strategy, linear regression is able to produce a Sharpe value of 0.19. The following figure indicates the trades and profits generated by our model. The blue triangles indicate time points at which the strategy bought Bitcoins worth 100 USD and the red triangles indicate the time points at which it sold the previously bought Bitcoins:

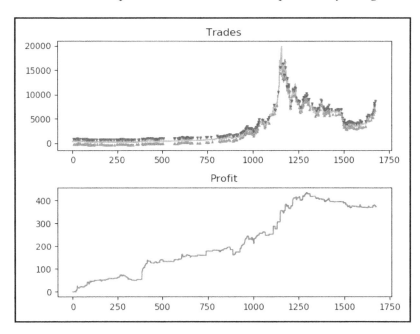

Profits and entry/exit points of our model

In the rest of this chapter, we will try to improve the MSE and Sharpe values by utilizing the ensemble methods we presented in the previous chapters.

The simulator

Here, we'll provide a brief explanation of how the simulator works. It is implemented as a function that accepts our standard Pandas DataFrame data and the model's predictions as inputs. First, we'll define the buying threshold and the stake size (how much money we invest in each buy), as well as placeholder variables. The variables will be used to store the true and predicted time series, as well as the profits of our model (`balances`). Furthermore, we define the `buy_price` variable, which stores the price at which we bought the Bitcoins. If the price is 0, we assume that we do not hold any Bitcoins. The `buy_points` and `sell_points` lists indicate the points in time when we bought or sold the Bitcoins and are used only for plotting. Furthermore, we store the starting index, which is equivalent to the sliding window's size as shown in the following example:

```
import matplotlib.pyplot as plt
import numpy as np
import pandas as pd

from sklearn import metrics

def simulate(data, preds):
 # Constants and placeholders
 buy_threshold = 0.5
 stake = 100

true, pred, balances = [], [], []

buy_price = 0
 buy_points, sell_points = [], []
 balance = 0

start_index = len(data)-len(preds)-1
```

Next, for each point, we store the actual and predicted values. If the predicted value is greater than 0.5 and we do not hold any Bitcoins, we buy 100 USD worth of Bitcoins. If the predicted value is less than -0.5 and we have already bought Bitcoins, we sell them at the current close value. We add the current profit (or loss) to our balances, cast the true and predicted values as NumPy arrays, and produce the plots:

```
# Calculate predicted values
 for i in range(len(preds)):

last_close = data.Close[i+start_index-1]
 current_close = data.Close[i+start_index]

# Save predicted values and true values
 true.append(current_close)
 pred.append(last_close*(1+preds[i]/100))

 # Buy/Sell according to signal
 if preds[i] > buy_threshold and buy_price == 0:
 buy_price = true[-1]
 buy_points.append(i)

 elif preds[i] < -buy_threshold and not buy_price == 0:
 profit = (current_close - buy_price) * stake/buy_price
 balance += profit
 buy_price = 0
 sell_points.append(i)

balances.append(balance)
 true = np.array(true)
 pred = np.array(pred)

# Create plots
 plt.figure()

plt.subplot(2, 1, 1)
 plt.plot(true, label='True')
 plt.plot(pred, label='pred')
 plt.scatter(buy_points, true[buy_points]+500, marker='v',
 c='blue', s=5, zorder=10)
 plt.scatter(sell_points, true[sell_points]-500, marker='^'
 , c='red', s=5, zorder=10)
 plt.title('Trades')

plt.subplot(2, 1, 2)
 plt.plot(balances)
 plt.title('Profit')
 print('MSE: %.2f'%metrics.mean_squared_error(true, pred))
```

```
balance_df = pd.DataFrame(balances)

pct_returns = balance_df.diff()/stake
  pct_returns = pct_returns[pct_returns != 0].dropna()

  print('Sharpe: %.2f'%(np.mean(pct_returns)/np.std(pct_returns)))
```

Voting

We will try to combine three basic regression algorithms by voting to improve the MSE of the simple regression. To combine the algorithms, we will utilize the average of their predictions. Thus, we code a simple class that creates a dictionary of base learners and handles their training and prediction averaging. The main logic is the same as with the custom voting classifier we implemented in Chapter 3, *Voting*:

```
import numpy as np
from copy import deepcopy

class VotingRegressor():

# Accepts a list of (name, classifier) tuples
  def __init__(self, base_learners):
  self.base_learners = {}
  for name, learner in base_learners:
  self.base_learners[name] = deepcopy(learner)

  # Fits each individual base learner
  def fit(self, x_data, y_data):
  for name in self.base_learners:
  learner = self.base_learners[name]
  learner.fit(x_data, y_data)
```

The predictions are stored in a NumPy matrix, in which each row corresponds to a single instance and each column corresponds to a single base learner. The row-averaged values are the ensemble's output, as shown here:

```
# Generates the predictions
  def predict(self, x_data):

# Create the predictions matrix
  predictions = np.zeros((len(x_data), len(self.base_learners)))

  names = list(self.base_learners.keys())

  # For each base learner
```

```
    for i in range(len(self.base_learners)):
    name = names[i]
    learner = self.base_learners[name]

  # Store the predictions in a column
   preds = learner.predict(x_data)
   predictions[:,i] = preds

  # Take the row-average
   predictions = np.mean(predictions, axis=1)
   return predictions
```

We chose to utilize a support vector machine, a K-Nearest Neighbors Regressor, and a linear regression as a base learners, as they provide diverse learning paradigms. To utilize the ensemble, we first import the required modules:

```
import numpy as np
import pandas as pd

from simulator import simulate
from sklearn import metrics
from sklearn.neighbors import KNeighborsRegressor
from sklearn.linear_model import LinearRegression
from sklearn.svm import SVR
from voting_regressor import VotingRegressor
```

Next, in the code we presented earlier, we replace the `lr = LinearRegression()` line with the following:

```
base_learners = [('SVR', SVR()),
  ('LR', LinearRegression()),
  ('KNN', KNeighborsRegressor())]

lr = VotingRegressor(base_learners)
```

By adding the two additional regressors, we are able to reduce the MSE to 16.22 and produce a Sharpe value of 0.22.

Improving voting

Although our results are better than linear regression, we can further improve them by removing the linear regression, thus, leaving the base learners as follows:

```
base_learners = [('SVR', SVR()), ('KNN', KNeighborsRegressor())]
```

This further improves the MSE, reducing it to 15.71. If we utilize this model as a trading strategy, we can achieve a Sharpe value of 0.21; considerably better than simple linear regression. The following table summarizes our results:

Metric	SVR-KNN	SVR-LR-KNN
MSE	15.71	16.22
Sharpe	0.21	0.22

Voting ensemble results

Stacking

Moving on to more complex ensembles, we will utilize stacking to combine basic regressors more efficiently. Using StackingRegressor from Chapter 4, *Stacking*, we will try to combine the same algorithms as we did with voting. First, we modify the predict function of our ensemble (to allow for single-instance prediction) as follows:

```
# Generates the predictions
def predict(self, x_data):

# Create the predictions matrix
predictions = np.zeros((len(x_data), len(self.base_learners)))

names = list(self.base_learners.keys())

# For each base learner
for i in range(len(self.base_learners)):
name = names[i]
learner = self.base_learners[name]

# Store the predictions in a column
preds = learner.predict(x_data)
predictions[:,i] = preds

# Take the row-average
predictions = np.mean(predictions, axis=1)
return predictions
```

Again, we modify the code to use the stacking regressor, as follows:

```
base_learners = [[SVR(), LinearRegression(), KNeighborsRegressor()],
                 [LinearRegression()]]
lr = StackingRegressor(base_learners)
```

In this setup, the ensemble yields a model with an MSE of 16.17 and a Sharpe value of 0.21.

Improving stacking

Our results are slightly worse than the final Voting ensemble, so we will attempt to improve them by removing the linear regression, as we did with the voting ensemble. By doing so, we can slightly improve our model, achieving an MSE of 16.16 and a Sharpe value of 0.22. Comparing it to voting, stacking is slightly better as part of an investing strategy (the same Sharpe value and a slightly better MSE), although it is unable to achieve the same level of predictive accuracy. Its results are summarized in the following table:

Metric	SVR-KNN	SVR-LR-KNN
MSE	16.17	16.16
Sharpe	0.21	0.22

Stacking results

Bagging

Usually, when fitting predictive models onto financial data, variance is our main problem. Bagging is a very useful tool to counter variance; thus, we hope that it will be able to produce better performing models compared to simple voting and stacking. To utilize bagging, we will use scikit's `BaggingRegressor`, presented in `Chapter 5`, *Bagging*. To implement it in our experiment, we simply call it using `lr = BaggingRegressor()` instead of the previous regressors. This results in an MSE of 19.45 and a Sharpe of 0.09. The following figure depicts the profits and trades that our model generates:

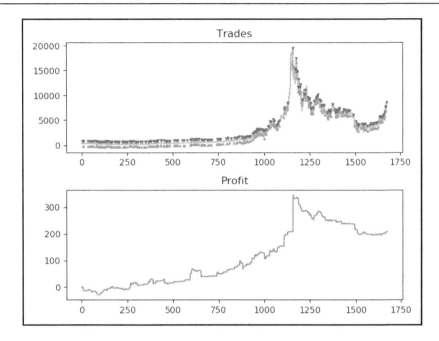

Bagging profits and trades

Improving bagging

We can further improve bagging as its performance is worse than any previous model. First, we can experiment with shallow trees, which will further reduce variance in the ensemble. By utilizing trees with a maximum depth of 3, using `lr = BaggingRegressor(base_estimator=DecisionTreeRegressor(max_depth=3))`, we can improve the model's performance, generating an MSE of 17.59 and a Sharpe value of 0.15. Further restricting the trees' growth to `max_depth=1`, allows the model to achieve an MSE of 16.7 and a Sharpe value of 0.27. If we examine the model's trading plots, we observe a reduction in the number of trades, as well as a considerable improvement in performance during periods in which Bitcoin's price significantly drops. This indicates that the model can filter noise from actual signals more efficiently.

The reduction in variance has indeed helped our model to improve its performance:

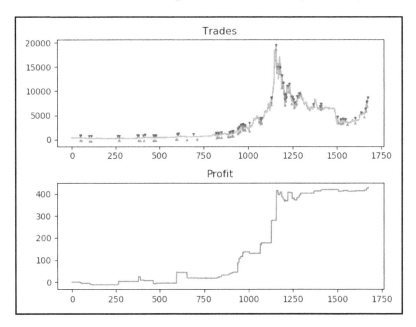

Final Bagging profits and trades

The following table summarizes the results for the various bagging models we tested:

Metric	DT_max_depth=1	DT_max_depth=3	DT
MSE	16.70	17.59	19.45
Sharpe	0.27	0.15	0.09

Table 3: Bagging results

Boosting

One of the most powerful ensemble learning techniques is boosting. It allows complicated models to be generated. In this section, we will utilize XGBoost to model our time series data. As there are many degrees of freedom (hyperparameters) when modeling with XGBoost, we expect some level of fine-tuning to be needed to achieve satisfactory results. By replacing our example's regressor with `lr = XGBRegressor()`, we can utilize XGBoost and fit it onto our data. This results in an MSE of 19.20 and a Sharpe value of 0.13.

Figure depicts the profits and trades generated by the model. Although the Sharpe value is lower than for other models, we can see that it continues to generate profit, even during periods in which the Bitcoin price drops:

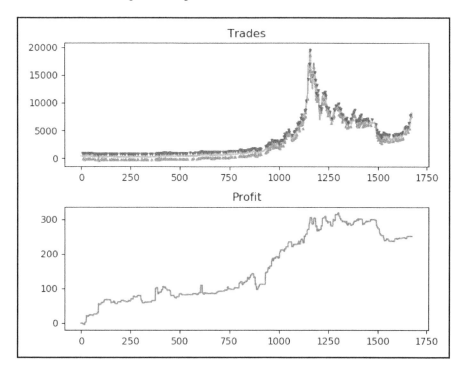

Trades generated by the Boosting model

Improving boosting

Due to the out-of-sample performance and the frequency at which boosting is bought and sold, we can assume it is overfitting the training data. Therefore, we'll will try to regularize its learning. The first step is to limit the maximum depth of individual trees. We start by imposing an upper limit of 2, using `max_depth=2`. This slightly improves our model, yielding an MSE of 19.14 and a Sharpe value of 0.17. Further limiting the overfitting capabilities of the model by using only 10 base learners (`n_estimators=10`), the model achieves additional improvement.

The MSE of the model is reduced to 16.39 and the Sharpe value is increased to 0.21. Adding an L1 regularization term of 0.5 (`reg_alpha=0.5`) only reduces the MSE to 16.37. We have come to a point where further fine-tuning will not contribute much performance to our model. At this point, our regressor looks like this:

```
lr = XGBRegressor(max_depth=2, n_estimators=10, reg_alpha=0.5)
```

Given the capabilities of XGBoost, we will try to increase the amount of information available to the model. We will increase the available feature lags to 30 and add a rolling mean of the previous 15 lags to the features. To do this, we modify the feature creation section of the code as follows:

```
def create_x_data(lags=1):
  diff_data = np.zeros((diff_len, lags))
  ma_data = np.zeros((diff_len, lags))

  diff_ma =
(data.Close.diff()/data.Close).rolling(15).mean().fillna(0).values[1:]
  for lag in range(1, lags+1):
  this_data = diffs[:-lag]
  diff_data[lag:, lag-1] = this_data

  this_data = diff_ma[:-lag]
  ma_data[lag:, lag-1] = this_data
  return np.concatenate((diff_data, ma_data), axis=1)

x_data = create_x_data(lags=30)*100
y_data = diffs*100
```

This increases the trading performance of our model, achieving a Sharpe value of 0.32—the highest of all of the models, while it also increases its MSE to 16.78. The trades generated by this model are depicted in figure and in the table that follows. It is interesting to note that the number of buys has greatly reduced, a behavior that bagging also exhibited when we managed to improve its performance as an investment strategy:

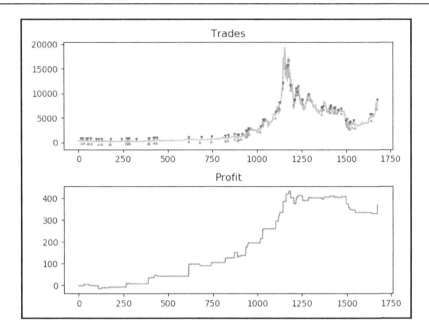

Final boosting model performance

Metric	md=2/ne=10/reg=0.5+data	md=2/ne=10/reg=0.5	md=2/ne=10	md=2	xgb
MSE	16.78	16.37	16.39	19.14	19.20
Sharpe	0.32	0.21	0.21	0.17	0.13

Metrics for all boosting models

Random forests

Finally, we will utilize random forests to model our data. Although we expect that the ensemble to be able to utilize the information from additional lags and the rolling average, we will start with only 20 lags and the return percentages as inputs. Thus, our initial regressor is simply `RandomForestRegressor()`. This results in a model that does not perform very well. Its MSE is 19.02 and its Sharpe value is 0.11.

The following figure depicts the trades that the model generates:

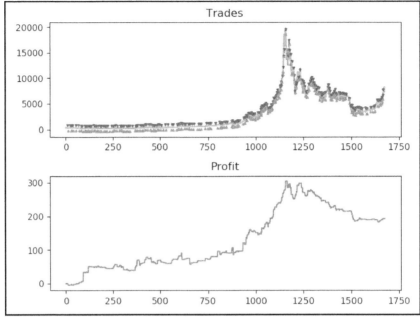

Trades of random forest model

Improving random forest

In an attempt to improve our model, we try to restrict its overfitting capabilities, imposing a maximum depth of 3 for each tree. This results in considerable performance improvement as the model achieves an MSE of 17.42 and a Sharpe value of 0.17. Further restricting the maximum depth to 2 improves the MSE score slightly more to 17.13, but reduces its Sharpe value to 0.16. Finally, increasing the ensemble's size to 50, using `n_estimators=50`, produces a considerably better model, with an MSE of 16.88 and a Sharpe value of 0.23. As we have only used the original feature set (20 lags of return percentages), we wish to also experiment with the expanded dataset we utilized in the boosting section. By adding the 15-day rolling average, as well as increasing the number of available lags to 30, the model can increase its Sharpe value to 0.24, although its MSE also increases to 18.31. The trades generated by the model are depicted in figure:

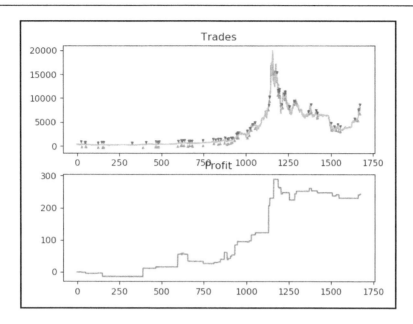

Random forest's results with the expanded dataset

The model's results are summarized in the following table:

Metric	md=2/ne=50+data	md=2/ne=50	md=2	md=3	RF
MSE	18.31	16.88	17.13	17.42	19.02
Sharpe	0.24	0.23	0.16	0.17	0.11

Metrics for all random forest models

Summary

In this chapter, we tried to model historical Bitcoin prices using all of the ensemble methods presented in earlier chapters of this book. As with most datasets, there are many decisions that affect a model's quality. Data preprocessing and feature engineering are some of the most important factors, especially when the dataset's nature does not allow direct modeling of the data. Time series datasets fall into this category, in which the construction of appropriate features and targets is required. By transforming our non-stationary time series to stationary, we improved the algorithm's ability to model the data.

To assess the quality of our models, we used the MSE of return percentages, as well as the Sharpe ratio (in which we assumed that the model was utilized as a trading strategy). When MSE is concerned, the best performing ensemble proved to be the simple voting ensemble. The ensemble consisted of an SVM and KNN regressor, without any hyperparameter fine-tuning, achieving an MSE of 15.71. As a trading strategy, XGBoost proved to be the best ensemble, achieving a Sharpe value of 0.32. Although not exhaustive, this chapter has explored the possibilities and techniques used in time series modeling using ensemble learning methods.

In the next chapter, we will leverage the capabilities of ensemble learning methods, in order to predict the sentiment of various tweets.

Evaluating Sentiment on Twitter

11

Twitter is a highly popular social network with over 300 million monthly active users. The platform has been developed around short posts (limited to a number of characters; currently, the limit is 280 characters). The posts themselves are called tweets. On average, 6000 tweets are tweeted every second, which equates to around 200 billion tweets per year. This constitutes a huge amount of data that contains an equal amount of information. As is obvious, it is not possible to analyze this volume of data by hand. Thus, automated solutions have been employed, both by Twitter and third parties. One of the hottest topics involves a tweet's sentiment, or how the user feels about the topic that they tweets. Sentiment analysis comes in many flavors. The most common approach is a positive or negative classification of each tweet. Other approaches involve a more complex analysis of positive and negative emotions, such as anger, disgust, fear, happiness, sadness, and surprise. In this chapter, we will briefly present some sentiment analysis tools and practices. Following this, we will cover the basics of building a classifier that leverages ensemble learning techniques in order to classify tweets. Finally, we will see how we can classify tweets in real time by using Twitter's API.

We will cover the following topics in this chapter:

- Sentiment analysis tools
- Getting Twitter data
- Creating a model
- Classifying tweets in real time

Technical requirements

You will require basic knowledge of machine learning techniques and algorithms. Furthermore, a knowledge of python conventions and syntax is required. Finally, familiarity with the NumPy library will greatly help the reader to understand some custom algorithm implementations.

The code files of this chapter can be found on GitHub:

```
https://github.com/PacktPublishing/Hands-On-Ensemble-Learning-with-Python/tree/
master/Chapter11
```

Check out the following video to see the Code in Action: `http://bit.ly/2XSLQ5U`.

Sentiment analysis tools

Sentiment analysis can be implemented in a number of ways. The easiest to both implement and understand are lexicon-based approaches. These methods leverage the use of lists (lexicons) of polarized words and expressions. Given a sentence, these methods count the number of positive and negative words and expressions. If there are more positive words/expressions, the sentence is labeled as positive. If there are more negative than positive words/expressions, the sentence is labeled as negative. If the number of positive and negative words/expressions are equal, the sentence is labeled as neutral. Although this approach is relatively easy to code and does not require any training, it has two major disadvantages. First, it does not take into account interactions between words. For example, *not bad*, which is actually a positive expression, can be classified as negative, as it is composed of two negative words. Even if the expression is included in the lexicon under positive, the expression *not that bad* may not be included. The second disadvantage is that the whole process relies on good and complete lexicons. If the lexicon omits certain words, the results can be very poor.

Another approach is to train a machine learning model in order to classify sentences. In order to do so, a training dataset has to be created, where a number of sentences are labeled as positive or negative by human experts. This process indirectly uncovers a hidden problem in (and also indicates the difficulty of) sentiment analysis. Human analysts agree on 80% to 85% of the cases. This is partly due to the subjective nature of many expressions. For example, the sentence *Today the weather is nice, yesterday it was bad*, can be either positive, negative, or neutral. This depends on intonation. Assuming that the bold word is intonated, *Today the weather is **nice**, yesterday it was bad* is positive. *Today the weather is nice, yesterday it was **bad*** is negative, while *Today the weather is nice, yesterday it was bad* is actually neutral (a simple observation of a change in the weather).

 You can read more about the problem of disagreement between human analysts in sentiment classification at: `https://www.lexalytics.com/lexablog/sentiment-accuracy-quick-overview`.

In order to create machine learning features from text data, usually, n-grams are created. N-grams are sequences of *n* words extracted from each sentence. For example, the sentence "Hello there, kids" contains the following:

- 1-grams: "Hello", "there,", "kids"
- 2-grams: "Hello there,", "there, kids"
- 3-grams: "Hello there, kids"

In order to create numeric features for a dataset, a single feature is created for each unique N-gram. For each instance, the feature's value depends on the number of times it appears in the sentence. For example, consider the following toy dataset:

Sentence	Polarity
My head hurts	Positive
The food was good food	Negative
The sting hurts	Positive
That was a good time	Negative

A sentiment toy dataset

Assume that we will only use 1-grams (unigrams). The unique unigrams contained in the dataset are: "My", "head", "hurts", "The", "food", "was", "good", "sting", "That", "a", and "time". Thus, each instance has 11 features. Each feature corresponds to a single *n*-gram (in our case, a unigram). Each feature's value equals the number of appearances of the corresponding *n*-gram in the instance. The final dataset is depicted in the following table:

My	Head	Hurts	The	Food	Was	Good	Sting	That	A	Time	Polarity
1	1	1	0	0	0	0	0	0	0	0	Positive
0	0	0	1	2	1	1	0	0	0	0	Negative
0	0	1	1	0	0	0	1	0	0	0	Positive
0	0	0	0	0	1	1	0	1	1	1	Negative

The extracted features dataset

Usually, each instance is normalized, so each feature represents the relative frequency, rather than the absolute frequency (count), of each *n*-gram. This method is called **Term Frequency (TF)**. The TF dataset is depicted as follows:

My	Head	Hurts	The	Food	Was	Good	Sting	That	A	Time	Polarity
0.33	0.33	0.33	0	0	0	0	0	0	0	0	Positive
0	0	0	0.2	0.4	0.2	0.2	0	0	0	0	Negative
0	0	0.33	0.33	0	0	0	0.33	0	0	0	Positive
0	0	0	0	0	0.2	0.2	0	0.2	0.2	0.2	Negative

The TF dataset

In the English language, some terms exhibit a really high frequency, while contributing little towards the expression's sentiment. In order to account for this fact, **Inverse Document Frequency (IDF)** is employed. IDF puts more emphasis on infrequent terms. For *N* instances with *K* unique unigrams, the IDF of unigram *u*, which is present in *M* instances, is calculated as follows:

$$IDF(u) = \log \frac{N}{M}$$

The following table depicts the IDF-transformed dataset:

My	Head	Hurts	The	Food	Was	Good	Sting	That	A	Time	Polarity
0.6	0.6	0.3	0	0	0	0	0	0	0	0	Positive
0	0	0	0.3	0.6	0.3	0.3	0	0	0	0	Negative
0	0	0.3	0.3	0	0	0	0.6	0	0	0	Positive
0	0	0	0	0	0.3	0.3	0	0.6	0.6	0.6	Negative

The IDF dataset

Stemming

Stemming is another practice usually utilized in sentiment analysis. It is the process of reducing words to their root. This lets us handle words that originate from the same root as a single unigram. For example, *love*, *loving*, and *loved* will be all handled as the same unigram, *love*.

Getting Twitter data

There are a number of ways to gather Twitter data. From web scraping to using custom libraries, each one has different advantages and disadvantages. For our implementation, as we also need sentiment labeling, we will utilize the `Sentiment140` dataset (`http://cs.stanford.edu/people/alecmgo/trainingandtestdata.zip`). The reason that we do not collect our own data is mostly due to the time we would need to label it. In the last section of this chapter, we will see how we can collect our own data and analyze it in real time. The dataset consists of 1.6 million tweets, containing the following 6 fields:

- The tweet's polarity
- A numeric ID
- The date it was tweeted
- The query used to record the tweet
- The user's name
- The tweet's text content

For our models, we will only need the tweet's text and polarity. As can be seen in the following graph, there are 800,000 positive (with a polarity 4) and 800,000 negative (with a polarity 0) tweets:

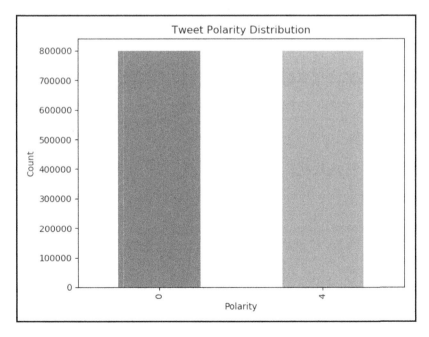

Polarity distribution

Here, we can also verify the statement we made earlier about word frequencies. The following graph depicts the 30 most common words in the dataset. As is evident, none of them bears any sentiment. Thus, an IDF transform would be more beneficial to our models:

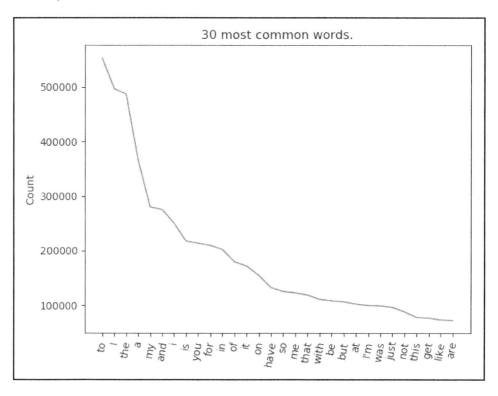

The 30 most common words in the dataset and the number of occurrences of each

Creating a model

The most important step in sentiment analysis (as is the case with most machine learning problems) is the preprocessing of our data. The following table contains 10 tweets, randomly sampled from the dataset:

id	text
44	@JonathanRKnight Awww I soo wish I was there to see...
143873	Shaking stomach flipping........god i hate thi...
466449	why do they refuse to put nice things in our v...

1035127	@KrisAllenmusic visit here
680337	Rafa out of Wimbledon Love Drunk by BLG out S...
31250	It's official, printers hate me Going to sul...
1078430	@_Enigma__ Good to hear
1436972	Dear Photoshop CS2. i love you. and i miss you!
401990	my boyfriend got in a car accident today !
1053169	Happy birthday, Wisconsin! 161 years ago, you ...

An outline of 10 random samples from the dataset

We can immediately make the following observations. First, there are references to other users, for example, @KrisAllenmusic. These references do not provide any information about the tweet's sentiment. Thus, during preprocessing, we will remove them. Second, there are numbers and punctuation. These also do not contribute to the tweet's sentiment, so they must also be removed. Third, some letters are capitalized while others are not. As capitalization does not alter the word's sentiment, we can choose to either convert all letters to lowercase or to convert them to uppercase. This ensures that words such as *LOVE*, *love*, and *Love* will be handled as the same unigram. If we sample more tweets, we can identify more problems. There are hashtags (such as #summer), which also do not contribute to the tweet's sentiment. Furthermore, there are URL links (for example https://www.packtpub.com/eu/) and HTML attributes (such as &amp which corresponds to &). These will also be removed during our preprocessing.

In order to preprocess our data, first, we must import the required libraries. We will use pandas; Python's built-in regular expressions library, re; punctuation from string; and the **Natural Language Toolkit (NLTK)**. The nltk library can be easily installed either through pip or conda as follows:

```
import pandas as pd
import re
from nltk.corpus import stopwords
from nltk.stem import PorterStemmer
from string import punctuation
```

After loading the libraries, we load the data, change the polarity from *[0, 4]* to *[0, 1]*, and discard all fields except for the text content and the polarity:

```
# Read the data and assign labels
labels = ['polarity', 'id', 'date', 'query', 'user', 'text']
data = pd.read_csv("sent140.csv", names=labels)

# Keep only text and polarity, change polarity to 0-1
data = data[['text', 'polarity']]
data.polarity.replace(4, 1, inplace=True)
```

As we saw earlier, many words do not contribute to a tweet's sentiment, although they frequently appear in text. Search engines handle this by removing such words, which are called stop words. NLTK has a list of the most common stop words that we are going to utilize. Furthermore, as there are a number of stop words that are contractions (such as "you're" and "don't") and tweets frequently omit single quotes in contractions, we expand the list in order to include contractions without single quotes (such as "dont"):

```
# Create a list of stopwords
stops = stopwords.words("english")
# Add stop variants without single quotes
no_quotes = []
for word in stops:
    if "'" in word:
        no_quotes.append(re.sub(r'\'', '', word))
stops.extend(no_quotes)
```

We then define two distinct functions. The first function, `clean_string`, cleans the tweet by removing all elements we discussed earlier (such as references, hashtags, and so on). The second function removes all punctuation or stop word and stems each word, by utilizing NLTK's `PorterStemmer`:

```
def clean_string(string):
    # Remove HTML entities
    tmp = re.sub(r'\&\w*;', '', string)
    # Remove @user
    tmp = re.sub(r'@(\w+)', '', tmp)
    # Remove links
    tmp = re.sub(r'(http|https|ftp)://[a-zA-Z0-9\\./]+', '', tmp)
    # Lowercase
    tmp = tmp.lower()
    # Remove Hashtags
    tmp = re.sub(r'#(\w+)', '', tmp)
    # Remove repeating chars
    tmp = re.sub(r'(.)\1{1,}', r'\1\1', tmp)
    # Remove anything that is not letters
    tmp = re.sub("[^a-zA-Z]", " ", tmp)
```

```
    # Remove anything that is less than two characters
    tmp = re.sub(r'\b\w{1,2}\b', '', tmp)
    # Remove multiple spaces
    tmp = re.sub(r'\s\s+', ' ', tmp)
    return tmp

def preprocess(string):
    stemmer = PorterStemmer()
    # Remove any punctuation character
    removed_punc = ''.join([char for char in string if char not in
punctuation])
    cleaned = []
    # Remove any stopword
    for word in removed_punc.split(' '):
        if word not in stops:
            cleaned.append(stemmer.stem(word.lower()))
    return ' '.join(cleaned)
```

As we would like to compare the performance of the ensemble with the base learners themselves, we will define a function that will evaluate any given classifier. The two most important factors that will define our dataset are the n-grams we will use and the number of features. Scikit-learn has an implementation of an IDF feature extractor, the TfidfVectorizer class. This allows us to only utilize the top *M* most frequent features, as well as define the n-gram range we will use, through the max_features and ngram_range parameters. It creates sparse arrays of features, which saves a great deal of memory, but the results must be converted to normal arrays before they can be processed by scikit-learn's classifiers. This is achieved by calling the toarray() function.

Our check_features_ngrams function accepts the number of features, a tuple of minimum and maximum n-grams, and a list of named classifiers (a name, classifier tuple). It extracts the required features from the dataset and passes them to the nested check_classifier. This function trains and evaluates each classifier, as well as exports the results to the specified file, outs.txt:

```
def check_features_ngrams(features, n_grams, classifiers):
    print(features, n_grams)

    # Create the IDF feature extractor
    tf = TfidfVectorizer(max_features=features, ngram_range=n_grams,
                         stop_words='english')

    # Create the IDF features
    tf.fit(data.text)
    transformed = tf.transform(data.text)
    np.random.seed(123456)

    def check_classifier(name, classifier):
```

```
        print('--'+name+'--')

        # Train the classifier
        x_data = transformed[:train_size].toarray()
        y_data = data.polarity[:train_size].values
        classifier.fit(x_data, y_data)
        i_s = metrics.accuracy_score(y_data, classifier.predict(x_data))

        # Evaluate on the test set
        x_data = transformed[test_start:test_end].toarray()
        y_data = data.polarity[test_start:test_end].values
        oos = metrics.accuracy_score(y_data, classifier.predict(x_data))

        # Export the results
        with open("outs.txt","a") as f:
            f.write(str(features)+',')
            f.write(str(n_grams[-1])+',')
            f.write(name+',')
            f.write('%.4f'%i_s+',')
            f.write('%.4f'%oos+'\n')

    for name, classifier in classifiers:
        check_classifier(name, classifier)
```

Finally, we test for n-grams in the range of [1, 3] and for the top 500, 1000, 5000, 10000, 20000, and 30000 features.

```
# Create csv header
with open("outs.txt","a") as f:
    f.write('features,ngram_range,classifier,train_acc,test_acc')
# Test all features and n-grams combinations
for features in [500, 1000, 5000, 10000, 20000, 30000]:
    for n_grams in [(1, 1), (1, 2), (1, 3)]:
    # Create the ensemble
        voting = VotingClassifier([('LR', LogisticRegression()),
                                   ('NB', MultinomialNB()),
                                   ('Ridge', RidgeClassifier())])
    # Create the named classifiers
    classifiers = [('LR', LogisticRegression()),
                   ('NB', MultinomialNB()),
                   ('Ridge', RidgeClassifier()),
                   ('Voting', voting)]
     # Evaluate them
     check_features_ngrams(features, n_grams, classifiers)
```

The results are depicted in the following diagram. As is evident, as we increase the number of features, the accuracy increases for all classifiers. Furthermore, if the number of features is relatively small, unigrams outperform combinations of unigrams and bigrams/trigrams. This is due to the fact that the most frequent expressions are not sentimental. Finally, although voting exhibits a relatively satisfactory performance, it is not able to outperform logistic regression:

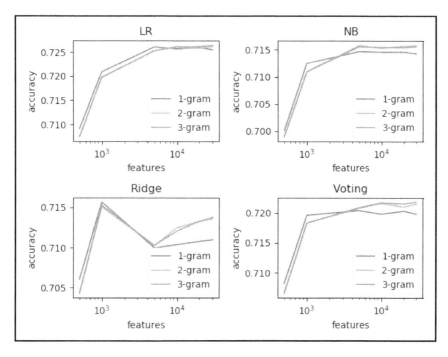

Results of voting and base learners

Classifying tweets in real time

We can use our model in order to classify tweets in real time using Twitter's API. In order to simplify things, we will make use of a very popular wrapper library for the API, `tweepy` (`https://github.com/tweepy/tweepy`). Installation is easily achieved with `pip install tweepy`. The first step to accessing Twitter programmatically is to generate relevant credentials. This is achieved by navigating to `https://apps.twitter.com/` and selecting **Create an app**. The application process is straightforward and should be accepted quickly.

Using tweepy's `StreamListener`, we will define a class that listens for incoming tweets, and as soon as they arrive, it classifies them and prints the original text and predicted polarity. First, we will load the required libraries. As a classifier, we will utilize the voting ensemble we trained earlier. First, we load the required libraries. We need the `json` library, as tweets are received in the JSON format; parts of the `tweepy` library; as well as the scikit-learn components we utilized earlier. Furthermore, we store our API keys in variables:

```
import pandas as pd
import json
from sklearn.ensemble import VotingClassifier
from sklearn.feature_extraction.text import TfidfVectorizer
from sklearn.linear_model import LogisticRegression, RidgeClassifier
from sklearn.naive_bayes import MultinomialNB
from tweepy import OAuthHandler, Stream, StreamListener
# Please fill your API keys as strings
consumer_key="HERE,"
consumer_secret="HERE,"

access_token="HERE,"
access_token_secret="AND HERE"
```

We then proceed to create and train our `TfidfVectorizer` and `VotingClassifier` with 30,000 features and n-grams in the *[1, 3]* range:

```
# Load the data
data = pd.read_csv('sent140_preprocessed.csv')
data = data.dropna()
# Replicate our voting classifier for 30.000 features and 1-3 n-grams
train_size = 10000
tf = TfidfVectorizer(max_features=30000, ngram_range=(1, 3),
                     stop_words='english')
tf.fit(data.text)
transformed = tf.transform(data.text)
x_data = transformed[:train_size].toarray()
y_data = data.polarity[:train_size].values
voting = VotingClassifier([('LR', LogisticRegression()),
                           ('NB', MultinomialNB()),
                           ('Ridge', RidgeClassifier())])
voting.fit(x_data, y_data)
```

We then proceed with defining our `StreamClassifier` class, responsible for listening for incoming tweets and classifying them as they arrive. It inherits the `StreamListener` class from `tweepy`. By overriding the `on_data` function, we are able to process tweets as they arrive through the stream. The tweets arrive in JSON format, so we first parse them with `json.loads(data)`, which returns a dictionary, and then extract the text using the `"text"` key. We can then extract the features using the fitted `vectorizer` and utilize the features in order to predict its polarity:

```
# Define the streaming classifier
class StreamClassifier(StreamListener):
    def __init__(self, classifier, vectorizer, api=None):
        super().__init__(api)
        self.clf = classifier
        self.vec = vectorizer
    # What to do when a tweet arrives
    def on_data(self, data):
        # Create a json object
        json_format = json.loads(data)
        # Get the tweet's text
        text = json_format['text']
        features = self.vec.transform([text]).toarray()
        print(text, self.clf.predict(features))
        return True
    # If an error occurs, print the status
    def on_error(self, status):
        print(status)
```

Finally, we instantiate `StreamClassifier`, passing as arguments, the trained voting ensemble and `TfidfVectorizer` and authenticate using the `OAuthHandler`. In order to start the stream, we instantiate a `Stream` object with the `OAuthHandler` and `StreamClassifier` objects as parameters and define the keywords we want to track with `filter(track=['Trump'])`. In this case, we track tweets that contain the keyword `'Trump'` as shown here:

```
# Create the classifier and authentication handlers
classifier = StreamClassifier(classifier=voting, vectorizer=tf)
auth = OAuthHandler(consumer_key, consumer_secret)
auth.set_access_token(access_token, access_token_secret)

# Listen for specific hashtags
stream = Stream(auth, classifier)
stream.filter(track=['Trump'])
```

That's it! The preceding code now tracks any tweet containing the keyword Trump and predicts its sentiment in real time. The following table depicts some simple tweets that were classified:

Text	Polarity
RT @BillyBaldwin: Only two things funnier than my brothers impersonation of Trump. Your daughters impersonation of being an honest, decent…	Negative
RT @danpfeiffer: This is a really important article for Democrats to read. Media reports of Trump's malfeasance is only the start. It's the…	Positive
RT @BillKristol: "In other words, Trump had backed himself, not Mexico, into a corner. They had him. He had to cave. And cave he did. He go…	Positive
RT @SenJeffMerkley: That Ken Cuccinelli started today despite not being nominated is unacceptable. Trump is doing an end run around the Sen…	Negative

Example of tweets being classified

Summary

In this chapter, we discussed the possibility of using ensemble learning in order to classify tweets. Although a simple logistic regression can outperform ensemble learning techniques, it is an interesting introduction to the realm of natural language processing and the techniques that are used in order to preprocess the data and extract useful features. In summary, we introduced the concepts of n-grams, IDF feature extraction, stemming, and stop word removal. We discussed the process of cleaning the data, as well as training a voting classifier and using it to classify tweets in real time using Twitter's API.

In the next chapter, we will see how ensemble learning can be utilized in the design of recommender systems, with the aim of recommending movies to a specific user.

12
Recommending Movies with Keras

Recommendation systems are an invaluable tool. They are able to increase both customer experience and a company's profitability. Such systems work by recommending items that users will probably like, based on other items they have already liked. For example, when shopping for a smartphone on Amazon, accessories for that specific smartphone will be recommended. This improves the customer's experience (as they do not need to search for accessories), while it also increases Amazon's profits (for example, if the user did not know that there are accessories available for sale).

In this chapter, we will cover the following topics:

- Demystifying recommendation systems
- Neural recommendation systems
- Using Keras for movie recommendations

In this chapter, we will utilize the MovieLens dataset (available at `http://files.grouplens.org/datasets/movielens/ml-latest-small.zip`) in order to create a movie recommendation system using the Keras deep learning framework and ensemble learning techniques.

We would like to thank the GroupLens members for giving us permission to use their data in this book. For more information about the data, please read the following relevant paper:

F. Maxwell Harper and Joseph A. Konstan. 2015. *The MovieLens Datasets: History and Context*. ACM Transactions on Interactive Intelligent Systems (TiiS) 5, 4, Article 19 (December 2015), 19 pages.

The paper is available at: http://dx.doi.org/10.1145/2827872

Technical requirements

You will require basic knowledge of machine learning techniques and algorithms. Furthermore, a knowledge of python conventions and syntax is required. Finally, familiarity with the NumPy library will greatly help the reader to understand some custom algorithm implementations.

The code files of this chapter can be found on GitHub:

```
https://github.com/PacktPublishing/Hands-On-Ensemble-Learning-with-Python/tree/
master/Chapter12
```

Check out the following video to see the Code in Action: `http://bit.ly/2NXZqVE`.

Demystifying recommendation systems

Although the inner workings of recommendation systems may seem intimidating at first, they are actually quite intuitive. Let's take an example of various movies and users. Each user has the option to rate a movie on a scale of 1 to 5. The recommendation system will try to find users with similar preferences to a new user, and will then recommend movies that the new user will probably like, as similar users also like them. Let's take the following simple example, consisting of four users and six movies:

User	Interstellar	2001: A Space Odyssey	The Matrix	Full Metal Jacket	Jarhead	Top Gun
U0	5	4		2	1	
U1		1		4	4	3
U2	4		4			1
U3		4	5	5	4	

Ratings for each movie from each user

As is evident, each user has rated a number of movies, although not all users watched the same movies and each user liked different movies. If we want to recommend a movie to **user two (U2)**, we must first find the most similar users. We can then make predictions in a **k-Nearest Neighbor (k-NN)** fashion, using the *K* most similar users. Of course, we can see that the user probably likes sci-fi films, but we need a quantitative method to measure it. If we treat each user's preferences as a vector, we have four vectors of six elements. We can then compute the cosine between any two vectors. If the vectors align perfectly, the cosine will be 1, indicating a perfect equality. If the vectors are completely opposite, it will be -1, indicating a perfect disagreement between the two users' preferences. The only problem that arises is the fact that not all movies have been rated by each user. We can fill empty entries with zeros, in order to compute the cosine similarities. The following graph shows the cosine similarities between the users:

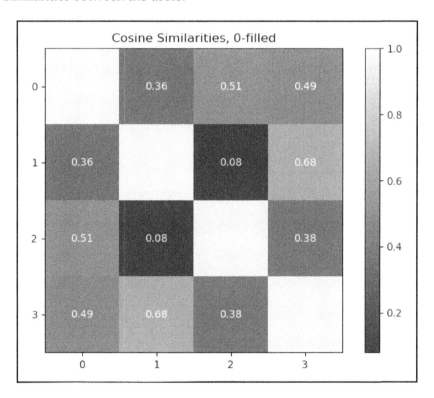

Cosine similarities between users

We notice that users U0 and U3 exhibit a high level of similarity with U2. The problem is that U0 also exhibits high similarity with U1, although their ratings are complete opposites. This is due to the fact that we fill any non-rated movie with 0, meaning all users who have not watched a movie agree that they do not like it. This can be remedied by first subtracting the mean of each user's ratings from their ratings. This normalizes the values and centers them around 0. Following this, we assign 0 to any movie the user has not yet rated. This indicates that the user is indifferent toward this movie and the user's mean rating is not altered. By computing the centered cosine similarity, we get the following values:

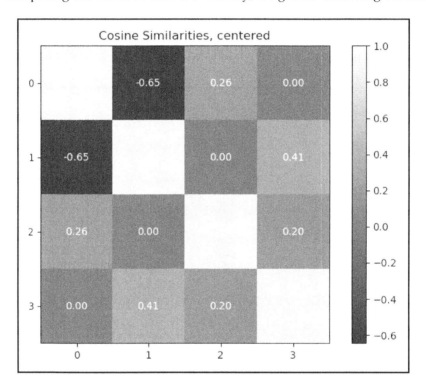

Centered cosine similarities between users

We can now see that U2 is similar to U0 and U3, while U1 and U0 are quite dissimilar. In order to compute a prediction about movies that U2 has not seen, but that the nearest K neighbors have seen, we will compute the weighted average for each movie, using the cosine similarities as weights. We only do this for movies that all similar users have rated, but that the target user has not rated yet. This gives us the following predicted ratings. If we were to recommend a single movie to U2, we would recommend *2001: A Space Odyssey*, a sci-fi film, as we speculated earlier:

Interstellar	2001: A Space Odyssey	The Matrix	Full Metal Jacket	Jarhead	Top Gun
-	4.00	-	3.32	2.32	-

Predicted ratings for user U2

This recommendation method is called **collaborative filtering**. When we search for similar users, as we did in this small example, it is called **user-user filtering**. We can also apply this method to search for similar items by transposing the ratings table. This is called **item-item filtering**, and it usually performs better in real-world applications. This is due to the fact that items usually belong to more well-defined categories, when compared to users. For example, a movie can be an action movie, a thriller, a documentary, or a comedy with little overlap between the genres. A user may like a certain mix of those categories; thus, it is easier to find similar movies, rather than similar users.

Neural recommendation systems

Instead of explicitly defining similarity metrics, we can utilize deep learning techniques in order to learn good representations and mappings of the feature space. There are a number of ways to employ neural networks in order to build recommendation systems. In this chapter, we will present two of the simplest ways to do so in order to demonstrate the ability to incorporate ensemble learning into the system. The most important piece that we will utilize in our networks is the embedding layer. These layer types accept an integer index as input and map it to an n-dimensional space. For example, a two-dimensional mapping could map 1 to [0.5, 0.5]. Utilizing these layers, we will be able to feed the user's index and the movie's index to our network, and the network will predict the rating for the specific user-movie combination.

The first architecture that we will test consists of two embedding layers, where we will multiply their outputs using a dot product, in order to predict the user's rating of the movie. The architecture is depicted in the following diagram. Although it is not a traditional neural network, we will utilize backpropagation in order to train the parameters of the two embedding layers:

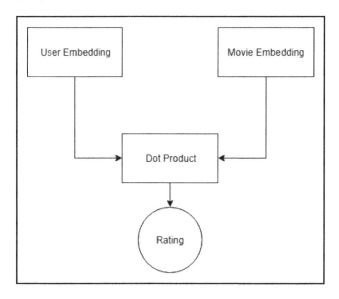

Simple dot product architecture

The second architecture is a more traditional neural network. Instead of relying on a predefined operation to combine the outputs of the embedding layers (the dot product), we will allow the network to find the optimal way to combine them. Instead of a dot product, we will feed the output of the embedding layers to a series of fully-connected (**dense**) layers. The architecture is depicted in the following diagram:

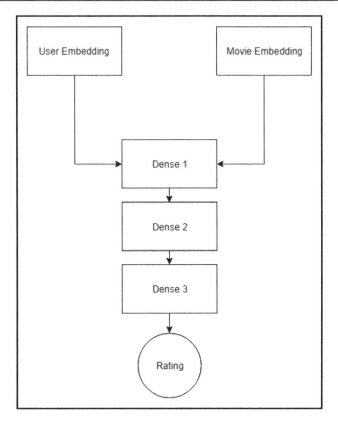

The fully connected architecture

In order to train the networks, we will utilize the Adam optimizer, and we will use the **mean squared error** (**MSE**) as a loss function. Our goal will be to predict the ratings of movies for any given user as accurately as possible. As the embedding layers have a predetermined output dimension, we will utilize a number of networks with different dimensions in order to create a stacking ensemble. Each individual network will be a separate base learner, and a relatively simple machine learning algorithm will be utilized in order to combine the individual predictions.

Using Keras for movie recommendations

In this section, we will utilize Keras as a deep learning framework in order to build our models. Keras can easily be installed by using either pip (`pip install keras`) or conda (`conda install -c conda-forge keras`). In order to build the neural networks, we must first understand our data. The MovieLens dataset consists of almost 100,000 samples and 4 different variables:

- `userId`: A numeric index corresponding to a specific user
- `movieId`: A numeric index corresponding to a specific movie
- `rating`: A value between 0 and 5
- `timestamp`: The specific time when the user rated the movie

A sample from the dataset is depicted in the following table. As is evident, the dataset is sorted by the `userId` column. This can potentially create overfitting problems in our models. Thus, we will shuffle the data before any split happens. Furthermore, we will not utilize the `timestamp` variable in our models, as we do not care about the order in which the movies were rated:

userId	movieId	rating	timestamp
1	1	4	964982703
1	3	4	964981247
1	6	4	964982224
1	47	5	964983815
1	50	5	964982931

A sample from the dataset

By looking at the distribution of ratings on the following graph, we can see that most movies were rated at 3.5, which is above the middle of the rating scale (2.5). Furthermore, the distribution shows a left tail, indicating that most users are generous with their ratings. Indeed, the first quartile of the ratings spans from 0.5 to 3, while the other 75% of the ratings lie in the 3-5 range. In other words, a user only rates 1 out of 4 movies with a value of less than 3:

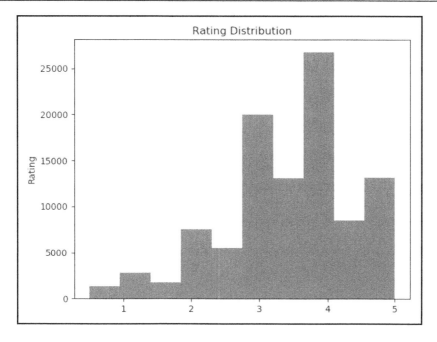

Ratings' distribution

Creating the dot model

Our first model will consist of two embedding layers, one for the movie index and one for the user index, as well as their dot product. We will use the `keras.layers` package, which contains the necessary layer implementations, as well as the `Model` implementation from the `keras.models` package. The layers that we will utilize are as follows:

- The `Input` layer, which is responsible for creating Keras tensors from more conventional Python data types
- The `Embedding` layer, which is the implementation of embedding layers
- The `Flatten` layer, which transforms any Keras n-dimensional tensor to a single dimensional tensor
- The `Dot` layer, which implements the dot product

Furthermore, we will utilize train_test_split and metrics from sklearn:

```
from keras.layers import Input, Embedding, Flatten, Dot, Dense, Concatenate
from keras.models import Model
from sklearn.model_selection import train_test_split
from sklearn import metrics

import numpy as np
import pandas as pd
```

Apart from setting the random seed of numpy, we define a function that loads and preprocesses our data. We read the data from the .csv file, drop the timestamp, and shuffle the data by utilizing the shuffle function of pandas. Furthermore, we create a train/test split of 80%/20%. We then re-map the dataset's indices in order to have consecutive integers as indices:

```
def get_data():
    # Read the data and drop timestamp
    data = pd.read_csv('ratings.csv')
    data.drop('timestamp', axis=1, inplace=True)

    # Re-map the indices
    users = data.userId.unique()
    movies = data.movieId.unique()
    # Create maps from old to new indices
    moviemap={}
    for i in range(len(movies)):
        moviemap[movies[i]]=i
    usermap={}
    for i in range(len(users)):
        usermap[users[i]]=i

    # Change the indices
    data.movieId = data.movieId.apply(lambda x: moviemap[x])
    data.userId = data.userId.apply(lambda x: usermap[x])

    # Shuffle the data
    data = data.sample(frac=1.0).reset_index(drop=True)

    # Create a train/test split
    train, test = train_test_split(data, test_size=0.2)

    n_users = len(users)
    n_movies = len(movies)

    return train, test, n_users, n_movies
train, test, n_users, n_movies = get_data()
```

In order to create the network, we first define the movie part of the input. We create an Input layer, which will act as the interface to our pandas dataset by accepting its data and transforming it into Keras tensors. Following this, the layer's output is fed into the Embedding layer, in order to map the integer to a five-dimensional space. We define the number of possible indices as n_movies (first parameter), and the number of features as fts (second parameter). Finally, we flatten the output. The same process is repeated for the user part:

```
fts = 5

# Movie part. Input accepts the index as input
# and passes it to the Embedding layer. Finally,
# Flatten transforms Embedding's output to a
# one-dimensional tensor.
movie_in = Input(shape=[1], name="Movie")
mov_embed = Embedding(n_movies, fts, name="Movie_Embed")(movie_in)
flat_movie = Flatten(name="FlattenM")(mov_embed)

# Repeat for the user.
user_in = Input(shape=[1], name="User")
user_inuser_embed = Embedding(n_users, fts, name="User_Embed")(user_in)
flat_user = Flatten(name="FlattenU")(user_inuser_embed)
```

Finally, we define the dot product layer, with the two flattened embeddings as inputs. We then define Model by specifying the user_in and movie_in (Input) layers as inputs, and the prod (Dot) layer as an output. After defining the model, Keras needs to compile it in order to create the computational graph. During compilation, we define the optimizer and loss functions:

```
# Calculate the dot-product of the two embeddings
prod = Dot(name="Mult", axes=1)([flat_movie, flat_user])

# Create and compile the model
model = Model([user_in, movie_in], prod)
model.compile('adam', 'mean_squared_error')
```

By calling `model.summary()`, we can see that the model has around 52,000 trainable parameters. All of these parameters are in the `Embedding` layers. This means that the network will only learn how to map the user and movie indices to the five-dimensional space. The function's output is as follows:

```
Layer (type)                  Output Shape        Param #     Connected to
=================================================================================
Movie (InputLayer)            (None, 1)           0

User (InputLayer)             (None, 1)           0

Movie_Embed (Embedding)       (None, 1, 5)        48620       Movie[0][0]

User_Embed (Embedding)        (None, 1, 5)        3050        User[0][0]

FlattenM (Flatten)            (None, 5)           0           Movie_Embed[0][0]

FlattenU (Flatten)            (None, 5)           0           User_Embed[0][0]

Mult (Dot)                    (None, 1)           0           FlattenM[0][0]
                                                              FlattenU[0][0]
=================================================================================
Total params: 51,670
Trainable params: 51,670
Non-trainable params: 0
```

The model's summary

Finally, we fit the model to our train set and evaluate it on the test set. We train the network for ten epochs in order to observe how it behaves, as well as how much time it needs to train itself. The following code depicts the training progress of the network:

```
# Train the model on the train set
model.fit([train.userId, train.movieId], train.rating, epochs=10,
verbose=1)

# Evaluate on the test set
print(metrics.mean_squared_error(test.rating,
      model.predict([test.userId, test.movieId])))
```

Take a look at the following screenshot:

```
Epoch 1/10
80668/80668 [==============================] - 13s 157us/step - loss: 11.8008
Epoch 2/10
80668/80668 [==============================] - 11s 142us/step - loss: 5.0013
Epoch 3/10
80668/80668 [==============================] - 12s 144us/step - loss: 2.6198
Epoch 4/10
80668/80668 [==============================] - 12s 145us/step - loss: 1.7814
Epoch 5/10
80668/80668 [==============================] - 12s 145us/step - loss: 1.3725
Epoch 6/10
80668/80668 [==============================] - 12s 151us/step - loss: 1.1442
Epoch 7/10
80668/80668 [==============================] - 12s 151us/step - loss: 1.0050
Epoch 8/10
80668/80668 [==============================] - 11s 140us/step - loss: 0.9137
Epoch 9/10
80668/80668 [==============================] - 11s 140us/step - loss: 0.8502
Epoch 10/10
80668/80668 [==============================] - 11s 139us/step - loss: 0.8049
```

Training progress of the dot product network

The model is able to achieve an MSE of 1.28 on the test set. In order to improve the model, we could increase the number of features each `Embedding` layer is able to learn, but the main limitation is the dot product layer. Instead of increasing the number of features, we will give the model the freedom to choose how to combine the two layers.

Creating the dense model

In order to create the dense model, we will substitute the `Dot` layer with a series of `Dense` layers. `Dense` layers are classic neurons, where each neuron gets, as input, all the outputs from the previous layer. In our case, as we have two `Embedding` layers, we must first concatenate them using the `Concatenate` layer, and then feed them to the first `Dense` layer. These two layers are also included in the `keras.layers` package. Thus, our model definition will now look like this:

```
# Movie part. Input accepts the index as input
# and passes it to the Embedding layer. Finally,
# Flatten transforms Embedding's output to a
# one-dimensional tensor.
movie_in = Input(shape=[1], name="Movie")
mov_embed = Embedding(n_movies, fts, name="Movie_Embed")(movie_in)
flat_movie = Flatten(name="FlattenM")(mov_embed)
```

```
# Repeat for the user.
user_in = Input(shape=[1], name="User")
user_inuser_embed = Embedding(n_users, fts, name="User_Embed")(user_in)
flat_user = Flatten(name="FlattenU")(user_inuser_embed)

# Concatenate the Embedding layers and feed them
# to the Dense part of the network
concat = Concatenate()([flat_movie, flat_user])
dense_1 = Dense(128)(concat)
dense_2 = Dense(32)(dense_1)
out = Dense(1)(dense_2)

# Create and compile the model
model = Model([user_in, movie_in], out)
model.compile('adam', 'mean_squared_error')
```

By adding these three Dense layers, we have increased the number of trainable parameters from almost 52,000 to almost 57,200 (an increase of 10%). Furthermore, each step now needs almost 210 microseconds, which increased from 144 us (a 45% increase), as is evident from the training progression and summary, as depicted in the following diagrams:

```
Layer (type)                    Output Shape         Param #      Connected to
=================================================================================
Movie (InputLayer)              (None, 1)             0

User (InputLayer)               (None, 1)             0

Movie_Embed (Embedding)         (None, 1, 5)          48620        Movie[0][0]

User_Embed (Embedding)          (None, 1, 5)          3050         User[0][0]

FlattenM (Flatten)              (None, 5)             0            Movie_Embed[0][0]

FlattenU (Flatten)              (None, 5)             0            User_Embed[0][0]

concatenate_7 (Concatenate)     (None, 10)            0            FlattenM[0][0]
                                                                   FlattenU[0][0]

dense_19 (Dense)                (None, 128)           1408         concatenate_7[0][0]

dense_20 (Dense)                (None, 32)            4128         dense_19[0][0]

dense_21 (Dense)                (None, 1)             33           dense_20[0][0]
=================================================================================
Total params: 57,239
Trainable params: 57,239
Non-trainable params: 0
```

Summary of the dense model

```
Epoch 1/10
80668/80668 [==============================] - 18s 226us/step - loss: 0.9361
Epoch 2/10
80668/80668 [==============================] - 17s 206us/step - loss: 0.7307
Epoch 3/10
80668/80668 [==============================] - 17s 213us/step - loss: 0.7022
Epoch 4/10
80668/80668 [==============================] - 16s 199us/step - loss: 0.6893
Epoch 5/10
80668/80668 [==============================] - 17s 211us/step - loss: 0.6775
Epoch 6/10
80668/80668 [==============================] - 17s 211us/step - loss: 0.6710
Epoch 7/10
80668/80668 [==============================] - 16s 200us/step - loss: 0.6648
Epoch 8/10
80668/80668 [==============================] - 16s 203us/step - loss: 0.6611
Epoch 9/10
80668/80668 [==============================] - 17s 209us/step - loss: 0.6574
Epoch 10/10
80668/80668 [==============================] - 17s 208us/step - loss: 0.6542
```

Training progression of the dense model

Nonetheless, the model now achieves an MSE 0.77 , which is 60% of the original dot-product model. Thus, as this model outperforms the previous model, we will utilize this architecture for our stacking ensemble. Moreover, as each network has a higher degree of freedom, it has a higher probability of diversifying from other base learners.

Creating a stacking ensemble

In order to create our stacking ensemble, we will utilize three dense networks, with embeddings consisting of 5, 10, and 15 features as base learners. We will train all networks on the original train set and utilize them to make predictions on the test set. Furthermore, we will train a Bayesian ridge regression as a meta learner. In order to train the regression, we will use all but the last 1,000 samples of the test set. Finally, we will evaluate the stacking ensemble on these last 1,000 samples.

First, we will create a function that creates and trains a dense network with n number of embedding features, as well as a function that accepts a model as input and return its predictions on the test set:

```python
def create_model(n_features=5, train_model=True, load_weights=False):
    fts = n_features

    # Movie part. Input accepts the index as input
    # and passes it to the Embedding layer. Finally,
    # Flatten transforms Embedding's output to a
    # one-dimensional tensor.
    movie_in = Input(shape=[1], name="Movie")
    mov_embed = Embedding(n_movies, fts, name="Movie_Embed")(movie_in)
    flat_movie = Flatten(name="FlattenM")(mov_embed)

    # Repeat for the user.
    user_in = Input(shape=[1], name="User")
    user_inuser_embed = Embedding(n_users, fts, name="User_Embed")(user_in)
    flat_user = Flatten(name="FlattenU")(user_inuser_embed)

    # Concatenate the Embedding layers and feed them
    # to the Dense part of the network
    concat = Concatenate()([flat_movie, flat_user])
    dense_1 = Dense(128)(concat)
    dense_2 = Dense(32)(dense_1)
    out = Dense(1)(dense_2)

    # Create and compile the model
    model = Model([user_in, movie_in], out)
    model.compile('adam', 'mean_squared_error')
    # Train the model
    model.fit([train.userId, train.movieId], train.rating, epochs=10,
verbose=1)

    return model

def predictions(model):
    preds = model.predict([test.userId, test.movieId])
    return preds
```

We will then create and train our base learners and meta learner in order to predict on the test set. We combine all three models' predictions in a single array:

```
# Create base and meta learner
model5 = create_model(5)
model10 = create_model(10)
model15 = create_model(15)
meta_learner = BayesianRidge()

# Predict on the test set
preds5 = predictions(model5)
preds10 = predictions(model10)
preds15 = predictions(model15)
# Create a single array with the predictions
preds = np.stack([preds5, preds10, preds15], axis=-1).reshape(-1, 3)
```

Finally, we train the meta learner on all but the last 1,000 test samples and evaluate the base learners, as well as the whole ensemble, on these last 1,000 samples:

```
# Fit the meta learner on all but the last 1000 test samples
meta_learner.fit(preds[:-1000], test.rating[:-1000])

# Evaluate the base learners and the meta learner on the last
# 1000 test samples
print('Base Learner 5 Features')
print(metrics.mean_squared_error(test.rating[-1000:], preds5[-1000:]))
print('Base Learner 10 Features')
print(metrics.mean_squared_error(test.rating[-1000:], preds10[-1000:]))
print('Base Learner 15 Features')
print(metrics.mean_squared_error(test.rating[-1000:], preds15[-1000:]))
print('Ensemble')
print(metrics.mean_squared_error(test.rating[-1000:],
meta_learner.predict(preds[-1000:])))
```

The results are depicted in the following table. As is evident, the ensemble is able to outperform the individual base learners on unseen data, achieving a lower MSE than any individual base learner:

Model	MSE
Base Learner 5	0.7609
Base Learner 10	0.7727
Base Learner 15	0.7639
Ensemble	0.7596

Results for individual base learners and the ensemble

Summary

In this chapter, we briefly presented the concept of recommendation systems and how collaborative filtering works. We then presented how neural networks can be utilized in order to avoid explicitly defining rules that dictate how unrated items would be rated by a user, using embedding layers and dot products. Following that, we showed how the performance of these models can be improved if we allow the networks to learn how to combine the embedding layers themselves. This gives the models considerably higher degrees of freedom without drastically increasing the number of parameters, leading to considerable increases in performance. Finally, we showed how the same architecture—with variable numbers of embedding features—can be utilized in order to create base learners for a stacking ensemble. In order to combine the base learners, we utilized a Bayesian ridge regression, which resulted in better results than any individual base learner.

This chapter serves as an introduction to the concept of using ensemble learning techniques for deep recommendation systems, rather than a fully detailed guide. There are many more options that can lead to considerable improvements in the system. For example, the usage of user descriptions (rather than indices), additional information about each movie (such as genre), and different architectures, can all greatly contribute to performance improvements. Still, all these concepts can greatly benefit from the usage of ensemble learning techniques, which this chapter adequately demonstrates.

In the next and final chapter, we will use ensemble learning techniques in order to cluster data from the World Happiness Report as we try to uncover patterns in the data.

13
Clustering World Happiness

In the final chapter of this book, we will look at utilizing ensemble cluster analysis in order to explore relationships in reported happiness around the world. In order to do so, we will leverage the `OpenEnsembles` library. First, we will present the data and its purpose. We will then construct our ensemble. Finally, we will try to gain more knowledge about structures and relationships within our data.

The following are the topics that we will cover in this chapter:

- Understanding the World Happiness Report
- Creating the ensemble
- Gaining insights

Technical requirements

You will require basic knowledge of machine learning techniques and algorithms. Furthermore, a knowledge of python conventions and syntax is required. Finally, familiarity with the NumPy library will greatly help the reader to understand some custom algorithm implementations.

The code files of this chapter can be found on GitHub:

```
https://github.com/PacktPublishing/Hands-On-Ensemble-Learning-with-Python/tree/
master/Chapter13
```

Check out the following video to see the Code in Action: `http://bit.ly/2ShFsUm`.

Understanding the World Happiness Report

The World Happiness Report is a survey of happiness in individual countries. It started from a United Nations meeting about well-being and happiness around the world. The survey generates happiness rankings using data from the Gallup World Poll, where people rate their overall quality of life (the variable containing the evaluations is the life ladder variable). The data can be found on the *World Happiness Report* website under the downloads section (`https://worldhappiness.report/ed/2019/`). Apart from the Life Ladder, the dataset also contains a number of other factors. The ones we will focus on are as follows:

- Log GDP per capita
- Social support
- Healthy life expectancy at birth
- Freedom to make life choices
- Generosity
- Perceptions of corruption
- Positive affect (average of happiness, laughter, and enjoyment)
- Negative affect (average of worry, sadness, and anger)
- Confidence in national government
- Democratic quality (how democratic the government is)
- Delivery quality (how effective the government is)

We can see how each one of these factors affects the life ladder by examining them on scatter plots. The following diagram depicts the scatter plots between each factor (*x* axis) and the life ladder (*y* axis):

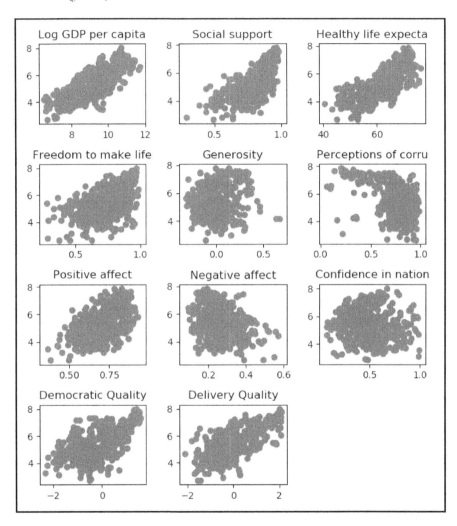

Scatter plots of the various factors against the Life Ladder

As is evident, **Log GDP per capita** and **Healthy life expectancy at birth** have the strongest positive and linear correlations with the life ladder. **Democratic quality**, **Delivery quality**, **Freedom to make life choices**, **Positive affect**, and **Social support** also exhibit positive correlations to the life ladder. **Negative affect** and **Perceptions of corruption** show negative correlations, while **Confidence in national government** does not indicate any significant correlation. By examining the Pearson's **correlation coefficient (r)** of each factor to the Life Ladder, we are able to confirm our visual findings:

Factor	Correlation coefficient (r)
Log GDP per capita	0.779064
Social support	0.702461
Healthy life expectancy at birth	0.736797
Freedom to make life choices	0.520988
Generosity	0.197423
Perceptions of corruption	-0.42075
Positive affect	0.543377
Negative affect	-0.27933
Confidence in national government	-0.09205
Democratic quality	0.614572
Delivery quality	0.70794

Correlation coefficient of each factor to the life ladder

Over the years, a total of 165 individual countries have been studied. The countries are organized in 10 different regions, according to their geographic location. The distribution of countries to each region for the latest report can be seen in the following pie chart. As is evident, Sub-Saharan Africa, Western Europe, and Central and Eastern Europe contain the most countries. This does not imply that these regions have the highest populations. It simply implies that these regions have the greatest number of separate countries:

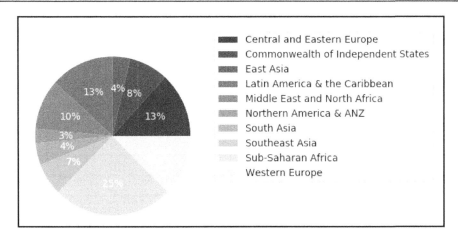

Distribution of countries to each region for 2018

Finally, it would be interesting to see how the Life Ladder progresses throughout the years. The following boxplot shows the Life Ladder's progression from 2005 to 2018. What we notice is that 2005 was a year with exceedingly high scores, while all other years are approximately the same. Given that there is not a global event that may explain this anomaly, we assume that something in the data collection process has influenced it:

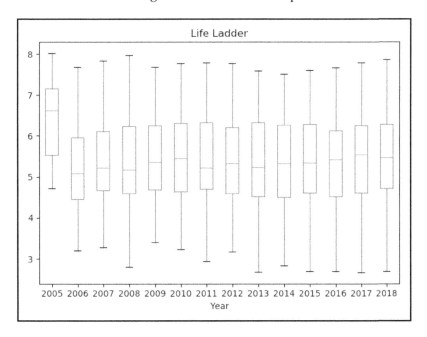

Boxplots of the Life Ladder for the various years

Indeed, if we examine the number of countries surveyed each year, we can see that 2005 has a very small number of countries compared to other years. There are only 27 countries for 2005, while 2006 has 89 countries. The number continues to increase up until 2011, when it stabilizes:

Year	Number of countries
2005	27
2006	89
2007	102
2008	110
2009	114
2010	124
2011	146
2012	142
2013	137
2014	145
2015	143
2016	142
2017	147
2018	136

Number of countries surveyed each year

If we only consider the initial 27 countries, the boxplots show the expected outcome. There are some fluctuations in the mean and deviation results; however, on average, the life ladder values are distributed around the same values. Furthermore, if we compare the average values with those of the previous boxplot, we see that, on average, these 27 countries are happier than the rest of the countries that were later added to the dataset:

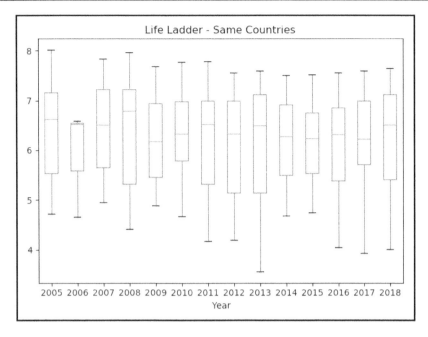

Boxplots for just the 27 countries that were part of the original 2005 dataset

Creating the ensemble

In order to create the ensemble, we will utilize the openensembles library that we presented in Chapter 8, *Clustering*. As our dataset does not contain labels, we cannot use the homogeneity score in order to evaluate our clustering models. Instead, we will use the silhouette score, which evaluates how cohesive each cluster is and how separate different clusters are. First, we must load our dataset, which is provided in the WHR.csv file. The second file that we load, Regions.csv, contains the region that each country belongs to. We will utilize the data from 2017, as 2018 has a lot of missing data (for example, **Delivery quality** and **Democratic quality** are completely absent). We will fill any missing data using the median of the dataset. For our experiment, we will utilize the factors we presented earlier. We store them in the columns variable, for ease of reference. We then proceed to generate the OpenEnsembles data object:

```
import matplotlib.pyplot as plt
import numpy as np
import openensembles as oe
import pandas as pd

from sklearn import metrics
```

```
# Load the datasets
data = pd.read_csv('WHR.csv')
regs = pd.read_csv('Regions.csv')

# DATA LOADING SECTION START #
# Use the 2017 data and fill any NaNs
recents = data[data.Year == 2017]
recents = recents.dropna(axis=1, how="all")
recents = recents.fillna(recents.median())

# Use only these specific features
columns = ['Log GDP per capita',
 'Social support', 'Healthy life expectancy at birth',
 'Freedom to make life choices', 'Generosity',
 'Perceptions of corruption','Positive affect', 'Negative affect',
 'Confidence in national government', 'Democratic Quality',
 'Delivery Quality']

# Create the data object
cluster_data = oe.data(recents[columns], columns)
# DATA LOADING SECTION END #
```

In order to create our K-means ensemble, we will test a number of *K* values and a number of ensemble sizes. We will test *K* values of 2, 4, 6, 8, 10, 12, and 14, and ensembles of size 5, 10, 20, and 50. In order to combine the individual base clusters, we will utilize co-occurrence linkage, as this was the most stable out of the three algorithms in Chapter 8, *Clustering*. We will store the results in the results dictionary, in order to process them later. Finally, we will create a pandas DataFrame from the results dictionary and arrange it in a two-dimensional array, in which each row corresponds to a certain *K* value and each column corresponds to a certain ensemble size:

```
np.random.seed(123456)
results = {'K':[], 'size':[], 'silhouette': []}
# Test different ensemble setups
Ks = [2, 4, 6, 8, 10, 12, 14]
sizes = [5, 10, 20, 50]
for K in Ks:
    for ensemble_size in sizes:
        ensemble = oe.cluster(cluster_data)
        for i in range(ensemble_size):
            name = f'kmeans_{ensemble_size}_{i}'
            ensemble.cluster('parent', 'kmeans', name, K)

        preds = ensemble.finish_co_occ_linkage(threshold=0.5)
        print(f'K: {K}, size {ensemble_size}:', end=' ')
        silhouette = metrics.silhouette_score(recents[columns],
        preds.labels['co_occ_linkage'])
```

```
        print ('%.2f' % silhouette)
        results['K'].append(K)
        results['size'].append(ensemble_size)
        results['silhouette'].append(silhouette)

results_df = pd.DataFrame(results)
cross = pd.crosstab(results_df.K, results_df['size'],
results_df['silhouette'], aggfunc=lambda x: x)
```

The results are depicted in the following table. As is evident, the silhouette score decreases as *K* increases. Furthermore, there seems to be a certain stability for *K* values up to six. Still, our data was fed to the clustering ensemble without any preprocessing. Thus, the distance metric can be dominated by features whose values are greater than others:

Size K	5	10	20	50
2	0.618	0.618	0.618	0.618
4	0.533	0.533	0.533	0.533
6	0.475	0.475	0.475	0.475
8	0.396	0.398	0.264	0.243
10	0.329	0.248	0.282	0.287
12	0.353	0.315	0.327	0.350
14	0.333	0.309	0.343	0.317

Results from the experimentation of different K values and ensemble sizes

In order to exclude the possibility that some features dominate over others, we will repeat the experiment by using normalized features, as well as **t-Distributed Stochastic Neighbor Embedding (t-SNE)** transformed features. First, we will test the normalized features. We must first subtract the mean and then divide by the standard deviation of each feature. This is easily achieved by using the standard pandas functions, as follows:

```
# DATA LOADING SECTION START #

# Use the 2017 data and fill any NaNs
recents = data[data.Year == 2017]
recents = recents.dropna(axis=1, how="all")
recents = recents.fillna(recents.median())

# Use only these specific features
columns = ['Log GDP per capita',
 'Social support', 'Healthy life expectancy at birth',
 'Freedom to make life choices', 'Generosity',
 'Perceptions of corruption','Positive affect', 'Negative affect',
```

```
    'Confidence in national government', 'Democratic Quality',
    'Delivery Quality']

# Normalize the features by subtracting the mean
# and dividing by the standard deviation
normalized = recents[columns]
normalized = normalized - normalized.mean()
normalized = normalized / normalized.std()

# Create the data object
cluster_data = oe.data(recents[columns], columns)
# DATA LOADING SECTION END #
```

We then test the same *K* values and ensemble sizes. As the following table shows, the results are quite similar to the original experiment:

Size K	5	10	20	50
2	0.618	0.618	0.618	0.618
4	0.533	0.533	0.533	0.533
6	0.475	0.475	0.475	0.475
8	0.393	0.396	0.344	0.264
10	0.311	0.355	0.306	0.292
12	0.346	0.319	0.350	0.350
14	0.328	0.327	0.326	0.314

Silhouette scores for the normalized data

Finally, we repeat the experiment with t-SNE as a preprocessing step. First, we import t-SNE with `from sklearn.manifold import t_sne`. In order to preprocess the data, we call the `fit_transform` function of `TSNE`, as shown in the following code excerpt. Note that `oe.data` now has `[0, 1]` as column names, since t-SNE, by default, only creates two components. Thus, our data will have only two columns:

```
# DATA LOADING SECTION START #

# Use the 2017 data and fill any NaNs
recents = data[data.Year == 2017]
recents = recents.dropna(axis=1, how="all")
recents = recents.fillna(recents.median())

# Use only these specific features
columns = ['Log GDP per capita',
  'Social support', 'Healthy life expectancy at birth',
```

```
    'Freedom to make life choices', 'Generosity',
    'Perceptions of corruption','Positive affect', 'Negative affect',
    'Confidence in national government', 'Democratic Quality',
    'Delivery Quality']

# Transform the data with TSNE
tsne = t_sne.TSNE()
transformed = pd.DataFrame(tsne.fit_transform(recents[columns]))
# Create the data object
cluster_data = oe.data(transformed, [0, 1])

# DATA LOADING SECTION END #
```

The results are depicted in the following table. We can see that t-SNE outperforms the other two approaches for some values. We are especially interested in 10 as the K value, due to the fact that there are 10 regions in the dataset. In the next section, we will try to gain insights into the data, using a K value of 10 and an ensemble size of 20:

Size K	5	10	20	50
2	0.537	0.537	0.537	0.537
4	0.466	0.466	0.466	0.466
6	0.405	0.405	0.405	0.405
8	0.343	0.351	0.351	0.351
10	0.349	0.348	0.350	0.349
12	0.282	0.288	0.291	0.288
14	0.268	0.273	0.275	0.272

Silhouette scores for t-SNE transformed data

Gaining insights

In order to gain further insights into our dataset's structure and relationships, we will use the t-SNE approach, with ensembles of size 20 and base **k-Nearest Neighbors (k-NN)** clusterers with a K value of 10. First, we create and train the cluster. Then, we add the cluster assignments to the DataFrame as an additional pandas column. We then calculate the means for each cluster and create a bar plot for each feature:

```
# DATA LOADING SECTION START #

# Use the 2017 data and fill any NaNs
```

```
recents = data[data.Year == 2017]
recents = recents.dropna(axis=1, how="all")
recents = recents.fillna(recents.median())

# Use only these specific features
columns = ['Log GDP per capita',
 'Social support', 'Healthy life expectancy at birth',
 'Freedom to make life choices', 'Generosity',
 'Perceptions of corruption','Positive affect', 'Negative affect',
 'Confidence in national government', 'Democratic Quality',
 'Delivery Quality']

# Transform the data with TSNE
tsne = t_sne.TSNE()
transformed = pd.DataFrame(tsne.fit_transform(recents[columns]))
# Create the data object
cluster_data = oe.data(transformed, [0, 1])

# DATA LOADING SECTION END #

# Create the ensemble
ensemble = oe.cluster(cluster_data)
for i in range(20):
    name = f'kmeans_{i}-tsne'
    ensemble.cluster('parent', 'kmeans', name, 10)

# Create the cluster labels
preds = ensemble.finish_co_occ_linkage(threshold=0.5)

# Add Life Ladder to columns
columns = ['Life Ladder', 'Log GDP per capita',
 'Social support', 'Healthy life expectancy at birth',
 'Freedom to make life choices', 'Generosity',
 'Perceptions of corruption','Positive affect', 'Negative affect',
 'Confidence in national government', 'Democratic Quality',
 'Delivery Quality']
# Add the cluster to the dataframe and group by the cluster
recents['Cluster'] = preds.labels['co_occ_linkage']
grouped = recents.groupby('Cluster')
# Get the means
means = grouped.mean()[columns]
# Create barplots
def create_bar(col, nc, nr, index):
    plt.subplot(nc, nr, index)
    values = means.sort_values('Life Ladder')[col]
    mn = min(values) * 0.98
    mx = max(values) * 1.02
    values.plot(kind='bar', ylim=[mn, mx])
```

```
    plt.title(col[:18])

# Plot for each feature
plt.figure(1)
i = 1
for col in columns:
    create_bar(col, 4, 3, i)
    i += 1
plt.show()
```

The bar plots are depicted in the following diagram. The clusters are sorted according to their average Life Ladder value, in order to easily make comparisons between the individual features. As we can see, clusters 3, 2, and 4 have comparable average happiness (Life Ladder). The same can be said for clusters 6, 8, 9, 7, and 5. We could argue that the ensemble only needs 5 clusters, but, by closely examining the other features, we see that this is not the case:

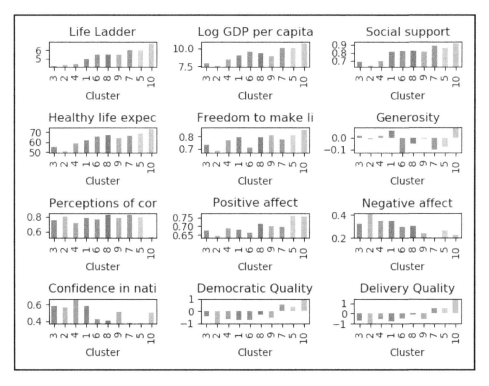

Bar plots of cluster means for each feature

By looking at *Healthy life expectancy* and *Freedom to make life choices*, we see that clusters 3 and 4 are considerably better than 2. In fact, if we examine every other feature, we see that clusters 3 and 4 are, on average, more fortunate than cluster 2. Maybe it is interesting to see how the individual countries are distributed among each cluster. The following table depicts the cluster assignments. Indeed, we see that clusters 2, 3, and 4 involve countries that have had to recently overcome difficulties that were not captured in our features. In fact, these are some of the most war-torn areas of the world. From a sociological point of view, it is extremely interesting that these war-torn and troubled regions seem to have the most confidence in their governments, despite exhibiting extremely negative democratic and delivery qualities:

N	Countries
1	Cambodia, Egypt, Indonesia, Libya, Mongolia, Nepal, Philippines, and Turkmenistan
2	Afghanistan, Burkina Faso, Cameroon, Central African Republic, Chad, Congo (Kinshasa), Guinea, Ivory Coast, Lesotho, Mali, Mozambique, Niger, Nigeria, Sierra Leone, and South Sudan
3	Benin, Gambia, Ghana, Haiti, Liberia, Malawi, Mauritania, Namibia, South Africa, Tanzania, Togo, Uganda, Yemen, Zambia, and Zimbabwe
4	Botswana, Congo (Brazzaville), Ethiopia, Gabon, India, Iraq, Kenya, Laos, Madagascar, Myanmar, Pakistan, Rwanda, and Senegal
5	Albania, Argentina, Bahrain, Chile, China, Croatia, Czech Republic, Estonia, Montenegro, Panama, Poland, Slovakia, United States, and Uruguay
6	Algeria, Azerbaijan, Belarus, Brazil, Dominican Republic, El Salvador, Iran, Lebanon, Morocco, Palestinian Territories, Paraguay, Saudi Arabia, Turkey, and Venezuela
7	Bulgaria, Hungary, Kuwait, Latvia, Lithuania, Mauritius, Romania, Taiwan Province of China
8	Armenia, Bosnia and Herzegovina, Colombia, Ecuador, Honduras, Jamaica, Jordan, Macedonia, Mexico, Nicaragua, Peru, Serbia, Sri Lanka, Thailand, Tunisia, United Arab Emirates, and Vietnam
9	Bangladesh, Bolivia, Georgia, Guatemala, Kazakhstan, Kosovo, Kyrgyzstan, Moldova, Russia, Tajikistan, Trinidad and Tobago, Ukraine, and Uzbekistan
10	Australia, Austria, Belgium, Canada, Costa Rica, Cyprus, Denmark, Finland, France, Germany, Greece, Hong Kong S.A.R. of China, Iceland, Ireland, Israel, Italy, Japan, Luxembourg, Malta, Netherlands, New Zealand, Norway, Portugal, Singapore, Slovenia, South Korea, Spain, Sweden, Switzerland, and United Kingdom

Cluster assignments

Starting with to cluster 1, we see that the happiness of people in these countries is considerably better than the previous clusters. This can be attributed to a better life expectancy (less wars), better GDP per capita, social support, generosity, and freedom to make choices regarding life changes. Still, these countries are not as happy as they could be, mainly due to problems with democratic quality and delivery quality. Nonetheless, their confidence in their governments are second only to the previous group of clusters we discussed. Clusters 6, 8, and 9 are more or less on the same level of happiness. Their differences are in GDP per capita, life expectancy, freedom, generosity, and confidence. We can see that cluster 6 has, on average, stronger economies and life expectancy, although people's freedom, generosity, and the government's efficiency seem to be lacking. Clusters 8 and 9 are less economically sound, but seem to have a lot more freedom and better functioning governments. Moreover, their generosity, on average, is greater than cluster 6. Moving on to clusters 7 and 5, we see that they, too, are close in terms of happiness. These are countries where we see a positive democratic and delivery quality, with sufficient freedom, economic strength, social support, and a healthy life expectancy. These are developed countries, where people, on average, live a prosperous life without fear of dying from economic, political, or military causes. The problems in these countries are mainly the perception of corruption, people's confidence in their governments, and the efficiency of the governments. Finally, cluster 10 contains countries that are better in almost every aspect, compared to the rest of the world. These countries have, on average, the highest GDP per capita, life expectancy, generosity, and freedom, while having sufficiently high confidence in their national governments and low perceptions of corruption. These could be considered the ideal countries to live in, given a compatible cultural background.

Summary

In this chapter, we presented the World Happiness Report data, providing a description of the data's purpose, as well as describing the data's properties. In order to gain further insights into the data, we utilized cluster analysis, leveraging ensemble techniques. We used co-occurrence matrix linkage in order to combine the cluster assignments of different base clusters. We tested various setups, with different ensemble sizes and numbers of neighbors, in order to provide a k-NN ensemble. After identifying that a t-SNE decomposition with a K value of 10 and 20 base clusters can be utilized, we analyzed the cluster assignments. We found that countries reporting the same happiness levels can, in fact, have different profiles. The most unhappy countries were, on average, developing countries who have to overcome many problems, concerning both their economies, and, in certain cases, wars. It is interesting that these countries had the most confidence in their governments, although these same governments are reported as dysfunctional. Countries that belong to clusters of medium happiness have either strong economies, but little freedom, or vice versa.

Developed countries with strong economies and life quality, but who perceive their governments as corrupt, are not able to achieve the highest happiness scores possible. Finally, the only countries that do not think their governments are corrupt have the strongest economies, democratic and delivery quality, and life expectancy. These are mostly countries in the European Union or the European Economic Area, along with Canada, Australia, New Zealand, Japan, South Korea, Costa Rica, Israel, Hong Kong, and Iceland.

In this book we have covered most ensemble learning techniques. After a short refresher on machine learning, we discussed about the main problems that arise from machine learning models. These problems are bias and variance. Ensemble learning techniques usually try to address these problems, through generative and non generative methods. We discussed both non-generative methods, such as Voting and Stacking, as well as generative methods, such as Bagging, Boosting, and Random Forests. Furthermore, we presented methods that can be utilized in order to create clustering ensembles, such as Majority Voting, Graph Closure, and Co-occurrence Linkage. Finally, we dedicated some chapters to specific applications, in order to show how some real-world problems should be handled. If there is a point that needs to be highlighted in this book, then it is that the data quality has a bigger impact on any particular model's performance than the algorithm used to create the model. Thus, ensemble learning techniques, such as any machine learning technique, should be used in order to address algorithmic weaknesses (of previously generated models) rather than poor data quality.

Another Book You May Enjoy

If you enjoyed this book, you may be interested in these other books by Packt:

Ensemble Machine Learning Cookbook

Vijayalakshmi Natarajan, Dipayan Sarkar

ISBN: 9781789136609

- Understand how to use machine learning algorithms for regression and classification problems
- Implement ensemble techniques such as averaging, weighted averaging, and max-voting
- Get to grips with advanced ensemble methods, such as bootstrapping, bagging, and stacking
- Use Random Forest for tasks such as classification and regression
- Implement an ensemble of homogeneous and heterogeneous machine learning algorithms
- Learn and implement various boosting techniques, such as AdaBoost, Gradient Boosting Machine, and XGBoost

Leave a review - let other readers know what you think

Please share your thoughts on this book with others by leaving a review on the site that you bought it from. If you purchased the book from Amazon, please leave us an honest review on this book's Amazon page. This is vital so that other potential readers can see and use your unbiased opinion to make purchasing decisions, we can understand what our customers think about our products, and our authors can see your feedback on the title that they have worked with Packt to create. It will only take a few minutes of your time, but is valuable to other potential customers, our authors, and Packt. Thank you!

Index

Made in United States
North Haven, CT
27 January 2022